How Does Jewish Law Work?

HOW DOES JEWISH LAW WORK?

A Rabbi Analyzes 95 Contemporary Halachic Questions

J. Simcha Cohen

JASON ARONSON INC.
Northvale, New Jersey
London

This book was set in 11 pt. Century by Lind Graphics of Upper Saddle River, New Jersey, and printed by Haddon Craftsmen in Scranton, Pennsylvania.

Library of Congress Cataloging-in-Publication Data

Cohen, J. Simcha.
   How does Jewish law work? : A rabbi analyzes 95 contemporary halachic questions / by J. Simcha Cohen.
     p. cm.
   Includes bibliographical references and index.
   ISBN 0-87668-155-0
   1. Responsa—1800–   2. Judaism—20th century. 3. Judaism—Customs and practices. I. Title.
BM522.27.03624 1993
296.3—dc20
                                                         93-19756

Manufactured in the United States of America. Jason Aronson Inc. offers books and cassettes. For information and catalog write to Jason Aronson Inc., 230 Livingston Street, Northvale, New Jersey 07647.

To

Zvika Ryzman

Good friend

Chavrutah

Baal Sevarah Yesharah

Patron of Torah

Contents

III
REPENTANCE AND REBUKE

IV
PARENTHOOD, MARRIAGE, AND CHILDREN

V
RITUALS, *SHABBAT*, HOLIDAYS, PRAYERS

Introduction

Jewish life, culture, and traditions are not the results of philosophical or ideological thoughts. They are, rather, the imprimatur of *halachah* – Jewish law – that molds our character and sets the contours of our life-style. *Halachah*, the distinctly unique Jewish legal system, crystallizes the guidelines of Judaism. It makes us into Jews and marks us as Jewish. As such, an understanding of the halachic process provides insight into the inner soul of Jewish life itself.

The key to any insight into Judaism or Jewish life is the recognition that Torah study is not just a means of acquiring knowledge to resolve questions or to perform *mitzvot*. It is a form of worship itself. Learning Torah is a *mitzvah*. As such, it becomes an exciting goal in its own right. It's a form of discerning the will of God. It's an all-absorbing and mind-boggling venture into the world of ideas. It's a means of hearing and sharing the thoughts of the sages of the past and seeking relevance to the problems of today. The resources are so vast that common usage describes it as "the sea of Talmud." This volume, hopefully, is a "swimming lesson"; a picture of how Torah analysis works in practice; a guide not only to decisions, but to the process of Torah decision making itself.

As I reflect on goals as an author and reactions to critical review, the thoughts of my paternal grandfather, HaRav HaGaon R. Shmuel HaKohen, tell it all. He was a rural community rabbi in the city of Shatava, Ukraine (Kaminetz Padolsk). He was also a famed author of halachic works that became classics in his lifetime and are utilized by rabbinic scholars as basic guides even today (*Minchat Shabbat* [on *Shabbat* laws], *Madanai Shmuel* [on

laws of Passover]). In his introduction to his volume on *Shabbat*
he made the following observations, which are definitely perti-
nent even today. I have taken the liberty of paraphrasing the
contents and expanding certain issues.

> Every serious person seeks to impact favorably the world
> itself; to in some way make a contribution that is lasting
> (*Tikun Olam*); to perform some action that may have a life of
> its own even beyond the frail limitation of one's own lifetime.
> Publishing Torah concepts seems to be a proper vehicle to
> accomplish this goal; for a quality volume has the potential of
> influencing future generations. As such, every publication is
> (in a way) a quest for immortality. Every volume gives an
> author an opportunity to live, again and again, in future eras.
> What a *zechut* (a religious privilege) it is to have one's Torah
> viewpoint discussed, and even perhaps helping to guide fu-
> ture leaders of Jewish people. For such reasons it is definitely
> understandable why an author seeks to share thoughts by
> publication.
>
> At issue is that initial common rabbinical reaction to halachic
> volumes is to deflate the egos of new authors by questioning
> their ability and sagacity or even their impudence to suggest
> that their works or thoughts should be guides for Jewish life.
> To such critics, I beg of you, do not dismiss the contents
> without sufficient analysis and thought. Should, after serious
> deliberation, it be determined that I erred, please inform me
> in writing of my errors. This will grant me an opportunity
> (while I have the ability to respond) to review all charges and
> defend my position. Moreover, after responding to you should
> I not satisfy your criticism, then I promise, as strength is
> within me, that in a future publication (for I will continue to
> write), I will publicly retract all errors I may have committed.
>
> The Chavat Yair writes that should a Torah volume contain
> but one good Torah thought, it serves as a guard and spiritual
> protector over the other parts. Hopefully so will be with this
> volume.

The *responsa* herein contained have a history. They were
weathered through a refining process. Many were first devel-

oped at lectures, seminars, and classes held at Congregation Shaarei Tefila, Los Angeles, California. Subsequently, they were published as weekly articles in the *Jewish Press* – the weekly periodical that prides itself on having the largest circulation of all Anglo-Jewish publications. My goal is *not* to proclaim that my thoughts are the *only* viable approach or final decision. No, that's not my purpose at all. Rather, it's to establish the realization that the thoughts noted herein may also have halachic validity.

God has been good to me. My previous *responsa* book, for example, has been praised. Scholars have looked on it with favor. May it be Thy will to have this volume also graced with favor and kindness.

The year 1993 marks the thirty-second anniversary of my marriage to my rebbitzen, Shoshana. Thirty-two is the numerical value of the Hebrew word *lev*, which means heart. Shoshana truly has a great Jewish heart that is full of love for our family and compassion for all. My ability to learn Torah is due, in the main, to her deep-seated viewpoint that Torah study is the prime role of the Jew and the guarantor of a Jewish spiritual life-style. May God grant us many years of health, happiness together, and continued devotion to our people.

As a *kohen*, I extend blessings to our wonderful children: Malkah, Matityahu (Chagit), Yehudah, Deena (Adam), and to our granddaughters, Ellin, Natalya, and Alexandra.

Special recognition must be extended to my mentors. My father, HaRav HaGaon R. Meir Cohen, may his memory be a blessing, former executive director of the Union of Orthodox Rabbis and author of halachic volumes entitled *Chelkat Meir* I and II; my mother, Rebbitzen Itka Cohen; my father-in-law, HaRav HaGaon R. Yaakov Nayman, the famed talmudic sage and disciple of the Brisker Rav and rabbi of Congregation Adat B'nai Yisrael, Chicago; my mother-in-law, Rebbitzen Chaya Nayman. Our Torah personality has been molded by their love of Torah coupled with their superb mastery of the art of hospitality and kindness.

To Congregation Shaarei Tefila, my deep appreciation and thankfulness to God for the privilege of serving as rabbi of such a prominent and illustrious community.

Part I

Charity

Charity to Fakers

QUESTION: Should one give charity to a person known to be a faker?

RESPONSE: No. The *Shulchan Aruch* rules that "should a person come and state 'feed me,' one does not check whether he is a faker, but one feeds him immediately" (*Yoreh De'ah* 251:10). This is based on the talmudic citation that "Claims for clothing one investigates but not claims for food" (*Bava Batra* 9b).

The very concept that certain categories of Jews are investigated logically implies, says the *Aruch HaShulchan*, that a person known to be a faker who misrepresents himself as a poor person is not to receive any charity at all. The Codes deal, rather, with a person unknown to the donor. In the event the request is for food, then such is provided even without an investigation as to the veracity of the claim. For perhaps the person is truly hungry and any delay might generate great pain or anguish. Should a request, however, be made for clothes, the claimant would have to await an assessment as to whether there is a realistic need (*Aruch HaShulchan, Yoreh De'ah* 251:12).

There is, however, a period of time when all requests for charity are honored even without any check as to the reality of the need. The *Shulchan Aruch* rules that on Purim, "all who stretch [out] a hand for charity are given," without any investigation (*Orach Chayyim* 694:2). The Bach cites Rashi, who says that on Purim one does not check out whether the claimant is a faker or truly in need (*Tur*, 694). In other words, no questions are asked claimants for charity funds on Purim. (During a seminar on charity laws, one student remarked that perhaps one does not assess people on Purim because most may be intoxicated; namely, under the influence of observing the *mitzvah* of drinking on that day.) The implication, of course, is that the donors are not able to make decisions; otherwise, should the donors be aware that the claimants are in no way in need of charity funds, then even on Purim one may withhold funds. This goes against the general impression that should a person request charity, then even if he is known to be a fake, one still must provide aid. This is simply not so.

Though the above deals with *halachah*, folklore generates an alternate orientation. It is told that a certain great sage made it his business to (*bedavka*) provide charity to a number of people who truly did not deserve such funds. When questioned concerning the propriety of his actions, he replied as follows: In one hundred and twenty years from now the Heavenly Court will judge my actions. I'm positive I will not live up to the holy standards. As such, any claims for heavenly rewards will be rejected. My retort will be that God must care for me as I cared for others. Just as in this world I gave charity to those who did not deserve it, so too should God reward me even though I too do not deserve it" (*midah keneged midah*, measure for measure).

Door-to-Door Charity Collectors

QUESTION: Many people are quite perturbed over the number of charity collectors and beggars who disturb family privacy and tranquillity by requesting aid at all hours of the day and night. As a reaction, one neighborhood wishes to set up the following program: Every household should contribute to a general communal charity fund. Beggars and/or charity collectors should not be permitted to go house to house to collect funds. Such a begging process is an invasion of privacy as well as a form of humiliation to the collectors. Instead, all who seek funds should go directly to the *gabbai* (agent) of the communal charity for proper distribution. Is this against *halachah*?

RESPONSE: Jewish communities had two major communal charities: the *"kupah"* and the *"tomchui."* The former granted funds each week to local poor, while the latter was set up to provide food for the poor from other areas who happened to visit the town (*Bava Batra* 8b). The Talmud reports that beggars who go from door to door to collect charity have a unique status. "A *Tanna* taught that a beggar who goes from door to door should not be granted funds from the *kupah* charity fund." Rashi notes that since such a person has learned how to beg, he does not need additional funds. The Talmud, however, concludes that we do in fact provide such beggars with communal charity funds. The distinction is that "we do not listen to his request for a large gift, but we do listen to his request for a small gift." Tosafot note that such people may acquire minimal funds from the communal charity fund (*Bava Batra* 9a).

HaGaon R. Moshe Feinstein (*z"l*) derives the following law from this citation. It is evident that the communal (*kupah*) charity fund was established to benefit the local poor. It was a fund set up to protect the integrity of the poor and shield them from humiliation. Yet, should a poor person disregard qualms over humiliation and integrity and opt for the potential greater amount of money to be earned at begging than through communal funds, he was permitted to do so. The community could not and would not outlaw begging door to door for charity. From this we see that communal charity programs are set up to help the poor and not to protect the sensitivities of the donors. Yet, the poor themselves are free to disregard any protection of their *kavod* to possibly acquire greater funds through personal embarrassment (see *Iggerot Mosheh, Yoreh De'ah* I, *Responsum* 149).

Tradition has it that when Rav Levi Yitzchok became Rav of Berditchev he informed the local leaders he was devoted to learning Torah. As such, he was not to be disturbed about old ordinances or issues but only for innovative concerns. The communal leaders once came to him with the following proposed ruling: To sustain a level of communal dignity, it was suggested that door-to-door begging be abolished and all poor should direct their needs to a special communal agency specifically set up to care for such problems. It is reputed that Rav Levi Yitzchok responded, "Didn't I say not to disturb me with old matters?

Your so-called new activity is as old as the Bible itself. It's simply a reenactment of the vicious rulings of Sodom, which did not permit poor people to go about the town collecting charity." Accordingly, one cannot withhold the poor person from his begging route.

A second concern relates to the amount *halachah* rules must be given to such collectors.

Tzedakah, charity, contains both a positive as well as a negative commandment. The Rogatchover Gaon, HaRav Yosef Rosen, makes a distinction between these commandments. He contends that the positive command to give charity "Open wide thy hand to thy poor" (Deuteronomy 15:11) is applicable even should no one request charity. This is an obligation imposed upon all Jews to give a certain amount each year. The negative commandment "Thou shalt not harden thy heart" (Deuteronomy 15:7) is generated only when one refuses an actual plea for help. A Jew may not turn down a request for help. Even if he has already given his requirement for the year, something must be given to the poor (see *Tzafnot Paanei'ach*, Rambam, Gifts to the Poor, chap. 7). This suggests that the donor must give something but that that amount may even be extremely minimal. The Rambam notes that should the proposed donor lack funds himself, then one should at least "appease the poor with words" (Rambam, Gifts to the Poor 10:5).

Priority in Charity, Part 1: Relatives versus Torah Scholars

QUESTION: Who is to receive priority in charity: a relative or a visiting rabbinic scholar?

RESPONSE: In a situation wherein there are numerous claimants for *tzedakah* and not sufficient funds to meet the needs, then the following priorities are recorded in the *Shulchan Aruch*: *kohen, levi, yisrael, mamzer,* convert. Namely, priority is granted first to the *kohen* and last to the convert. Should the *mamzer*, for example, be a Torah scholar, then he takes precedence even over a *kohen gadol* who is ignorant of Torah (*Horayut* 13a, *Yoreh De'ah* 251:9). Thus, *Torah* knowledge grants precedence *over lineage (yichus).*

The Rema rules that a scholar who requires clothing takes precedence even over an ignorant person who seeks food (*Horayut* 13a, *Yoreh De'ah* 251:9). This law establishes great powers to Torah learning. In fact, it seems almost contrary to logic and common sense. Why? For the law is that "one is obligated to feed the hungry before clothing the naked" (*Yoreh De'ah* 251:7). Without the Rema's remarks it might be assumed that a Torah scholar has priority over another person who has a similar need— both seek food or clothing. In the event, however, that an illiterate or ignorant Jew is hungry and a rabbi requires clothing, then the need to feed the hungry should normally take precedence over all other needs, even that of a Torah sage. The Rema's ruling, however, indicates that Torah takes precedence not only over lineage but also over need. When a Torah scholar is impoverished, he gains priority regardless of the need of others.

Of interest is that the Codes detail the priorities of family relationships and geography. For example, priority is granted to parents, children, brothers, relatives, and even neighbors over others. Also, the poor of one's city have priority over the poor of another city. The poor of Israel have priority over nonlocal poor (*Yoreh De'ah* 251:3).

At issue is whether Torah is deemed so important that it takes priority over even poor family members.

The Rambam rules that "a relative has priority over all persons" (*Matanot Aniyim* 7:13). The terminology suggests to the Chacham Tzvi that a relative has priority over even a Talmud scholar.

The logic is that the obligation to support a *rav* or Torah scholar is incumbent upon the community at large. The mandate to support a relative, however, is a personal particular obligation of the family member himself. No one else has such an obligation. An important limitation is that this priority to relatives, further suggests the Chacham Tzvi, relates to the distribution of the personal funds of a donor. Should one distribute communal funds, however, then family relationships have no practical bearing on the issues. In such a case, Torah takes precedence except for a parent or a *rebbe*, who always has priority (Chacham Tzvi, *Responsum* 70).

Priority in Charity, Part 2: Relatives versus Other Poor

QUESTION: When does a poor relative take priority over other poor?

RESPONSE: The Torah states, "If amongst you there be a *poor person*" (Deuteronomy 15:7). The biblical word used to describe a poor man is the term *evyon*, which the Sifre states: "*Evyon*, a person who desires; priority [is granted] to the greater desire or need." Probably based on this *Sifre*, Rav Samson Raphael Hirsch translates the biblical word relating to a poor person to be "a necessitous man." Commenting on the *Sifre*, HaGaon HaRav Pinchas Hurowitz (the Baal HaFla) contends that the general *halachah* is that local poor have priority over the nonlocal poor (*Yoreh De'ah* 251:3). This law suggests that when two people have an equal need, the claim of the local poor has priority. In the event, however, that the local poor already have basic sustenance and the poor of another city do not, then the nonlocal poor have precedence, for their need is greater than that of the local poor. This is based on the principle that priority is granted to the greatest need.

The *Sifre* also elaborates on the personal pronoun of the verse. It states, "If amongst *you* [there be a poor person]," the word *you* means "within you, namely within your family, there is poverty, they take priority over the local poor." Note, suggests Rav Hurowitz, that the pronoun indicating care for poor family members is located in the verse prior to any mention of the necessitous (poor) person. This teaches us that the family poor take priority even over the local poor who have greater needs. Family members always have priority (*Panim Yafot*, Deuteronomy, *Parashat Re'eh*, also cited by *Responsa* Chatam Sofer, *Yoreh De'ah* 231). The Chatam Sofer (in his commentary on the Pentateuch) provides the following additional rationale. He notes that should a person always be required to give priority to the greatest need or desire, then the rich who become poor would always take precedence over the poor who never tasted affluence. Accordingly, such poor would never have an opportunity to survive. On the other hand, should poor relatives take precedence over even those with greater needs, a fairer distribution may emerge (*Torat Moshe*, Deuteronomy, *Re'eh*).

HaRav Unterman, former chief Ashkenazic rabbi of Israel, contends that family obligations have priority over others *only* in the event that there is no imminent danger to life (*sakkanah*).

Priority to support relatives (*Yoreh De'ah* 251:3) is granted because there is an underlying assumption that others (within the community) will come to the aid of those in need. In case there is no time for others to come to the aid of the person in need, then priority is *not* given to family relationships but rather to lineage and Torah scholarship. For this reason the Talmud (*Horayut* 13a) does not even mention the priority to help family relations. The Talmud was dealing with life-threatening, dangerous cases. As such, it listed only categories of lineage and Torah (HaRav Unterman: "Levels of Priority in Saving People, Ransoming Captives, Charity and Loans According to Halachah," pp. 56–58; see Yad Shaul memorial volume in honor of HaRav Dr. Sol Weingart, ed., Rabbi Dr. Y. Weingart and Rabbi Pinchas Biberfeld, Tel Aviv, 1953).

The Pitchai Teshuvah cites scholars (*Yoreh De'ah* 251:3) who claim that local poor take precedence even over the claims of a *talmid chacham*. This ruling is questioned seriously by the Chofetz Chayyim. Local poor have priority only when the need is comparable to the nonlocal poor. Should, however, the local poor need to be clothed and the nonlocal poor require food, the nonlocal poor have priority (previously cited ruling of the Chatam Sofer). Yet, when it comes to Torah personalities, the *Shulchan Aruch* rules that a Torah scholar who needs clothes has priority even over one who requires food (*Yoreh De'ah* 251:9). As such, the Torah scholar is not to be compared to ordinary needs. His request should be responded to with a greater mandate than that to the poor of a local town. And yet, a relative still has priority over a *talmid chacham* (Chacham Tzvi, *Responsum* 70).

Charity to Only One Person

QUESTION: Is it permissible to designate one person to be the sole recipient of all of one's charity obligations?

RESPONSE: The *Shulchan Aruch* specifically rules "one should not give all of one's charity funds to only one poor person" (*Yoreh De'ah* 257:9). The Shach, however, adds a phrase that somewhat alters the simple, clear-cut *halachah*. Commenting on the words "one poor person" he states, "or to one relative and [thus] leave other relatives (without any charity funds at all) (*Yoreh De'ah* 257:19). The implication, says HaGaon Rav Moshe Feinstein (*z"l*) is that one may be permitted to solely grant charity funds to a relative should no other relatives be poor. In other words, the prohibition according to the Shach is not to grant exclusivity to any poor person within a specific category and thus neglect others. In the event, however, that no one in a category is being excluded, then one may provide such a person with all of one's charity funds. This means that, for example, should a person have only one *rebbe* who is poor, he may be the sole recipient of all of one's charity funds.

The difficulty is that the Talmud appears to support the general rule that no one person should receive the total charity funds of another, regardless of relationship or category. In *Eruvin*, the Talmud says that one verse notes King David was punished for deciding halachic matters, and in another verse he is lauded for the same behavior. R. Hamnuna contends that David was punished for ruling in the era of his *rebbe*, Ira HaYairi, and praised for making such halachic decisions after Ira's death. R. Aba Bar Zavda added that a verse stating that Ira was David's personal *kohen* meant that King David gave all his presents to Ira (the *kohen*). To the extent that Scripture notes a famine took place in the land teaches us "one should not give all one's presents to a single *kohen*" (*Eruvin* 63a). The basic interpretation is that Ira was both King David's *rebbe* and his personal *kohen*. At that time there is no knowledge of King David having any other *rebbe* (which means he was the only person in that category); yet the Talmud still states that one should not give all one's presents to a single person. This appears to refute the Shach. Perhaps, suggests HaGaon R. Moshe, R. Hamnuna and R. Aba Bar Zavda disagree as to whether Ira was, in fact, King David's *rebbe*. The former would accept Ira as the king's *rebbe*; the latter would reject that role and reserve for Ira solely the function as *kohen*. Accordingly, Ira had no special relationship to the king. He was simply a *kohen* to whom the king gave presents. In the event, however, that a poor person has a distinctly unique relationship (that is, a *rebbe*) maybe such a person could receive all funds. Though this may be the rationale for the Shach's ruling, the simple meaning of the text appears to not support the Shach's view. HaGaon R. Moshe concludes that in practice one should not exclusively provide charity funds to one person. Why? It's a form of *Chilul HaShem* (profaning God's Name). People may contend that this person simply supports his family and doesn't give charity at all. Thus, though a large percentage may be given to a poor relative or to a *rebbe*, it is best to give to other charities; other poor people, including support of *yeshivot* (see *Iggerot Mosheh, Yoreh De'ah* I, *Responsum* 144).

Charity to a Parent

QUESTION: In the event a parent is poor, may a child support the parent from funds designated for distribution to charity?

RESPONSE: This question was posed to the famed Chatam Sofer of Pressburg. His response was that such a child not only has halachic permission to utilize his charity funds to support his parents but is under a mandatory obligation to so exclusively utilize the charity funds.

The logic is as follows: In *Kiddushin* the Talmud discusses a case wherein the *mitzvah* of honoring parents can be fulfilled only through the expenditure of funds. At issue is whether a child is required to spend money in order to honor his (her) parents. The halachic conclusion is that a child is required to provide service to a parent, but *not* funds. So should, for example, a parent be thirsty and request a drink, the parent must provide the funds to pay for the item requested, but the child must expend service (*Kiddushin* 32a; *Yoreh De'ah* 240:5). Should the parent be impoverished, however, the Codes rule that the child is required to support the parent (ibid.).

The Chatam Sofer contends that the latter law falls under the aegis of charity. His reasoning is that a child is not required to spend money and thus detract from his personal resources to observe the *mitzvah* of *kibud av* (honoring a father). But what about a situation where there is not a loss of funds to the child? Namely, the child uses funds already set aside for charity. As such, the funds no longer belong to the child. The son has only the right of distribution. He may select the poor person of choice to receive his charity. In such a case, says the Chatam Sofer, he *must* give the funds to his father. The *mitzvah* of *kibud av* directs the son and limits his choice of recipients. The money is charity, but the *mitzvah* that directs the action is *kibud av*. In such a circumstance the son is obliged to give all to the parent (Chatam Sofer, *Yoreh De'ah, Responsum* 229).

This suggests that the *mitzvah* of honoring parents directs a child's course of action and limits his discretionary behavior.

Jewish Maids and Charity

QUESTION: When a person hires a maid, should any preference be given to a Jew over a Gentile?

RESPONSE: Many women contend that they prefer hiring a Gentile maid, rather than a Jewess. Their argument is that domestic housework involves arduous labor. It disturbs the fine sensitivities of Jewish women employers to have a Jewish woman crawling on the ground cleaning floors. It's not right or suitable for one Jewish woman to work in such an undignified manner for another. As such, many will simply not hire a Jewish woman to provide housework.

This so-called moral standard goes against the precepts of *halachah*. The *Shulchan Aruch* rules, "Your home should have poor people" (*Yoreh De'ah* 251:6). The source, say the commentaries, is the Rambam, who notes "The sages commanded that poor and orphans should [serve] a household rather than slaves. It is best to use the service of Jews rather than those from a strange seed so that [at least] the children of Abraham, Isaac, and Jacob should receive benefit and some enjoyment from Jewish property. An increase of slaves generates sin. Having Jews work in a household increases *mitzvot* (Rambam, *Matanot Aniyim* 10:17).

In other words, just the opposite of what women contend reflects Jewish sensitivity. Giving a Jewish woman or man a job is a basic principle of Judaism. The Shach adds a nuance of importance. He contends that the engagement of a Jewish employee (who needs a job) is deemed as if the employer observed the *mitzvah* of *tzedakah* (251:10). So, not only is the housework being well cared for by a Jew, but the Jewish woman employer also acquires the *mitzvah* of *tzedakah*. The principle underlying the preceding *halachah* is that there is no shame in honest labor. Certain professions or trades may have a higher status than others, but no necessary labor is to be denigrated.

Throughout the history of immigration, domestic house labor was generally provided by the most recent immigrant group. In America different cultures were prominent as maids, including the Irish and the Jews. Yes, Jewish women served as maids for other Americans. The key to the *halachah* is that should a Jew need a job, preference is to be granted to b'nei Avraham, Yitzchak, and Yaakov – no matter what the job entails.

Charity to Friends

QUESTION: Are friends who seek charity to be granted priority over strangers?

RESPONSE A: The *Shulchan Aruch* lists a number of priorities for the distribution of charity. The Rema, for example, notes that a brother has priority over other relatives and such relatives over *neighbors* (*shecheinav*) and neighbors over residents of one's town and townspeople over residents from other cities (*Yoreh De'ah* 251:3).

Of these priorities, one seems difficult to define. It's the category of neighbors. Now what does this term mean? What are the parameters of the category? I assume that a person who lives directly next door is classified as a neighbor. But, what about a person who lives in the same neighborhood? Of greater concern is whether a person may claim priority as a neighbor who simply does not know the donor at all. Namely, he lives physically near the donor but has never had any communication. Would physical, spatial proximity without a personal relationship still grant the person priority to receive charity?

The Imrei Ash questions whether the term "neighbors" refers altogether to actual residents who live in close proximity and suggests that, perhaps, it relates to people who are personally close to the donor; namely friends. Indeed, in an instance of determining the intent of a gift of a dying person, the *Shulchan Aruch* rules that in certain situations a neighbor has priority. To this the Rema rules that the neighbor must refer to one who has a personal relationship, not just a spatial residential proximity (*Choshen Mishpat* 253:29). The Imrei Ash suggests that so too one may perhaps relate to the term "neighbor" as it pertains to charity (see Imrei Ash, *Siman* 101; see also *Daat Torah, Yoreh De'ah* 251:3).

Based upon the foregoing, those who maintain personal relationships with the donor may also have priority to receive charity funds over total strangers.

Just as an obligation is owed to fellow residents of one's town prior to that of strangers, so too, perhaps, is an obligation to support those friends who are currently in need.

RESPONSE B: The *Mishnah* rules that a person confronted with the choice of either returning a lost item to his father or to his *rebbe* (teacher) should grant priority to his *rebbe*. The talmudic reasoning is that "the father brought him [the son] to this world while the *rebbe* [by teaching Torah] brings him to the world to come" (*Bava Metzia* 33a). The Rema restricts this principle to a situation wherein the father does not provide payment to the *rebbe* for teaching Torah to his son. In an instance, however, where the father actually expends funds to the *rebbe* so that his son may learn Torah, then the priority is reversed and the father (not the *rebbe*) is granted preference (*Shulchan Aruch, Yoreh De'ah* 242:34).

This rule requires clarification as to why payment to a *rebbe* alters the respect owed him for teaching Torah to a young boy.

HaGaon Rav Yitzchok Hutner suggests that the general rationale for granting priority to a *rebbe* entails two vital components. One, a *rebbe* is granted *kavod* for actually teaching Torah. Two, the process of learning Torah generates an obligation of appreciation to the *rebbe* for the Torah taught. By paying funds to the *rebbe*, the obligation of appreciation is transferred from the *rebbe* to the father. The son now owes his own father a debt of gratitude for ensuring that he acquired Torah knowledge. The father is owed not only a debt of gratitude for giving physical life to the child, but also a moral debt for the *chesed* (kindness) of giving him Torah. As such, the father takes priority in this instance over a *rebbe*. This principle implies that an act of kindness takes precedence over the *kavod* due Torah scholars. An act of kindness crystallizes a lien of appreciation comparable to a debt of money. Each must be repaid. A loan of funds requires repayment. An act of kindness obligates a repayment of kindness. Accordingly, the needs of one who previously extended graciousness to a person has priority even over the request of a Torah scholar who is a stranger (*Pachad Yitzchok, Rosh HaShanah, Maamar* 3:1).

Charity Recipients and Chanukah

QUESTION: Are recipients of charity required to spend funds to observe Chanukah?

RESPONSE: The Rambam notes that the *mitzvah* of Chanukah is special and dear to K'lal Yisrael (*havivah hi me'od*). It is
deemed so important that "even if one has not what to eat except
from charity [i.e., a person is supported by charity], he should
borrow or [even] sell his garment in order to acquire oil and/or
candles [so that] he may kindle [the Chanukah *menorah*]" (*Hilchot Chanukah* 4:12).

The Magid Mishneh directs attention to the source for the
preceding ruling. He contends that it is a logical derivative from
a comparable law dealing with the *mitzvah* to drink four cups of
wine at the Pesach *seder*. The law at Pesach is that even a person
who is the "poorest of the poor" is to be granted by those who
dispense poverty funds additional means to acquire the necessary four cups of wine (*Hilchot Chametz uMatzah* 7:7; see also
Pesachim 99b).

The reason, suggests the Magid Mishneh, is that the
mitzvah of drinking the four cups of wine is categorized as a
mitzvah wherein *pirsum hanes* (popularizing the *mitzvah*) is an
integral aspect. Since the *mitzvah* is so important that it requires
to be publicized, then even a poverty-stricken person is obliged to
observe it.

Now, reasons the Magid Mishneh, as follows: If a person is
required to sell his garment to acquire the *mitzvah* of the four
cups of wine, he certainly should be obligated to sell his garment
in order to observe the *mitzvah* of lighting the Chanukah *menorah*.

Of concern is the logic of the Magid Mishneh that Chanukah
is a greater degree of *pirsum hanes* than the *mitzvah* of drinking
four cups of wine on Pesach. Why is one more public than
another?

The Avnei Nezer suggests that the *pirsum hanes* of Chanukah is greater than that of Pesach for on Pesach a person is
mandated to publicly manifest the *mitzvah* to his household. The
seder is in the privacy of one's home.

On Chanukah, however, the Jew is required to kindle his
menorah so that all who pass his home will observe the *mitzvah*.
Such a communal role involves more people than just a private

household, as at Pesach (*Responsa, Avnei Nezer, Orach Chay-yim*, vol. 2, *Responsum* 501).

Biblical and Rabbinic Responses to Charity

QUESTION: Judaism classifies charity as not only a moral, humane response to the poor, but also as a basic *mitzvah*. Are there specific biblical and rabbinic guidelines as to how one should care for the poor? Are there any distinctions between biblical obligations and the rabbinic responses?

RESPONSE:

Biblical Source

A major and unique source of the rabbinic response to poverty is the interpretation given to a biblical verse. It is written,

> If, however, there is a needy person among you, one of your kinsmen in any one of your settlements, in the land the Lord your God is giving you, do not harden your heart and shut your hand against your needy kinsman (Deuteronomy 15.7). Rather, you must open your hand and lend him sufficient for whatever he needs (Deuteronomy 15.8).[1]

Or, for purposes of analysis, a more literal translation,

> If there be among you a needy man, one of thy brethren, within any of thy gates, in thy land which the Lord thy God giveth thee, thou shalt not harden thy heart, nor shut thy

hand from thy needy brother; but thou shalt surely open thy
hand unto him, and shalt surely lend him *sufficient for his
need (in that) which is wanting unto him.*[2]

Ancient rabbinic sources interpret the words, "sufficient for
his need," to mean one is obligated to provide sustenance to the
needy but not to make him wealthy.[3] The latter phrase "which is
wanting unto him" is considered extraneous, for the verse has
meaning without it. Its inclusion is believed by tradition to teach
a unique understanding of the concept of charity. The term "unto
him" is considered a directive that not all grants to the poor are
equal. Each person must receive a gift according to his needs.
The phrase "which is wanting" teaches that not only food and
drink must be given but all that he requires according to his
previous standards.[4]

The meaning of this tradition is further articulated in the
following specific talmudic and pretalmudic laws.

If he was accustomed to be fed, one actually is required to
feed him. If he was accustomed to a certain quality of clothing,
one is required to provide such clothing.[5] If he needs a house or
furniture, one is required to provide him with such possessions.
If he needs a wife, one is obligated to acquire a mate for him. An
orphan is provided with a home, furniture, essential utensils, and
a mate.[6]

To demonstrate that the laws were actually put into effect,
actual cases are provided in the Talmud that give insight into the
realization and specificity of the biblical tradition.

1. If the poor person needed a horse to ride upon and a slave
to run before him, such items were required to be provided to
him. It is said that Hillel, the Elder, once acquired for a poor man
of a good family (*ben tovim*) a horse to ride upon and a slave to run
before him. One time, Hillel was not able to find a slave to run
before a poor person, so he, himself, ran before him three *milin* (a
talmudic measure of space).[7] (Variants of this case contend that
Hillel gave the poor person his own horse and slave,[8] or rented
for the poor person a horse and slave.[9] A further variant deletes
the ending of Hillel running before the poor man.[10])

2. A story is told of the people of Galil, that they acquired for a poor person of a good family a measure of meat every day even though it was quite costly and difficult to obtain.[11]

The Jerusalem Talmud deletes the fact that the needy man was of a good family and suggests the reason for such a grant was that the individual was accustomed to a life of grandeur and a rich diet.[12] The direct implication is that a luxury is provided only if such was the style prior to poverty.

3. A person came before Raba and not only requested sustenance but informed the rabbi that his custom was to eat stuffed chicken and old wine. Raba asked the poor person whether he was concerned with the great difficulty he was imposing upon the community with such an unusual diet. To this query, the man countered by saying that he was not eating food taken from man but, rather, from the Lord. Since it is written "and thou gives to them their food in his time [in its time of need]"[13] rather than the more grammatical term "in their time," it implies that the Lord provides to each man his own type of food according to his custom. While this discussion took place, the sister of Raba came to visit with him, after an absence of thirteen years, and brought as a present a stuffed chicken and old wine. When Raba noted the coincidence, he gave the poor the present.[14]

4. A person came to Rabbi Nechemia and requested sustenance. The rabbi made an inquiry concerning the poor man's diet and was told that the poor person was accustomed to fat meat and old wine. Since the rabbi was a vegetarian, he gave the poor person a diet similar to his own and the poor person died. When questioned as to whether the rabbi was responsible for the death of the poor man, the Talmud maintains his innocence by stating that the poor person was alone accountable for his own death for he should not have accustomed himself to such a rich diet.

The first three cases appear to reinforce by actual practice the biblical definition of poverty. They suggest that poverty is a personal condition of need. The definition of the need is the previous standards of the individual prior to his fallen status.

Yet, the fourth case[15] suggests a contradiction of the biblical law rather than its actualization in practice.

One method of harmonizing this case with the others is the suggestion that the obligation to provide the luxurious needs of the poor refer only to those individuals accustomed to luxury from early childhood. Such individuals cannot be personally held accountable for luxurious habits or diets. As a result, whatever the need, an obligation exists to meet it. Should, however, a person not be from such a family (*ben tovim*) and acquired by himself luxurious habits, then there is no requirement to provide that person with luxury when he is poor. The cases of Hillel and the people of Galil refer to poor from good families. The case of R. Nechemia was one wherein the poor person assumed himself a total luxurious habit and was, therefore, personally responsible for the results. The case of Raba was one where the poor person enjoyed a rich diet but on numerous occasions maintained whatever diet provided him,[16] or simply was a member of the so-called good families. Though this interpretation harmonizes the laws, it severely limits the scope of the biblical command. It suggests that childhood habits are so ingrained in an individual that life is meaningless unless those standards are constant. As a result, those standards are to be reconstructed should such a person become poor. On the other hand, it demeans the progress and affluence of the self-made man. It appears to contend that affluence is a transitory experience that may be nullified. Any person who changes his status—from poor to rich and down again—has had experience with a nonluxurious life and should be able to assume the transition without trauma. The biblical command would, therefore, be saying, give a person his luxurious needs only when he is not at fault for their acquisition.

A further consideration is that no one is required to provide to a poor person a standard above the custom of the donor. R. Nechemia's custom was to eat vegetables—not meat—therefore, he was under no obligation to provide the poor person with a standard above his own.[17] This qualification appears logical. The biblical command appears as a dual process of balances. The recipient's poor status must be reversed. His level of consumption must be upped to either his former status—if such was lower than the standard of the present donor—or at least equal to the status of the donor if his previous standard was higher than that of the donor. With this interpretation the rabbinic dictum that one "is required to sustain the poor, not make him wealthy,"[18] is totally understandable. It means, do not provide the poor with a standard above that of the donor nor above that of his previous status.

Yet, this qualifying aspect of the biblical law necessitates a reinterpretation of the previous cases.

Case 1–The story of Hillel would assume, as one variant reading does, that he, himself, possessed such a standard.[19]

Case 2–The people of Galil provided an expensive item of meat to a poor person even though it may have been above the normal custom prevailing in the city. This incident is interpreted to refer to a poor person who was ill and required such food for recovery and strength. To the extent that this incident related to matters of health or life and death, the community was required to provide such assistance until the invalid would resume good health. However, a healthy person would in no way obtain anything above the standard of the community.[20] It is also possible that this interpretation of the biblical command would maintain that the correct variant of case two is the source that does not mention the standard of the community.[21] Thus, the poor person received his allotment simply because it was not only his standard but also the standard of the community.

Case 3–Raba, perhaps, would not have given the poor the food he requested if not for the coincidental visit and present from his sister. The grant was merely an act of piety.

As such, all laws would be colored by this definition to limit grants to the standard of the donor. Indeed, even the law that states that he who is accustomed to be fed should be so fed is limited to a situation wherein the donor possessed that standard or the recipient was sick and, therefore, required such unusual treatment.[22]

A third qualifying theory of the biblical command is that it refers only to an individual whose poverty is not publicly known. Such an individual is provided with luxurious items to maintain his standard in order that his present poverty should not become a matter of public knowledge. Any individual, even one of former great affluence, of whom the community is aware of his condition of poverty, receives no special consideration and shares the grants alloted to the average poor.[23] The case of R. Nechemia would simply relate to a person who was known to be poor and, as a result, no special considerations were to be granted.

An astounding factor of the above three qualifying considerations of the biblical command is that they are not even mentioned in the Codes. In fact, only case one is noted by the general commentators of the Babylonian Talmud[24] and case two is mentioned only in the Jerusalem Talmud.[25] This suggests that the text of the Talmud may have had variant editions that simply deleted the cases other than that of Hillel. This then permits the biblical command to remain without limitation.

Maimonides states that one is obligated to give to the poor man according to his needs. Should he require clothing, household furnishings, or a mate, it was incumbent upon the donor to provide these items. If when wealthy, prior to the poor man's change in status, he was accustomed to have a horse to ride upon and a slave to run before him, there is an obligation to meet that need. Source—the biblical command to provide the poor "sufficient for his need (in that) which is wanting unto him."[26] In the authorized codes of R. Yaakov Ben Asher and R. Yosef Caro, the biblical command is defined in terms similar to that found in Maimonides. They even embellish the law by quoting the ancient source that states that one is required to actually spoon-feed the poor and provide warm bread if such was the poor man's custom prior to his poverty.[27]

Thus the biblical law is presented without any major limiting qualification. The only minor requirement was that the poor person should manifest needs that were evident prior to his condition of poverty. Needs developed while poor were not considered as obligatory to be provided. However, needs, even of a luxurious nature, if practiced while affluent, were required to be provided.

The vital implication is that the requirement was a personal obligation upon individuals and not upon communal funds. The story of Hillel serves as a prime example of an individual response to a need.[28]

The community had no requirement to meet the total needs of the poor and restore them to their previous state of affluence. Of course, the individual requirement to provide total needs relates only to individuals who possess the means to accomplish such a task. Indeed, the rabbis of the Talmud even put a limitation upon the total amount that a person should give each year to the poor. The Talmud relates that in Usha it was decreed that no more than one fifth of possessions should be given each year to the poor in order not to become also in need.[29] However, after the first year, one fifth of one's profit, not principal, is required to be granted to the poor.[30] (The Jerusalem Talmud maintains that this law was an ancient tradition that was forgotten through the passage of time and later reenacted in Usha.)

Yet, another decision is noted in the Codes that maintains that the obligation to provide the needs of a needy person according to the biblical command is not upon the individual but only upon the agent of the community or the community in unison. A person in need should inform the community or its agent of his need. Only a community is required to restore the prior status of affluence of a poor person. The obligation of the individual to maintain the biblical command is only when he is alone and does not live with his brethren.[31] This theory is further qualified to obligate the individual when the communal funds are insufficient to meet the demand and the individual has great affluence. The story of Hillel is, therefore, interpreted to imply a lack of funds on the part of the community.[32] (Indeed, this interpretation of communal responsibility stimulates a wide variety of interpretations of the case of Hillel, who was known not to be an agent of communal poverty funds. The variant that states that Hillel rented a horse and slave for the poor man,[33] rather than purchase one, is simply because only a community is required to actually purchase such an item for a poor person. An individual such as Hillel, therefore, only rented the items.[34] Also, the act of Hillel was not a requirement but an act of piety.[35] Indeed, one variation even notes that it was the slave who refused to run before the poor person and, therefore, Hillel himself provided the service for the poor.[36] It would, therefore, mean that Hillel wished not only to provide a service to the poor, but desired to teach his slave humility.)

Both interpretations of the biblical command appear to imply that either the community or the individual was required to supplant the poor with his former customs even if they were of a luxurious nature. Yet, even this assumption finds an alternative view in the commentaries. A medieval scholar maintains that the biblical command relates only to bare essential, nonexpensive items. The communal responsibility to purchase a home or clothing for poor orphans refers only to essential, nonexpensive items. The requirements of a horse to ride upon or a slave to run before the poor man are also qualified. They relate to a poor person who must make a journey or who finds that his community cannot sustain him and wishes to journey to a larger community. In such a case, his trip is made as comfortable as possible.[37] Perhaps a horse was provided to show the future community that he was a person of means and required substantial support. Luxury is to be provided only when essential to health. No needs are to be provided that are above the standards of the donor or the community. Even, moreover, the little extras provided to a poor person are only to be granted to one who previously had a status of wealth.[38] Thus, several alternative orientations existed for fulfillment of the biblical command.

The Beggar

Neither the community nor the individual was required to provide the needs of a poor person who went about from house to house to beg for sustenance. The biblical command was considered inapplicable to such a person. A communal agent of funds was not required to provide such a person with total needs, or even the fourteen-meal grant given to local poor once a week.[39] A mere token gift was given to him. Some contend that he received sufficient funds for at least one meal.[40] The same law applies to an individual's obligation to such a beggar.[41] Thus, the biblical command to provide total needs of the poor was reserved for those poor who were ashamed to go from house to house to publicly beg for sustenance. Beggars appeared to have sufficient means to acquire sustenance and needed neither communal funds nor special consideration. Also, since the beggar had acquired the habit of sustaining himself through such a vehicle, that sustenance is considered sufficient for his needs.[42]

This law is certainly a severe limitation of the biblical command. In fact, there is no alternative viewpoint noted. It lends, moreover, credence to the theory advanced by Rashi[43] that the *kupah* (citywide charity fund) was developed to care for the poor of good families (*b'nei tovim*). For this reason, perhaps, those who did not come from such families begged from house to house; the others, received *kupah* support. Also, the *kupah* provided funds for a week's sustenance; the beggar had such sustenance.

The biblical command to provide the needs of the poor thus had an objective and subjective factor. The objective factor was the actual previous condition of the poor man. That standard provided the amount of funds he was to receive. However, there was also a psychological social factor of shame or humiliation. The requirement of restoring a previous status was a process of providing dignity to the poor person. As long as he behaved in a dignified fashion and refused to humiliate himself by begging, then the community or individuals were required to provide him with the social ingredients of dignity. Once the individual manifested his personal lack of dignity – by begging – then the requirement to provide articles of dignity were not applicable.

Pe'ah, Leket, Shikchah

In ancient times, certain portions of the agricultural harvest were allotted to the poor. Based on biblical verses, rabbinical law designated three major grants at the annual harvest of grain: *pe'ah, leket,* and *shikchah.*[44]

Pe'ah was the requirement to leave to the poor one sixtieth of the field[45] at the conclusion of the harvest.[46]

Leket refers to the one or two ears of corn or grain that fell to the ground from the sickle or hand at the time of harvest.[47]

Shikchah was a sheaf of grain forgotten by workers and owner and left in the field.[48] These were considered a bounty to the poor and could not be retaken for the possession of the owner of the field.

In addition, several tithes were required of the owners of land at the time of the harvest. The first tithe, called *trumah*, was one fiftieth of the harvest that was given to the *kohen*, the descendant of Aaron the High Priest. After that distribution, one tenth of the remainder, called *maaser*, first measure (tithe) was given to any descendant of the tribe of Levi (who was not a *kohen*). From the remainder, one tenth was to be designated as the second *maaser* and was to be utilized during a pilgrimage to Jerusalem. Such was the procedure during the first, second, fourth, and sixth years of the calendar cycle. On the third year, however, instead of collecting the second tithe, used for the owner's benefit, a special poor man's *maaser* was collected. This was the same amount as the second *maaser* but was to be distributed solely to the poor. In lands owned by Jews outside of Israel, the poor man's tithe was given even on the seventh year.[49]

The Rabbinic Legal Response to Poverty

The rabbinic communal response to poverty was the establishment of two basic and several auxiliary funds.

Kupah—When Collected and Distributed

The basic fund was called *kupah*. The term refers to the rubber or straw box, or basket, used for the collection of funds and signified probably by its limited nature the necessity for immediate distribution.[50] Funds for the *kupah* were collected throughout the week and distributed the Friday afternoon prior to the Sabbath.[51]

Collection of Funds—Amounts Collected

The amount collected from each member of the community appears to have been based upon a prior communal assessment of

the financial ability of the donor.[52] As a result, the communal
agents had no permission to collect either more or less than the
assessed amount.[53] Yet, another source suggests two additional
alternatives for collecting funds. Either all communal members
gave to the *kupah* an approximately equal share or each gave an
amount voluntarily decided by the donor.[54]

The latter methods of collection appear to provide the communal agents with a degree of influence in the carrying out of
their task. To the extent each member of the community is not
assessed on the basis of personal wealth, it would suggest that
the agents may attempt by persuasion to increase the level of
each individual's contribution.

Number of Agents Required

In talmudic times a team of two individuals would serve as
collectors for the *kupah*, and a singular agent was not permitted
to be designated for this role. This was due to the communal
authority that these collectors possessed. The *kupah* collectors
had the right to force an individual to give to the *kupah* by taking
possession of some item of value equal to the amount required for
the *kupah*. Such communal authority was deemed by Jewish
traditions as too vital to be entrusted to a singular person.[55]

To the extent that sources reveal three alternative methods
of collecting funds, it would be logical to assume that the power of
coercion would directly relate to the vehicle of collection. In the
instance of assessment based on personal ability, the agents
would have the right to seek the total assessed *kupah* tax. When
all communal members gave equal sums, the agents would have
authority only equal to the amount given by others irrespective
of the personal wealth of the donor. In the situation of voluntary
amounts of contribution, then, it would appear that the agent
would have the greatest problem in ascertaining the amount to
be forcibly taken. The only logical consideration would be that an
amount equal to the lowest contribution of others would be
proper. Indeed, in such a situation, the individual could relieve
himself of all problems by giving merely a token contribution.

An Egyptian medieval rabbi noted that in his time most Jewish communities appointed only one person to serve as the *Kupah* collector. He contends that this does not violate Jewish tradition in that *kupah* collectors no longer in his time had the authority to lay claim to possessions of those who refused to contribute. As a result, the purpose of the requirement of two agents no longer had validity.[56] Yet no reference is made by European scholars of either the change in the number of *kupah* collectors required nor of the rescinding of authority of such collectors.

Residency Requirements for *Kupah* Collection and Distribution

Any person who moved into a town with intention to remain as a permanent citizen was required immediately to contribute to the weekly *kupah* fund on the first Friday after his arrival.[57] In addition, anyone who lived in a town for thirty days, even though he had no intention of permanently settling in that town, was required to contribute at that time to the *kupah*.[58] The thirty-day residency requirement for collection appears to be based on the requirement for distribution. *Kupah* funds were not granted to the poor from other towns. It was a specific grant to the local poor. The assumption was that anyone who lived in a town for thirty days had sufficient residency to qualify for receipt of *kupah* funds as a local poor citizen. Since a thirty-day residence would obligate the town to provide assistance, that period was considered sufficient to obligate an individual to contribute.[59]

In the Talmud, however, the residency requirement obligating contribution to the *kupah* was noted as three months. The thirty-day residency was utilized for another fund.[60] According to this custom, the residency requirement of the poor in order to receive *kupah* funds is not clear. Was it still thirty days to receive *kupah* funds even though contributions were not required until a three-month residency? In fact, the specific requirement of the poor to receive *kupah* funds is quite ambiguous. The Talmud and Codes merely stipulate that *kupah* funds be given only to the poor of the city and not to those who reside elsewhere.[61] Yet, clarity is not made on the residency requirement that enables one to be considered a member of the town. Since, however, even according to the talmudic version, there is another communal required response at thirty days, perhaps that time limit is sufficient residency for receipt of funds.

All previous discussion relates to customs prior to medieval times for the Codes note that in medieval times the custom was to utilize the thirty-day residency requirement for all funds and social matters.[62]

Kupah Distribution

Every Friday evening, prior to the Sabbath, each poor person was given funds to purchase sufficient food for one week.[63] The amount given was equal to that which would provide sufficient food for fourteen meals. In fact, he who had sufficient funds to provide fourteen meals was not permitted to take from the *kupah*.[64] The assumption was that poor people would have sufficient food for three required meals on the Sabbath–Friday night, Saturday morning, and Saturday afternoon just prior to evening–and then have two meals each day, morning and evening, and a morning meal on the following Friday. Thus, when the *kupah* funds would be distributed on the following Friday, the poor would then require another week's sustenance.[65]

Should an individual possess food for only twelve meals, he was permitted to receive *kupah* funds; for since he lacked a week's sustenance and *kupah* funds were distributed only on Friday afternoon, he would miss out on two meals were he required to await the following week's distribution.[66]

Rashi suggests a unique reason for the establishment of the *kupah*. He contends that it was enacted to sustain poor who were *B'nei tovim*. This term literally means sons of the good, or children of good people. It would imply poor of good families or those possessing good qualities. Such poor were ashamed to acquire their sustenance from a daily dole presented in the city. Therefore, a *kupah* fund was enacted that made a weekly distribution of funds sufficient for a week's sustenance.[67] The poor were thus shielded from the embarrassment of daily contacts with communal agents and would meet the agent only once a week.

It is suggested that the following is a preliminary motivation behind Rashi's unique concept. It was previously noted that a man who possessed less than fourteen meals was permitted to obtain funds from the *kupah*. It should also be noted that there was an additional communal fund, not the *kupah*, that provided meals on a daily basis to the poor.[68] It is possible that Rashi required an explanation as to why *kupah* agents had to be bothered with an individual who possessed funds for twelve meals. Could not these individuals sustain themselves for six days, and on the seventh receive food from the daily fund? In other words, the communal agents could put off involvement with such individuals for an entire week. It is, perhaps, for this reason that Rashi suggests the element of embarrassment in seeking food from the other source. The daily dole was set up for the poor who were strangers to the town.[69] Only those who had less than sufficient funds for two meals could utilize such a fund.[70] Thus, the fund dealt with only the most destitute. This fund, Rashi assumed, involved a stigma of degradation. As a result, the so-called "gentle poor" would be shielded from such involvement and permitted to receive funds from the weekly *kupah*.

Yet it appears that Rashi limits the *kupah* distribution to a certain class of people. If this be so, then the stipulation that the *kupah* was for local poor[71] is further qualified to mean local poor who come from good families or who possess certain high personal standards of conduct. Everyone else, including local citizens residing in the town on a permanent basis, would be directed to the daily dole. Thus the criterion for *kupah* was based not on need but on standard of stature and personal conduct. This would suggest that the communal agents not only had to discern the needs of those requesting *kupah* funds[72] but also which individuals had the personal standard that merited such consideration. The daily dole would be not specifically for strangers but for all who lacked the personal standards necessary for the *kupah*.

Thus, all previous mention of residency requirements would apply only to the citizens of virtue. Even they had to reside in town at least thirty days.

Yet, no mention is made of Rashi's theory in the Codes or the Commentaries. It could be assumed that the situation of a man possessing thirteen meals poses no serious question to them. The *kupah* was set up for local poor. The daily dole was set up for strangers. Anyone who lacked the residency requirement was directed to the daily communal dole. Citizens were given preferential treatment over strangers. The *kupah* was their agency for poverty funds. Whether it was for one meal or fourteen, local citizens had only the *kupah* to look to for assistance.

Daily *Tomchui*

To clearly note the distinctions between the *kupah* and the daily dole, some clarification must be presented.

The first distinction is that the *kupah* distributed funds, not food.[73] The daily dole distributed food, not funds.[74] Indeed, the term designated for the daily dole was *tomchui*. This was a dish used to collect food sometimes already cooked, fruit, etc., and distributed for the poor to eat on it.[75] Thus, the *tomchui* was not a communal fund but rather a communal process. Agents collected food in the morning and distributed it the same day in the afternoon.[76] It was set up for the poor "of the world."[77] This generally is interpreted to mean the poor from other cities, or those who do not fulfill the residency requirements for the *kupah*. The agents required similar degrees of trustworthiness and fame as those who collected for the *kupah*.[78]

A Comparison of the Collection and Distribution of the *Tomchui* and the *Kupah*

The number of the agents necessary for the *tomchui* differed somewhat from that required by the *kupah*. A minimum of two *kupah* agents could collect funds,[79] but a minimum of three was necessary for the distribution of the funds.[80] The requirement of the three for distribution was that it was considered necessary for the agents to make decisions on the amounts to be given to each individual. Such decisions were considered sufficiently important to be judged a monetary matter that required a court of three.[81] Thus the agents provided a judicial role. Just as in monetary cases, a court may take from one to give to another; so too, in the distribution of poverty funds, the court would perhaps increase the amount given to a person.[82] This discretion required the authority of a court of law. No individual was provided such authority. In Jewish law the minimum number necessary for a court of law was three judges.

Though the *tomchui* also required three judges (agents) for the distribution, it also required three agents for the collection.[83] There are two basic reasons for this requirement.

1. The amount of food daily collected from each individual had to be personally assessed by the agents themselves. Since a judgment was necessary, a court of three was required. In comparison with the three previously mentioned methods of collecting funds for the *kupah*, the *tomchui* collectors had greater discretion.[84]

2. The *kupah* collectors could not influence the amount granted. That was assessed by others. The *tomchui* agents made personal assessments based on the wealth of the donor. The second method of *kupah* collection was an equal amount from all citizens. In this case, the *tomchui* collection was personalized, with the collectors making the assessments. The third method of *kupah* collection was a voluntary amount given by all. The donor had the choice of selecting the amount given, not the agent. In the *tomchui* situation, the agents actually made daily assessments that could be taken by force should the donor not desire to give the amount selected.[85]

It is suggested that the *tomchui* agents were given greater authority, for they dealt with conditions of immediate urgency. Only those who had less funds or food to provide for two meals were permitted to utilize the *tomchui*.[86] Thus, if the agents failed to acquire the proper amounts necessary, people would immediately not eat. Also, it appears that many poor would merely be traveling from town to town.[87] In fact, it is suggested that the two-meal requirement was an amount given travelers in addition to one meal eaten immediately. Thus, the traveler had one day's food for his journey.[88] By providing the poor with an immediate dole, the poor would be able to move on and not remain in town. Thus, the agents would not wish to add to the burden of the town and, therefore, would attempt to immediately meet the needs of such poor and enable them to depart. Only poor strangers who remained in town overnight were required to be given, by the agent, sustenance for the evening, in addition to two meals. Such sustenance was a bed, a pillow, and oil. Also, the distribution on Friday was for three Sabbath meals rather than the daily two-meal grants.[89] Thus, the wandering poor who remained in town increased both qualitative and quantative services necessary to be provided by the *tomchui* agents.

Another reason for the requirement of three agents for the collection of the *tomchui* was a practical matter of expediency. Since food was collected each day and on the same day distributed by three agents, the community required an additional agent in the collection so that the agents should always be prepared for distribution and not delay matters by seeking out a third person.[90]

According to this practical requirement, it is possible that the *tomchui* agents had no greater discretion or power than the *kupah* collectors. One dealt with the local, poor, the other with the noncitizens. According to Rashi, one was involved with the elite poor, the other with the most destitute.

Residency Requirements

Citizens who lived in town for thirty days (even if not desirous of remaining permanent residents) were required to contribute to the *kupah*, while a three-month residency was necessary to obligate *tomchui* responsibility.[91] In the Talmud, the issue is reversed: three months for *kupah* and thirty days for *tomchui*.[92]

According to the former custom, it would appear that communal responsibility was primarily for the local citizenry. The community was more interested in providing funds for the local poor than for outsiders. In fact, Maimonides states that every Jewish community of record prior to and including his period of time always had a *kupah* fund. Yet, some communities possessed a *tomchui*, while others did not.[93] Thus, the deep-rooted historical tradition was a local fund for local citizens. Indeed, the *tomchui* was but a means of providing daily communal sustenance to the nonlocal poor. Such response was not necessary. Such poor could beg, could accumulate funds on a personal basis from door to door. This may have been the reason why all Jewish communities did not establish a *tomchui*.[94]

According to the talmudic version necessitating *tomchui* responsibility at thirty days, the assumption was that *kupah* was a luxury, an accommodation provided for the local poor. *Tomchui* was the necessity, for should funds not be collected, people would starve. Whether local or not, anyone living in a town for thirty days must support the daily poor—prior to any other obligation. Also, should the nonlocal poor not be cared for and sent away, the town could conceivably be inundated with the ranks of the poor who could not acquire the means to depart.

Thus, each fund had its necessity. However, it cannot be denied that the *kupah* fund catered to a more elite element than the *tomchui*.

Further *Kupah* Considerations

The *kupah* fund was an estimation of the amount of funds necessary to sustain each individual for a week, providing him with fourteen meals. In other words, three meals a day was not a necessity. Typical allotments were probably based on local normal eating habits. In fact, the requirement of three meals on the Sabbath is not based on habit but on biblical verses wherein both the term Sabbath and the word eat are mentioned three times.[95]

An alternative theory may be that everyone ate three meals a day, but it was not considered vital to so provide the poor. They were given just enough to keep them healthy.

Another consideration was that each person individually required a fourteen-meal diet. The fourteen-meal distribution was not a family total. It did not include the amount required by a man's wife.[96] The communal agents, therefore, had to assess a family total based on an individual family's needs.[97]

What is unique about this is that each family received funds, not food. Therefore, it was up to the family to decide how much to actually utilize for food, how many meals to eat, and where to spend the money. Thus, each family had discretion in the allocation of their own funds given to them. Of course, the assumption is that minimal amounts were given. But, should one member of the family skip a meal and utilize the funds for personal reasons, good or bad, it was his right to do so. The poor were not denied the right to beg and receive personal contributions of either food or funds. This again may permit the family to acquire certain aspects of necessity. As long as when the next Friday came along the individual still had not sufficient funds for fourteen meals, he was still provided again with funds.

The Poverty Line

The Talmud maintains that the possession of 200 *zuzim* (a form of money) disqualifies a person from taking LSP (*leket*, *shikchah*, and *pe'ah*) as well as the poor man's tithe.[98] This financial standard is extended in the Codes to prohibit any individual having 200 *zuzim* or more from receiving any form of charity.[99] One theory is that it was believed that 200 *zuzim* were sufficient for sustenance of food and clothing for one year.[100]

The difficulty with this theory is that it is not clear whether the 200-*zuzim* amount was the sum total available to a family or to an individual. Yet, previous sums noted as requirements for receipt of *kupah* and *tomchui* funds were personal amounts for each individual member of the family.[101] So, the 200-*zuzim* poverty line was not, perhaps, a family but a personal need of each family member. Also, since the sum was not altered by the degree of family size, it appears difficult to assume that the 200-*zuzim* sustenance was the criterion of family needs.[102]

Another theory is that the sum of 200 *zuzim* was a biblical standard for poverty. This theory is based on an analysis of biblical verses.

In the Leviticus chapter of vows it is written that the valuation of a male aged twenty to sixty was 50 *shekels* of silver.[103] Considering the situation of an individual who lacked this sum the Bible states that should a person be *mawch*, which is translated as "too poor for thy valuation," then the priest shall assess him personally based on his means.[104] Rashi interprets the Hebrew word *mawch* to mean he lacks the above noted sum of fifty *shekels* of silver.[105] In fact, even in the chapter on charity the term describing poverty is again the Hebrew word *mawch*. See, for example, "and if thy brother be waxen poor, and his means fail with thee; then thou shalt uphold him."[106]

Furthermore, in a talmudic discussion concerning the amount necessary for a slave owner to give his slave at the time of freedom R. Shimon states that the amount should be 50 *selas* (*sela'im* in Hebrew). R. Shimon's source appears to be a similarity of biblical terms. In one verse it states that a person who is *mawch*–poor–is sold into slavery.[107] In another verse it is written that one who is *mawch*–poor–lacks 50 *shekels* for valuation purposes.[108] Therefore the person was sold into slavery for he lacked 50 *shekels*, for such appears to be the definition of poverty. Consequently, at the time of freedom one is required to eliminate the cause of slavery by providing the former slave with 50 *selas*. Thus, the man is no longer poor.[109]

The preceding talmudic theory of R. Shimon interchanges the biblical monetary coin of *shekel* with the talmudic monetary coin of *sela*. In fact, there is a tradition that such coins were interchangeable.[110] Assuming each *sela* to contain 4 *zuzim*, the biblical poverty line of 50 *shekels*, or 50 *sela'im*, would equal 200 *zuzim*.[111]

Therefore, the poverty line was an ancient standard irrespective of social conditions or family size.

Yet, such a theory, in addition to being a somewhat strained biblical interpretation, lacks basic substantiation. Maimonides contends that a *sela* was worth 4 *dinarim*, and each *dinar* was equal to 6 *zuzim*.[112] Thus a *sela* would equal 24 *zuzim*. Even if it would be accepted that the biblical poverty line was 50 *sela'im*, then in terms of *zuzim* the amount would be 1,200 rather than 200.

Yet, it is possible that in early times the monetary coins *zuz* and *dinar* were also interchangeable. In the *Mishnah* it is written that a person who possesses 200 *zuzim* was not permitted to partake in the agricultural allotments to the poor. "If he possessed 200 [*zuzim*] less a *dinar*, he may take [from the agricultural allotment] even 1,000 at one time."[113] If a *dinar* was worth 6 *zuzim*, as contended by Maimonides, then the law appears somewhat difficult to understand. For if 200 *zuzim* was the poverty line, then anything less than 200 *zuzim* permitted the individual to accept poverty funds. Why present an example of 194 *zuzim*? Should, however, *zuz* equal a *dinar*, then the law is totally understandable. A person having even one *zuz* less than the poverty line may accept poverty funds.

Thus, the origin of the 200-*zuzim* poverty line is not clear. However, the rabbis did make qualitative distinctions concerning which assets of a person were included in the 200-*zuzim* poverty line.

Personal Belongings

The first distinction is that not all personal belongings were included in the 200 *zuzim* to invalidate a person from receiving poverty funds. Exceptions were made.

In one mishnaic law it overtly states that if a person possessed 200 *zuzim* he was not permitted to take part in the agricultural tithes set aside for the poor. Yet, "he is not required to sell either his home nor his utensils."[114] This law is quoted with no alternative viewpoint. In the Jerusalem version of the Talmud, it is even noted that if he had two garments, one for the Sabbath and one for the rest of the week, he was not required to sell his garments.[115] Thus, the 200-*zuzim* poverty level was for sustenance independent of essential possessions. Yet, in a different section of the Talmud another law is posed as contradictory to this law. It is stated that if a man was accustomed to golden utensils, he should (if poor) use only silver utensils; if he was previously accustomed to silver utensils, he should make do with only copper ones.[116] The implication was that a person who became poor was required to sell his possessions and accustom himself with less luxurious habits. To this question the Talmud provides two responses. The first is that only purely luxurious items such as a silver comb used in a bathhouse[117] were required to be sold; however, essential items (even if expensive) may be retained even though the individual collected funds allotted to the poor. The second response is that retention of personal items was permitted only prior to taking from the "dole." Once a person took from the "dole," then sale of possessions was required.[118] The latter response was further articulated by post-talmudic commentators. The basic interpretation was that as long as the person received support privately from a few individuals, he was not required to sell possessions; however, should the individual seek communal *kupah* funds, then no allotment was provided unless possessions were sold.[119] Maimonides and the Codes clarify this interpretation. They contend that in such a case sale is required of expensive items even of an essential nature, such as beds and tables, in order to purchase simple practical items.[120] Thus, the poor may have possessions, but nothing of great value in order to qualify for communal funds.

Both talmudic responses were considered noncontradictory and were placed into law.[121] Thus, an individual who received private charity was required to sell his nonpractical items. He was permitted to maintain essential utensils even of extreme value. Once he, however, requested communal funds, he was required to subsist on only those items that were practical and inexpensive. The reason behind this law was that once an individual submits to communal funds, he is vying for money that belongs to the poor. At that time, he has no right to take such funds unless he is similar to them in general possessions. He must sell personal possessions before he can decrease the *kupah* fund.[122] Any attempt to acquire *kupah* funds when considered above the poverty line may be considered as an act of theft of money belonging to the poor.[123]

Other interpretations of the second response in the Talmud provide a variety of legal implications and variant customs. Rashi suggests that no sale of possessions was required for any individual who had less than 200 *zuzim* apart from the value of his essential items. Such a person could take from the agricultural tithes as much as any poor person. However, should the court ascertain that the individual possessed 200 *zuzim* and yet still took the agricultural tithes, then the court may repossess that which he took illegally. The talmudic term *grevoi* is interpreted not as "dole" but as repossessing. Should an individual illegally acquire from the dole, then the court has a right to sell his possessions and force the individual to make do with inexpensive items.[124]

According to Rashi, acceptance of *kupah* funds was not a demeaning process that required the recipient to be equal to other poor people. As previously noted, Rashi maintained that the original establishment of the *kupah* was to provide help for the poor of good families.[125] The other poor could seek their help from the daily *tomchui* dole. As a result, no effort should be made to restrict their possessions and thus further demean their status. No concern should be made over decreasing the funds available to the poor. *Kupah* funds were a polite method of caring for those of status who were in need.

A third interpretation is that of Rabbeinu Tam. He contends that prior to acquiring communal funds a person is obligated to sell his expensive possessions if worth more than 200 *zuzim*. Once a person takes from communal funds and subsequently somehow acquires expensive items, he is then not obligated to sell his possessions.[126] The implication is that the poor man is judged at the time he requires public poverty funds. Should at that moment his total possessions be less than 200 *zuzim*, then he may obtain the funds. Any additional acquisition after that date does not invalidate the receipt of poverty funds. He is under no obligation to repay such funds to the community. This is comparable to the case of a poor man who became wealthy and is under no obligation to repay poverty funds collected.[127]

A fourth interpretation is noted by R. Channiel.[128] He maintains that sale of property is required only if a person accepts funds from the *kupah*. However, if he takes from the agricultural tithes he need not sell any possessions.[129] According to this interpretation, a poor individual may publicly acquire the agricultural tithes. In fact, the agricultural tithes are not equated with the communal *kupah* funds. Agricultural tithes were personal requirements of any individual who possessed land. They were in no way a communal endeavor. No community taxes were collected. This interpretation differs from the first in that it permits publicity as long as collection is not from a communal source. The first interpretation is that anything available to the general poor, even agricultural tithes, are not to be permitted to a man who has major assets. Also, the first interpretation has the implication that permission to collect funds from individuals should not be done in a public manner. Indeed, the theory is presented that *kupah* funds are distributed by three agents of the community and have a public nature to them and, therefore, are prohibited. The only permissible funds are those acquired privately, at night.[130]

Though the first interpretation is codified into law,[131] the others provide insight into the various ramifications of the law. They suggest the difficulty of harmonizing two distinct ancient traditions: the requirement that the poor must sell personal property and the sensitivity that the poor should be able to retain possessions.

Capital Assets

The 200 *zuzim* did not refer to all types of people. Persons who were in business and possessed 50 *zuzim* were not permitted to acquire funds from the *kupah*.[132] The reason was that those with business acumen were able to earn 200 *zuzim* with an investment of only 50 *zuzim*. Thus, the 200-*zuzim* poverty line referred only to those who were idle and not able to increase their principal amount.[133]

A situation could occur wherein one person possessed 199 *zuzim*, lacked business or investment ability, was idle the whole year, and could still acquire poverty funds. Yet, another would possess 50 *zuzim*, work at his business to sustain himself to provide the 200 *zuzim* during the year, and could not acquire anything from poverty funds. It appears that the business effort expended by one or the idleness of the other in no way disturbed the administrators of the poverty laws. The poverty line was geared to ability. The person who couldn't increase his investment was to be sustained. No mention is made of training him to be adept at business. Each person was judged on personal merit, and two distinct poverty lines were developed.

The 200-*zuzim* poverty line was further qualified to refer to those funds apart and independent from monies pledged to a creditor or to a wife as part of a marriage contract to be given at divorce.[134] To the extent that such monies were pledged to others, the person is considered poor.[135] The Jerusalem Talmud contends that the law refers even to a creditor who is not pressing the debtor for his funds. This inference is based on the juxtaposition of the case of creditor to the case of the marriage contract. The latter refers to a contract signed at marriage to provide the bride with a stipulated sum of money in the event of a divorce. To the extent that prior to a divorce such funds are exempt from the poverty line, even though there is no obligation to give such funds to a woman while married to her, it clearly demonstrates that pledged funds are exempt from inclusion in the poverty line without regard to any consideration concerning the immediacy of repayment.[136]

The aforementioned qualification of the Jerusalem Talmud creates an ambiguity to this law. To the extent that the pledged funds need not be immediately repaid, it does appear logical that a distinction should be made as to whether the individual is able to do business and earn money or lacks investment and business ability. In the former situation the poverty level should be 50 rather than 200 *zuzim*, as the previous law stated. This logical distinction is maintained by a later commentary that acknowledges that no mention of this item is found in the codes.[137]

A further difficulty is that the aforementioned law relates to a married man and yet still discusses the poverty line of 200 *zuzim*. This suggests that the 200 *zuzim* was a family total rather than a need of an individual. A possible answer may be that the law relates only to the needs of the male member of the household. The female or any other member of the family was judged independently of the male.[138]

Nonpersonal Property

All previous distinctions noting that property need not be sold in order to acquire communal poverty funds refer only to such property used by an individual as a residence. However, land and real estate valued 200 *zuzim* and more that are not utilized as a residence for the individual must definitely be sold in order to acquire poverty funds.[139] Anyone possessing such property is not considered a poor person and the acquisition of poverty funds would be an act of theft of money belonging to the poor.[140] Yet, even such property was not sold under terms detrimental to the seller. Based on market conditions the following qualifications were made.

In a circumstance where land generally has a higher market value in the spring than in the fall—example: worth 200 *zuzim* in the spring and only 100 *zuzim* in the fall—the individual, in the fall, is in a quandary. He is neither rich nor poor. He is not considered poor, for his assets will definitely be worth 200 *zuzim* in a few months. He is not rich, for at present, in the fall, his property is not worth 200 *zuzim*.[141] Since seasonal fluctuations (in those times) did not decrease more than one half of the standard market value,[142] the individual was permitted to acquire communal poverty funds in the fall up to one half the value of his property.[143] Thus he receives 100 *zuzim* from poverty funds and may sell his property for 100 *zuzim* and thus be invalidated from future poverty funds.

Another interpretation of the law is that in a seasonal low market the individual is never required to sell at a loss. Such a person must be sustained by communal funds until the market changes. If the seasonal fluctuation of price brought the property to less than 200 *zuzim*, then he is definitely within the status of the poor and may acquire even 1,000 *zuzim* from poverty funds. Should the property be valued more than 200 *zuzim* even in the fall, he is still permitted to obtain poverty funds. In such a case, however, he may not obtain any amount given him, but only up to one half the value of the property price in the spring. No attention is made concerning the actual drop in price. Since general fluctuations are no more than one half of the market value in the spring, that amount is the total permitted to be given him from both communal and private poverty funds.[144] Such funds, moreover, were given on a day-to-day basis.[145]

A variant of this interpretation is that the individual is permitted to acquire as much funds as he receives until he is able to acquire a purchaser willing to buy the property at one half of its spring market value.[146] According to this variation, the rabbis merely did not want the seller to lose more than the normal 50 percent decrease of market value. As long as no such purchaser was available, the seller could acquire as much as was given to him. Once a purchaser was available, he could receive nothing.

In a circumstance wherein general property values were high but a person's property values were down simply because all knew he was in need of cash then, the individual may obtain poverty funds in any amount until such a time when he is able to sell his property at the regular market price.[147]

A nonaccepted variant of this law is that under such a circumstance, the individual should not be permitted to receive anything from poverty funds. By publicly seeking funds, he is at fault for personally depressing his own market and is, therefore, not to receive poverty funds.[148]

Spatial Dimension of Poverty

A further qualification is that poverty had a spatial dimension.

It is written that a traveler in need may acquire the agricultural bounty set aside for the poor (LSP) in the area where his need developed.[149] The assumption is that he has spent his funds and is not able to acquire food for sustenance.[150] Yet the source states that when the individual returns to his home, wherein it is assumed he possesses assets above the poverty line, there is a debate as to whether he is obligated to repay that which he acquired in his moment of need. R. Eliezer maintains repayment is required. The sages contend that "at the time of need he was poor" and, therefore, he has no requirement of repayment.[151]

R. Eliezer's view is qualified in the Jerusalem Talmud to be an obligation to repay the value not to any poor person, nor to any communal fund but to the poor of the area from which he acquired poverty funds.[152] The obligation is not viewed as a generous act of piety, but a legal obligation[153] and that the poor of that specific town may even initiate court action to coerce repayment.[154] However, a variant reading does not state "when he returns to his home," but only "when he returns he is required to repay."[155] This variant is interpreted to mean that repayment is required when the individual returns to the city wherein he acquired funds.[156] This may mean that should he never return to that city, then no repayment is required.

In the Codes, the opinion of the sages is enacted as law and the view is considered applicable not only to agricultural bounty but also to poverty funds.[157]

The view of the sages is further articulated to be comparable to a person who was poor–collected poverty funds–and later became wealthy. Such a person is not obligated to repay poverty funds.[158] The implication is that the traveler also lacked the ability to borrow money. For, if he were able to acquire funds through other vehicles rather than through communal poverty funds, then he was not permitted to acquire communal funds.[159]

Even though the comparison is not perfect, for the traveler does possess funds in another area, he is still considered to have the status of a poor person, for at present he has an immediate need. Maimonides does mention that while a legal requirement of repayment does not exist, some form of repayment in the realm of gracious piety should be considered.[160] Yet, in the Codes even this obligation is not mentioned.[161]

An interesting observation not reflected in the Commentaries is the reason presented for the need of the traveler for communal funds. The original source merely states that the traveler is required to accept communal funds. Yet, no mention is made as to the reason for such a requirement.[162] Later commentaries codify into the law the statement that the traveler has "depleted his money and lacked funds for sustenance."[163] The implication is that there is an immediate need of urgency.

An alternative interpretation is that the traveler depleted his funds for business purposes and lacked 200 *zuzim*. R. Eliezer's requirement of repayment is due when the wares are sold and funds are received upon return of the traveler home.[164]

According to this interpretation, lack of funds is not a spatial limitation but a dimension of time. The traveler has not the availability of assets. In some fashion he may be comparable to the debtor who cannot utilize his assets because of a requirement of repayment and to a real estate owner who lacks funds due to adverse market conditions. This case relates to business investments. He may be rich in assets but poor in cash. He is and is not poor at the same period of time. To some extent he is responsible for his condition. For this reason, R. Eliezer requires repayment when his cash is obtained. Permission to obtain communal poverty funds is a form of a loan that must be repaid. The sages' view enacted into law is that poverty is a status of immediacy irrespective of future speculations.

Yet, the Codes of Jewish Law appear to reject the preceding considerations by maintaining that the motivation for the traveler's need was an immediate requirement for food. This suggests the spatial dimension of poverty. The fact that assets or cash may be in abundance at a place inaccessible to the individual does not invalidate a condition of poverty. Thus, a person is poor who merely lacks access to funds.

It is possible that this law is based on the consideration of yet another principle.

In addition to the *kupah* and *tomchui*, there were other communal funds. In fact, a person who resided in a town for at least six months was required to contribute to a special fund to provide clothing for the poor. Should he reside in a town for nine months, then he was required to also contribute to a burial fund to provide the burial needs of the poor.[165] This assessment was obligatory only on residents but not on businessmen whose family resided in another area.[166]

The Talmud relates a debate of scholars regarding the investigation of the requests of the poor. R. Huna maintains that a poor person who says he is hungry and needs sustenance must be investigated prior to any grant to discern the validity of his request. However, should he be naked and request clothing, then he must be immediately clothed to eliminate the shame of his exposure or tattered condition. R. Yehudah disagrees and maintains a request for food implies a condition of physical want and pain and must be immediately cared for. A request, however, for clothing, must be investigated.[167] The view of R. Yehudah is enacted as law, yet a further qualification is made. Should the individual be prominent or well known, then even a request for clothing is granted immediately without any investigation.[168] The clothing given to such a person would be in accordance to his status.[169]

Thus, not everyone requesting aid was cared for. The possibility of misrepresentation or falsehood to acquire communal funds must have been sufficiently evident to require formal investigation of claims. Yet, an investigation concerning a request for clothing in no way involved a danger to the poor. However, a request for food implied an immediate danger to the health of the individual. Hence, no time was wasted and the poor was cared for immediately.[170]

It is, perhaps, for this reason that the commentaries maintain that the traveler (in the previous law) depleted his funds and had not food for sustenance. Such an individual would not be investigated prior to granting him his needs. In fact, in the ancient times of the agricultural bounty, such a person would be permitted to acquire not only 200 *zuzim* but as much as he could obtain from the fields. As was previously noted, once a person was under the poverty line, he was permitted to accept even 1,000 at one time.[171] Hence, only after the claimant acquired his agricultural bounty was an investigation made, and it was noted that the individual possessed assets in another locale. Yet, the wording in the Codes is that a person maintaining hunger is fed. Whether this limits the grant to merely a meal or more is not clear.

Basis of Communal Funds

The basis of the rabbinic tradition of communal funds was the belief and the tradition that any donation or grant to the poor should be accomplished with the least element of embarrassment to the poor. Maimonides lists eight levels of charity. The highest level is the support of an individual through loans, gifts, business, or partnership prior to a man's fall from affluence. It is the essential help of another by sustaining him in a way so that he should not even become poor.[172] The second highest level is the situation wherein the donor knows not the recipient and the recipient knows not the donor. An example of such charity was the silent treasury fund of the ancient Temple. The righteous gave silently, and the poor of good families were supported silently. Comparable to that ancient fund (and in the same category) are the communal *kupah* funds.[173]

The ancient fund was called the silent fund because of the manner by which funds were contributed and distributed.[174] A tradition also maintains that each ancient city had a similar fund.[175] This ancient fund was considered on a somewhat higher level than the *kupah*. For in the former, the agent of the fund knew not the contributor, while in the *kupah* the contributor was known.[176] However, in the *kupah* still neither the donor knew the recipient nor the recipient the donor. With such a tradition, it is understandable that the rabbis assumed that all grants to the poor should be channelled through the vehicle of agents to protect the integrity of the poor.

A Critical Analysis of Biblical and Rabbinic Traditions

A key to the understanding of the rabbinic traditions may be noted by a law in the *Tur* of Rabbi Yaakov ben Asher, a fourteenth-century codification of Jewish law. He writes that the 200-*zuzim* poverty line was not applicable in his time. Indeed, such a measurement of poverty referred only to ancient times wherein the agricultural bounty (LSP) and the poor tithe as well as *kupah* and *tomchui* funds existed. At that time it was established that he who had 200 *zuzim* should not be permitted to obtain communal funds or the agricultural bounty, for such was sufficient to sustain a person for a year. (Should the person's funds be depleted after the year, then the agricultural bounty that was always available could be provided.) Since the agricultural bounty was no longer available, a person may obtain poverty funds as long as he did not possess sufficient principal that provides a profit and the person was able to sustain himself from such profit. The fact that the law maintains that one who possesses 50 *zuzim* that can bring a profit was invalidated from acquiring poverty funds shows that the law pertained to a specific time and place wherein it was possible to sustain oneself for a year with the normal profit of 50 *zuzim*. Yaakov R. ben Asher concludes that in his time it was impossible to support oneself with the profit earned on 50 *zuzim*.[177] This radical change in law was reported in the authoritative Codes of R. Yosef Caro (known as "*Shulchan Aruch*," 1564). Indeed, he even further qualifies the law by stating that poverty funds may be obtained as long as a person does not have principal that provides a sufficient profit to support himself and his family.[178] The original source for this law appears to be a ruling by R. Shlomo ben Aderet, a thirteenth-century talmudist who maintained all depended on one's needs.[179] To the extent that R. Moshe b. Yisrael Isserles (the venerated sixteenth-century scholar whose notes on Caro's Codes established the law for the European Ashkenazic communities) made no comment on this law,[180] it appears to have been an accepted fact at that time by all phases of Jewish cultural influence. Yet, the third major codification of law, the earlier work of Maimonides in the twelfth century, makes no reference in his consideration of the poverty line between ancient or modern (meaning medieval) times. The poverty line was fixed by Maimonides as 200 *zuzim*. Also, it is contended that the compendium of Rabbi Mordecai ben Hillel, a thirteenth-century halachist (scholar of Jewish law), maintains that the 200-*zuzim* poverty line was applicable in his period of time.[181]

Thus, we note that a shift of thinking concerning the poverty line developed in the thirteenth century, and from the fourteenth to the sixteenth century it became widely accepted that it was a figure proper only to a particular historical period of time. This suggests that prior to talmudic times it is possible that 200 *zuzim* was not the poverty line at all.

This would mean that prior to talmudic times one of three alternative poverty lines existed. One, the 200-*zuzim* figure was extremely ancient in origin, dating back to the Bible. The change occurred only after the Jews were exiled or had no land to provide the agricultural bounty. This position would appear contrary to logic. Just as social conditions in later generations altered the feasibility of the 200-*zuzim* poverty line, so too would changing conditions prior to talmudic times. (A suggestion that social conditions remained constant from biblical to talmudic times cannot be maintained.)

A second possibility was that prior to talmudic times the poverty line was not 200 *zuzim* but, rather, some objective standardized criteria. Just as the 200-*zuzim* poverty line was applicable to all, so too were all previous poverty lines. Each generation established objective criteria to define poverty. Also, the 200 *zuzim* was merely that minimum amount determined that could sustain a person for a year. Therefore, ability to sustain oneself for a year according to certain minimum requirements may have been the constant poverty line. The exact amount of such minimum yearly requirement would depend on social and economic conditions. The contention that a sustenance for a year was the constant poverty line appears not to be noted in the revision of the law articulated in the Codes of R. Yaacov ben Asher and R. Yosef Caro. In fact, Caro merely states that a person should have sufficient profit for family sustenance. Nowhere is it mentioned that the duration of the sustenance should be for a year. Also, no mention or clarification is made as to objective criteria to determine an individual's minimum needs. The implication is that each person is the sole judge of his own needs. This argument is somewhat substantiated by the language that is directed to the individual, rather than to the communal agents.[182] This radical departure from objectivity suggests that such a form may have occurred in the past. Thus, the second alternative is not rejected but is a possible understanding of the history of the poverty line. Yet, a discussion of the third alternative will disclose that the second alternative is not plausible and is also not substantiated by documentation.

The third alternative is that in biblical times poverty had no objective criteria. It was a relative state of affairs, a personal condition of need based probably on the relative standard of one's community. Nowhere in the Bible is a poverty line articulated. Nowhere in the Bible is poverty explicitly defined. In the passage of the Bible obligating one to help the poor the Hebrew word used is *evyon*.[183] This term is generally translated to mean a "needy person." Rashi defines *evyon* as one who is desirous of things.[184] Probably based on Rashi, Samson Raphael Hirsch in his translation of the Bible calls the *evyon* "a necessitous man."[185] The poor person was not the destitute man, the person without the means to actually exist who, without a grant, would starve. Such people definitely were helped. Indeed, the biblical command to not harden one's heart to the pleas of such people would appear superfluous. The Bible is talking to all men, not to the cruel and arrogant. Who is he who would withhold himself from the plea of a starving man? The Bible, rather, is addressing a unique form of poverty, a poverty defined by the needs of the poor person himself. The individual himself establishes his status by his own perception of his needs.

This concept corresponds to the ancient definition of wealth noted in the moral maxims of the *Ethics of the Fathers*. Ben Zoma said, "Who is wealthy? He who is happy with his lot."[186] If wealth is a sense of satisfaction, then the converse must define poverty. Poverty could be a personal state of dissatisfaction and desire.[187]

This definition provides a major distinction between biblical and rabbinic law. Biblical law defined poverty in terms of personal relative needs; rabbinic law defined poverty in terms of objective economic needs.

This distinction between biblical and rabbinic responses may be noted in a reference made by Rabbi Moses ben Yosef Mitrani, a sixteenth-century contemporary of R. Yosef Caro. In his famous treatise, which provides a summation of the laws of Maimonides and the sources for such laws, he makes the following terse comments. The establishment of communal poverty agents and their process of collection and distribution were developed by rabbinic law. Biblical law requires a response to the needs of the poor at a time when the poor has such a need. The rabbis, however, decreed by the establishment of communal agents that funds should be available for a time of need. Also, biblical law permits a poor person to obtain all that he needs. Scriptural law would not require a person to sell his golden utensils even if he obtained poverty funds.[188] Thus the previously mentioned contradictory laws regarding the sale of personal assets and the numerous observations on that law basically reflect two distinct orientations to poverty,[189] a biblical and a rabbinic response.

Yet, these notes of this scholar provide still a further major distinction between the two traditions. The scriptural response was to individuals solely and not to any institutionalized communal agents. The Bible speaks to each man. Just as other commandments throughout the Pentateuch were directed to the individual, so too was the response to the biblical dimension of poverty. Indeed, nowhere in Scripture is found an obligation for a community to care for the poor. No reference or even hint is suggested that a community establish a communal fund. The agricultural bounty was a personal obligation of each person who owned land. The entire scope of the biblical response was a personal relationship between the donor and the recipient. A contemporary scholar contends that the source of the obligation to establish a *kupah* is not the commandment of charity but, rather, the inherent right of a community to establish laws for its own betterment.[190]

Talmudic or traditional rabbinic law is an attempt to interpret biblical law. The Pentateuch serves as a guide or standard for all legal discussions, and all rabbinic decrees or interpretations must be compatible with scriptural law or traditional practices. Whenever a law is discussed that appears to contradict a biblical passage, some means of harmonizing the biblical quote with the law discussed is presented.

An example of this would be the talmudic debate concerning the standardized greeting made before a bride. The School of Hillel maintained that all should make a statement praising the bride's charm and beauty. Immediately, the problem is posed concerning a bride not known for her beauty. If one praises her beauty, is it not a violation of the biblical injunction against telling a lie? The implication is that a falsehood or white lie is always wrong regardless of the circumstance. The Talmud answers this question by stating that the biblical injunction does not apply when the withholding of the complete truth creates family harmony and peace.[191] The original law is thus qualified and limited.

The numerous charity customs may have been a result of the need to harmonize the biblical definition and response to the rabbinic communal institutionalized approach. On the one hand a tradition to provide a man with even superfluous needs irrespective of his assets, on the other hand an obligation to provide subsistence only if he lacked 200 *zuzim*. The biblical law could not be simply discarded. That was alien to the rabbinic mind. It had to have relevance yet could not contradict current practices.

The first major[192] modification was the definition of need or poverty. Poverty meant less than 200 *zuzim*. Anyone who possessed more than that amount was simply not poor. The biblical command to help the needy meant only for one who lacked 200 *zuzim*. The second emendation was that the response was limited to basic necessities. The biblical command of providing needs such as a horse to ride upon related only to one who previously possessed such a standard.[193] To the others, only basics were provided. The third clarification was that the obligation of luxury was incumbent upon the community and not the individual. It was a relationship of the community to the recipient and not of the individual to the recipient. A poor person is not one with needs or desires but one who lacks objectively determined criteria essential for existence. Once a person has sufficient for existence, communal funds should not be squandered on the attainment of personal luxuries. The tradition of not selling assets was modified to apply only when he does not acquire communal funds. The communal response was considered a means of protecting the integrity of the poor. A beggar who sought sustenance from house to house was considered to be involved in a most humiliating practice. As a result, the community had no responsibility to him. Not only was there no need to protect his pride (for what pride had a beggar), there was also no need to provide funds. The beggar not only negatively valued his level of consumption, but also his former status.

Biblical and Rabbinic Responses

At issue is the rationale for setting up a rabbinic response. Why was it necessary? It is our contention that meaning to the divergent biblical and rabbinic responses to poverty may be gleaned from an understanding of a shift in mentality that took place as Jews altered their original modes of residence.

Numerous verses in Deuteronomy state that biblical law was to be actualized upon the inheritance of the land of Canaan.[194] Indeed, the specific command to help the needy relates the law to the land to be given to the Hebrew people. "If there be among you a needy man, one of thy brethren, within any one of thy gates, in thy land which the Lord thy God giveth thee . . . thou shalt open thy hand unto him, and shalt surely lend him sufficient for his needs."[195] Thus, the response to poverty was to be actualized in ancient Israel (Canaan).

Upon entering Canaan a process of land distribution occurred. The land was divided between the tribes of Israel and further subdivided according to the major families of each tribe.[196] This process was based on a biblical stipulation.[197] Thus, each person basically lived in the geographical domain of his tribe and the local domain of his family. The social relationship was, therefore, one based upon family ties.

An example of the utilization of family ties may be noted in the story of Avimelech, son of Gideon. Gideon had seventy sons from several wives. One son, Avimelech, was born to a woman from the city of Shechem. Upon the death of Gideon, Avimelech went to his mother's family in Shechem and told them to ask the people to decide whether they wished seventy rulers or one; also, to have them mention, "I am your bone and flesh." The family spoke to the people, and it is recorded that "their hearts inclined to follow Avimelech; for they said: 'He is our brother.' "[198]

In addition, the people were tied to the land through agriculture. This is noted through the various commandments relating to the harvest,[199] as well as the entire history of the people.[200] The dispersion of the Jews from the land occurred in great measure when the Assyrian and Babylonian kings uprooted a certain portion of the people from the land and scattered them throughout the world. Also, a portion was dispersed due to voluntary reasons for purposes of business and trade. It is suggested that this occurred in the times of Solomon when certain groups began to be concerned with sea trade. Yet, throughout history, "the vast majority . . . (of Jews) in Israel were bound to the soil."[201]

The conquests of various kings resulted in the development of two distinct communities: a Jewish Diaspora and a Jewish homeland.

It is maintained that Jewish economic life in the Diaspora in the Hellenistic period (323–330 B.C.E.) was not the one-sidedness of ghetto life in the Middle Ages. The people were not engaged in business alone. They were governmental officials, merchants, farm laborers, and so forth. They were involved in almost every rank of social life. They lived in large cities as well as in rural towns.[202] Though they had comparable professions to the Jews in Judea, a major economic distinction existed between the two communities. In Judea, the decisive majority of the people were tillers of the soil; the merchants and others were a comparatively small minority. In the Diaspora, the merchants and nonagricul-

tural professions were the majority and the farmers a distinct
minority. The Jews of the Diaspora were, therefore, primarily
concerned with nonindustrial trades, while the Jews of Judea
were basically concerned with agriculture.[203] (It is interesting to
note that the oral tradition was put into the complete written
form called the *Mishnah* by Rabbi Yehudah the Prince in the
early part of the third century C.E.[204] The *Amora'im*, the
teachers who developed, elaborated, and discussed the laws of
the *Mishnah*, are found in a work called *Gemara*. The Palestinian
Gemara, based on the research of Palestinian scholars, was
compiled at the end of the fourth century C.E., and the Babylonian
Gemara, with research by the Babylonian scholars, was completed in the beginning of the fifth century C.E.[205] The *Mishnah*
and *Gemara* together are called Talmud.)

Thus the Babylonian Talmud, which is the major resource of
Jewish law, was completed in an era wherein the majority of
people were not involved in agriculture. Even the minority in
agriculture were not living in their homeland.

The ancient Jew, after the division and distribution of land in
Canaan, lived a form of rural agricultural life that may be
characterized by the theoretical model of a *Gemeinschaft*. To
articulate this view it is necessary to describe the typological
distinctions between *Gemeinschaft* and *Gesellschaft* suggested
by Tonnies.

Gemeinschaft

Tonnies contends that "all intimate, private and exclusive living
together" is life in a *Gemeinschaft*. In such a world, "one lives
from birth on, bound to it in weal and woe."[206] It is a natural form
of relationship based on feelings of family ties, kinship (blood
relations), and friends and is characterized by a common
habitat.[207] A relationship of brothers is a natural *Gemeinschaft*
relationship for it is based on origin rather than on motive.[208] It
is a situation wherein the existence of the relationship (kinship,
friendship) is not dependent on rational will. It is, rather, the act
of birth that determines the relationship.[209] The basis of com-

munal relationships are oft-repeated customs, folkways, and mores. Where clan and community coincide, the community itself is viewed as one large family.[210] The positive task of such traditions is to affirm and nurture individual relationships and make friendly action and aid a duty.[211] Alms in a *Gemeinschaft* is an expression of a natural general sympathy for the recipient, a general duty, and a simple desire to help.[212] The normal manifestation of its mentality is in the house, village, and small town, the town being the highest or most complex form of social life. When the town develops into a city, *Gemeinschaft* relationships are almost entirely lost.[213]

Gesellschaft

A *Gesellschaft* "is public life." One enters into it "as one who goes into a strange country."[214] It is based on the rational exchange principle that "I give so that you give." The relationship is based on the end result motivated by a rational transaction. Thus, the process or the relationship itself is of no real concern or merit.[215] It is not a natural form of human relationship but a mechanical construct.[216] There is not total involvement with another. Spheres of activity with others are limited, and total knowledge of others is not found. Its relationships are segmented. Intrusion into private spheres of activity are characterized as hostile acts. Property acquires an aura of exclusivity.[217] Every person seeks those actions that provide personal gain and affirms the actions of others only insofar as they further his interests.[218] The more extensive the arena of trade, the more the society tends to be a *Gesellschaft*.[219] The giving of alms is based on a rational reason: either to rid the unpleasant sight of the beggar or to show generosity and thus sustain a role of generosity.[220]

Thus, a *Gemeinschaft* or *Gesellschaft* relationship creates the framework of a response to the needs of another. In a *Gemeinschaft*, the existence of the relationship between the donor and the recipient precedes the immediate social interaction. A family member, because of his familial ties, requires a positive response regardless of the merits of the individual. The relationship is total and such must be the response. The tie of kinsmanship is sufficient to demand a response. In a *Gesellschaft*, the response will depend on the merit of the recipient. All relationships are limited and segmental and, therefore, such will be the response. It is incumbent upon the recipient to substantiate his claim.

The biblical definition of poverty and its requirement of providing total needs to a recipient may be considered the classic formalization of a *Gemeinschaft* response. Indeed, it is the existence of a blood relationship or kinsmanship that creates the unique response. The Bible, in fact, specifically qualifies the obligation of responding total needs by stating that the recipient has a unique status: he is not any man, he is your brother. As it is written, "If there be among you a needy man, *one of thy brethren.*"[221] Thus, the motivation for the specific response is the existence of a familial tie. Under such a circumstance there is no shame or humiliation dealing with the poor on a personal basis. The poor person is a member of the family living within the community. His total life experiences are shared and known. His total life is firmly interwoven into the fabric of mutual experiences and shared values. Such a person must be restored to a position of value. For in a fashion the feelings of shame or needs of the needy person are a reflection of the status of the entire family. The poor is a part of a whole that must be cared for to bring about total living. The *Gemeinschaft* is a form of organic living and resembles the functioning of organic life. As a result, a diseased cell creates havoc to the entire system. In the *Gemeinschaft*, the definition of poverty is relative to the standards of the community. A poor person is one whose standards are below his community; no matter how affluent such standards may be. An investigation of the poor person's assets is a totally irrelevant requirement. He is known, he was born into the community, and he is a member of a status of kinsmanship. One doesn't investigate a brother; one knows him and responds to his needs.

In addition, an assumption may be made that the number of the poor in the original *Gemeinschaft* Jewish community was quite minute. It was the unusual, rather than the frequent, occurrence. People had land. Tribes and families were given equal portions. It was the alien, the Gentile, who may have been landless. The Jews all started out on an equal basis. As a result, total needs could be provided. If the communal standard was a horse to ride upon or a slave to run before oneself, such could be provided to a minute number of needy brothers. Yet, materialism could not be forced upon another. The recipient had to acknowledge his desire for communal social standards. He had to reject his minimal standard of consumption.

Indeed, the concept of brotherhood served as the stimulus for the entire response to poverty and provided its underlying theme. This may be noted in the following talmudic observations.

Rabbi Yehoshua ben Korcha stated in the Talmud that he who withheld himself from giving charity was considered comparable to one who worshiped idols.[222] This statement is interpreted to mean that one who has no mercy for his brother negates the unity of brotherhood. Such a person could not accept the unity of a divinity. The unity of the Lord is comparable to the unity of Israel. A negation of the unity of man is a direct reflection of a negation of the Almighty.[223]

The concept of brotherhood as a stimulus for response finds its greatest articulation in a talmudic dialogue between Rabbi Akiva and the governor of Judea, the Roman General Tineius Rufus.

R. Meir used to say: "The critic [of Judaism] may bring against you the argument, 'If your Lord loves the poor, why does he not support them?' If so, answer him, 'so that through them we may be saved from the punishment of *Gehinnom.*'" This question was actually posed by Tineius Rufus to R. Akiva: "If your God loves the poor, why does He not support them?" He replied, "so that we may be saved through them from the punishment of *Gehinnom.*"

"On the contrary," said the other, "it is this which condemns you to *Gehinnom.* I will illustrate by a parable. Suppose an earthly king was angry with his servant and put him in prison and ordered that he should be given no food or drink, and a man went and gave him food and drink. If the king heard, would he not be angry with him? And you are called servants, as it is written, 'For unto me the children of Israel are servants.' "

R. Akiva answered him: "I will illustrate by another parable. Suppose an earthly king was angry with his son, and put him in prison and ordered that no food nor drink should be given to him, and someone went and gave him food and drink. If the king heard of it, would he not send him a present? And we are called sons, as it is written, 'Sons are ye to the Lord your God.' "[224]

Thus, the brotherhood of man and the fatherhood of God are closely intertwined. Recognition of the fatherhood of God implies a common identity of man. This creates an obligation of mutual concern.

Yet, the kinship or brotherhood relationship of a *Gemeinschaft* carries within it an extreme limiting factor: it excludes from consideration the stranger or alien. It reserves a response to the members of the *Gemeinschaft* and excludes all others. Perhaps for this reason the Bible constantly repeats itself with admonitions against harsh treatment of the stranger.[225] Perhaps each poor person originally was required to seek basic help within the domicile of his family. It was to his kinsmen that a biblical obligation was issued. Also, in a situation wherein people are tied to the land, the basic domicile was within the boundary of one's familial threshold.

Yet, the *Gemeinschaft* principle could be extended to include all who possessed some element of basic kinsmanship. This, of course, would preclude any consideration to the Gentile. Such a person lacked the bond of familial or tribal relationship and, therefore, was not to be provided with total needs.

Indeed, one interpretation of the previous dialogue between R. Akiva and the Roman general makes the following observation. It appears that R. Akiva agrees that one is prohibited to sustain the poor of those who are not called "children of God." Since only Israel is called such in the Bible, Jews are thus prohibited to care for the needs of the Gentile poor.[226] This is an extreme, harsh, but logical implication of the *Gemeinschaft* principle.

In theory, it is, however, possible to conceptualize a universal *Gemeinschaft* principle, a principle that would relate to the universal brotherhood of man. Our relationship to any man must be conditioned by the fact of his existence and not by the actual services he renders. Help must be provided any man simply because he is a human being and that kinship relationship predates any experience, social condition, or personal problem. R. Akiva would, therefore, require aid to any human, for all are children of God. This form of human endeavor would appear to be the answer to Cain's question, "Am I my brother's keeper?"[227] The *Gemeinschaft* response is that one is the keeper of one's brother because of the brotherhood. I am he and he is I.

Though such a theoretical approach may be conceptualized, in fact, the *Gemeinschaft* appears rooted in a localized in-group characterized by kinship, habitat, and local traditions. It, perhaps, draws its strength and appeal from the very nature of its limiting factors. The response to the relationship is intense for not all possess the unique relationship. It has the attraction of membership in a secret society not open to all. Not everyone is a member of my family. Not everyone has shared with me total life experiences. Not everyone can join my family except through kinship and birth. Once the *Gemeinschaft* is destroyed, the specific response of providing total needs loses its special, potent *raison d'être*.

Gesellschaft Responses to Charity

In a *Gesellschaft* urban setting, life experiences are ordained by rational considerations. Domicile is conditioned not by producing something from the land but by exchanging services for profit. People are not rooted in total generational family traditions. It is basically as scholars maintain, an arena providing a wider range of alternatives for individuals than found in nonurban areas of any given nation in any given time.[228] In such a setting experiences are segmental. The total man is not exposed. Primary to all considerations is the motive for the exchange of services. A *Gesellschaft* society must, therefore, create its own responses to poverty. To the people not rooted in the soil, not sharing total life and generational experiences, both the provision of total needs to a poor person and the *Gemeinschaft* kinship bonds providing such an obligation are alien concepts. The *Gesellschaft* is a community of strangers bound by rational considerations. There is no feeling of unity or equality with other citizens. There is no theoretical organic destruction of the whole by the lack of a few. The concept of providing total needs of the poor is antagonistic to the roots of a *Gesellschaft*. No man has an inherent right to affluence. Affluence is the reward or profit received in exchange for services rendered. The poor man has no claim to receive *gratis* the high standards of the community. Also, it is incumbent on the poor man to substantiate his claim. He is not known. He is a stranger living in a unique fashion among strangers. He has no family. An investigation must be made to ascertain the reality of his need. Such an investigation must, of necessity, be a dehumanizing, degrading process. The poor person is put into the position of providing the motive for the response. Prove your need! In a *Gesellschaft*, such response, even after an investigation, must be in the nature of subsistence and not relative affluence. Affluence is the reward of success, not failure.

In addition, time spent in such a process of investigation is not a worthwhile effort of the *Gesellschaft* mentality. It is the end result that is the major concern. A poor person must not starve. A community must care for its citizens. Whether for biblical mainstream traditions or practical communal pride or personal distaste, a poor man must be helped. A practical solution is to assign the investigatory task to communal agents. Such a process would limit the public shame of the recipients. Such a process would remove the poor from a relationship with the wealthy. The agents would represent the community and have funds collected from assessments or individual contributions. Poverty would be defined in terms of an objective criterion and localized in the hands of communal agents. It is a *Gesellschaft* type of mentality that extolls the role of indirect grants to the poor. A practical concern becomes sublimated into a form of human dignity and a high level of charity.

The poor person who refuses to accept the *Gesellschaft* response and personally seeks a door-to-door relationship with the affluent is denied even the general communal response. Legally, both the communal agents and the individual are obligated to provide no more than a token response. Efforts at personalizing the response to poverty are, thus, considered alien and disgraceful for the poor.

Communal funds are established. The *tomchui* is set up to provide a day's subsistence for the nonresident poor with the hope that they will leave the city. The *kupah* is established for the resident poor. To them, the more dignified allocation of funds for one week's subsistence is provided. The city, thus, cares for its own.

Ancient tradition incorporated into the Codes the following priorities in responding to the needs of the poor. The first response was to sustain oneself. After that came an obligation to provide support to one's parents, then came elder children, afterwards brothers, then relatives, then neighbors, then members of one's city, and finally, citizens from another town.[229]

Thus we see the true *Gemeinschaft* relationship incorporated into law. In fact, the *Gesellschaft* response of communal funds was prohibited to be given to a poor person whose family had the means of supporting him, even though the family contributed to the communal fund.[230] The derivation of this latter law is based on a talmudic statement that "anyone who falls, falls not to the communal poverty agent first."[231] This is interpreted to mean that the primary obligation of supporting a poor person is on the family of the poor.[232] An additional insight is the view that this comment describes the process of caring for the poor. When a man becomes poor, the family supports him while the communal agent investigates whether the family has the means to provide such support. Only if the family cannot provide support does the poor person come under the jurisdiction of the communal agent.[233] Thus, communal responsibility is only when familial relations are not present or are not able to provide a response.

It is certain that when the family cares for its own there is no shame in such a relationship. Indeed, there is greater humiliation in seeking outside support. The *Gesellschaft* response enters when the condition for *Gemeinschaft* (kinship-family) is no longer present. It is a new response based on urban conditions of people not tied to the land. In such a situation even the ideal of a *Gemeinschaft* is not present. It is colored and transformed by the reality of the *Gesellschaft*. The latter defines the need in terms of objective criteria. It formulates poverty as a lack of 200 *zuzim*. Yet, the response of the family to its poor is not articulated. Nowhere is this response delineated. The family is obligated to respond according to their own method of response. They must sustain the poor according to their own definition of sustenance. This is contrasted to the specific detailed objective response provided by the communal agent.

Indeed, the fusion of both mental orientations provides a unique new form of *Gemeinschaft* obligation. The Codes provide that total needs are to be granted to a poor person if such was his custom prior to poverty. He must be restored to his former position of affluence.[234]

This law is unique in that it appears to favor the *status quo* of wealth. The poor person who never had affluence is not able to acquire the standards of his community. Yet, the wealthy person is assured that either individuals or the community will guarantee his status. This is basically the kinsmanship of wealth that develops within a *Gesellschaft*. A new relationship develops that can command a response similar to the blood ties of the *Gemeinschaft*. It is the bond of class and equality of style of living. This now assumes the fervor and vitality of the old *Gemeinschaft* relationship. This kinsmanship of wealth serves as the obligation for the response and, therefore, provides a response with all the embellishments of a pure *Gemeinschaft*. Thus, a pure *Gemeinschaft* community may decay, but the concept may be kept alive and revitalized by creating a new bond for a response.

It was, therefore, perhaps only to the good families (*ben tovim*) that the community felt an obligation to respond to needs as a community. Such families had, in addition to sheer geographical domicile within a town, also the bond of similar values. Such individuals had to be shielded from disgrace. Since they had no family to support them, the community assumed the obligation because of the family name. Others could acquire a daily dole of food and needed no special considerations.

The *Gesellschaft* mentality had always to create a reason (a motive) for a response. The modern *Gesellschaft* mind would consider poverty in terms of loss of productivity to society. The ancient mind, however, created artificial bonds of kinship and limited responses to those who fell within the sphere of their limitation. The basic bond was style of life. For this reason, those who did not observe Jewish ceremonial and traditional laws were excluded from the obligation of communal support. Some even suggest that it was prohibited to support flagrant violaters of Jewish religious law.[235] Thus the bond of kinship was developed as the brotherhood of religious observance.

Also, the codes maintained that the priority of response should be to the needs of scholars.[236] Later commentaries suggest that this law refers only to the response of the communal agent. The individual still is obligated to provide sustenance to his family members, who may be illiterates, rather then to a scholar who is not a family member.[237] The *Gesellschaft* status establishes scholarship as a bond that demands communal support. It is, of course, a *Gesellschaft* rather than a *Gemeinschaft* response.

Thus, the biblical and rabbinic definitions of poverty reflect the evolution of society from a *Gemeinschaft* to a *Gesellschaft*. Ideas representing distinct social structural conditions fused into a holistic approach of divergent practices as society tended to manifest both orientations.

The End of the Communal Response

It was noted that the development from rural agricultural life to urban experiences stimulated a radical change in the response to poverty. Thus, the meaning of poverty was dependent on the social substructure. A basic consideration constant in both schemes of response was the communal ability to care for its needy. Poverty was a minority concern. An affluent majority can actualize its concern for the needy by either a total private philanthropy or an objectivized, institutionalized communal response. When, however, the needy increase to such an extent that they become the majority, a qualitatively distinct orientation develops. Just as a *Gemeinschaft* response was inapplicable to a *Gesellschaft* condition, so too was the rabbinic communal response unrealistic to a condition of poverty as a majority concern. When the overwhelming majority of citizens need support, the communal funds derived from the affluent simply have not the means of providing a viable response. A reference to such a situation is found in the Codes of Caro. He states the following law: "In a case where the poor are plentiful and the wealthy maintain that the poor should beg, and the average citizen contends that the poor should not beg but seek support from the communal fund, the law is as the average citizen contends. The poor should be supported from communal sources."[238] The source for this law is the *responsa* of a thirteenth-century scholar.[239] The interpretation of this law is that in the thirteenth century the *kupah* and *tomchui* were still in existence. Yet the condition of the poor so radically changed that they tended toward achieving a majority status. The wealthy, therefore, maintained that since the *kupah* fund could not sustain all the poor, it should be eliminated. There was no purpose to contribute to a fund that could not accomplish a total task. The poor should be on their own to seek individual sources of sustenance. The average citizen, however, contended that the *kupah* should be maintained. At least some role could be accomplished. Those who would not receive *kupah* funds could beg. The law was considered to be the viewpoint of the average citizen. Yet, at that time, different customs began to emerge.[240] Coupled with this change in status was a change in the standard of living. People needed more than 200 *zuzim* to sustain themselves.[241]

These factors must have led to the total dissolution of the communal institutionalized approach. A communal response was the recognition that the response would care for the need. Once that condition changed, the motivation for the response lost its validity.

Part II

Jewish Sensitivities

Covering the Jewish Head

QUESTION: Why does a Jew cover his head?

RESPONSE: The Talmud (*Kiddushin* 31a) notes that Rav Huna, son of Rav Yehoshua would not walk four cubits bareheaded, saying, "The Divine Presence is above my head." Thus, the head covering is a manifestation of the constant presence of God. As the Psalmist states (23:4), "Yea, though I walk through the valley of the Shadow of death, I shall fear no evil, for Thou art with me." God is shown to be always above the Jew. The hat (*yarmulkah*) is a constant reminder that the Jew is never alone. He walks with God. It's a feeling of assurance and comfort. At the same time it's an ever-present conscience to withhold one from going astray.

The head covering has another role. It's a symbol of humility. How enlightening it is that the Talmud presents the concept of covering one's head directly subsequent to a statement prohibiting one from "walking with arrogance."

The most human quality of man is his mind. It's his essence. Yet it must be controlled. It is constantly covered as a shield against arrogance. The greatest treasure of a person – his mind – is withheld from total public scrutiny; hidden like a priceless heirloom; controlled by the presence of God. The bareheaded man is a symbol of pride, perhaps even hautiness. His head is covered to remind him of his limits, frailties, and ever-dependence upon God. The hat or *yarmulkah* is the daily implementation of the rule in Proverbs (1:7) that "the fear of God is the beginning of knowledge." It is the intertwining of religion and wisdom.

Since the presence of God permeates our existence, tradition has it that the Jewish head is covered throughout all pursuits of life in and out of the synagogue, at home, and at one's place of business.

71

The Talmud considers the covering of one's head to be as natural to the Jew as rising in the morning and getting dressed. In *Berachot* (60b) the Talmud contends that each process of awakening has a concomitant *berachah*. For example; "When he opens his eyes, he should say: 'Blessed is He *who* opens the eyes of the blind.' . . . When he dresses he should say, 'Blessed is He who *clothes* the naked.' . . . When he *places a covering on his head*, he should say, 'Blessed is He who crowns Israel with glory.' "

In other words, the covering of one's head is part of the process of awakening and getting dressed each morning. It's inconceivable to the Talmud that a Jew would not place a covering on his head. Indeed, the significance of the *berachah* for daily covering one's head may relate to the primary religious role of the hat (or *yarmulkah*) itself.

The Jew makes numerous *berachot* (blessings) throughout each day. Prior, for example, to the performance of ritual *mitzvot*, the Jew acknowledges its sanctity by chanting a blessing. Of concern is that the all-pervasive *mitzvah* of believing in God has no special *berachah*. Why? A partial response is that blessings were instituted as introductory statements prior to specific religious actions (not thoughts). Blessings were never set up for the obligations of the heart or the mind. Yet, there is a specific action that relates to the essence of belief. The covering of the Jewish head is a dramatic and concrete action manifesting the presence of God. It's an action of belief. Accordingly, the blessing for covering one's head may, in reality, be the *berachah* of belief; for God is definitely the glory of the Jew.

It is no wonder that the Jew covers his head. It's his tag of identification; it overtly stamps him as a believing Jew.

K'lal Yisrael

QUESTION: Does the concept of *K'lal Yisrael* (the organic totality of Israel) generate any pragmatic halachic ramifications?

RESPONSE: Yes. The *Chumash* reports that Yosef made the children of Israel swear an oath that they would bring his bones to Israel when they departed from Egypt. Rashi (citing a *Mechilta*) says that Yosef was insistent that the brothers take an oath that they would make certain that their children will also swear to bring Yosef's bones to Israel (see Exodus 13: 19, Rashi). The Maharal of Prague was concerned over the exact meaning of this oath. What difference was there between the oath of the brothers and the oath of yet another generation, their children? If the oath of parents was not powerful enough to commit their children, then the oath of Yaakov's grandchildren also should have no impact upon their children or the generations that follow. As such, only one oath should take place, namely the vow of Yosef's brothers.

Answering his poignant questions, the Maharal suggests that there is a qualitative distinction between an oath vowed by Yosef's brothers and an oath expressed by a succeeding generation. At the time Yosef requested an oath from his brothers, it was impossible to receive a commitment from the totality of *K'lal Yisrael* (the Jewish people), for eleven tribes (or brothers) do not make up *K'lal Yisrael*. This entity requires twelve brothers, which simply were not available to make such an oath. Accordingly, when the children made such a vow, it represented the totality of *K'lal Yisrael*. Once that transpired, it was not necessary to remake the oath in succeeding generations (see Commentary, Maharal, *Gur Aryeh*, Exodus 13:19).

Commenting upon this Maharal, HaGaon HaRav Yitzchok Hutner (*z"l*), *rosh hayeshivah*, Rabbi Chaim Berlin Rabbinical Academy, noted that it is apparent from the Maharal's commentary that *K'lal Yisrael* has an existence and a role distinctly apart from the function and capacity of each Jew. Just as a Jew may obligate himself via a personal commitment, so too may *K'lal Yisrael*. The totality of Jews as an entity may obligate itself to observe certain commitments. Such commitments generated through the authority of *K'lal Yisrael* itself have meaning, impact, and relevance for future generations. There is, moreover, no need to reaffirm such commitments in the future. For this

reason, once the oath of the children occurred, no additional oath
was necessary.

Of interest is that an obligation set up by *K'lal Yisrael* is
different from one mandated through only a segment of the
Jewish community. In the latter case, continuous devotion of
future generations is guided by the concept of "Forsake not the
teaching of thy mother" (*Al Titosh*; Proverbs 1:8—see *Pesachim*
50b). When, however, a principle is developed by *K'lal Yisrael*,
there is no distinction between one generation or another. It's as
if every generation made a personal oath. When *K'lal Yisrael*
does something it impacts everyone and all generations. It uni-
fies the past, present, and future.

Of concern is whether the principle of *K'lal Yisrael* is yet
viable after the Assyrian exile of the ten tribes. Just as eleven
brothers (of Yosef) could not effectuate a commitment of *K'lal
Yisrael*, so too, perhaps, would be the fate of the two and a half
tribes that remained Jewish after the disappearance of the ten
tribes. In other words, the concept of *K'lal Yisrael* may have
been eliminated when a large number of our tribes were simply
lost.

Indeed, the festival of Purim is the first holiday historically
to take place after the exile of the ten tribes. Yet, it is deemed as
if *K'lal Yisrael* ordained this event. The reason must be that
Judaism considers the status of the two and a half tribes remaining comparable to the sanctity of the original twelve tribes.
As such, the commitment was for all generations and for all
times. There is no distinction between the obligation of the Jews
of Persia in the times of Esther and Mordechai and the Jews of
today (see Rav Hutner, *Pachad Yitzchok*, Purim, *Maamar* 14).

This may be the reason for the talmudic dictum that the
Jewish people in the time of Mordechai renewed their commitment to observe the Torah that was made at Sinai (see *Shabbat*
68a). Perhaps it was to demonstrate that a commitment made by
just two and a half tribes was comparable to the commitment
made by *K'lal Yisrael* at Sinai. The Jewish people will forever
endure. So, too, does the concept of *K'lal Yisrael*. It cannot be
ruptured nor erased by a loss of Jews. To demonstrate this

feature, perhaps, the Jews of Persia recommitted themselves to their obligations made at Sinai: They wished to manifest that even though part of Jewry disappeared through the exile of the ten tribes, the concept of *K'lal Yisrael* still permeates our essential being. This also suggests the rationale for the *midrash* that the souls of all Jews were present at Sinai. A commitment of *K'lal Yisrael* interweaves all generations. It is a commitment made by all of us today and not just as obligations of the past made by our ancestors.

Commitment to K'lal Yisrael

QUESTION: Does a Jew have a special obligation to share the plight and fate of the Jewish people?

RESPONSE: Yes.
This concept may be derived from the following text:

> If at the present time a man comes [desires] to become a proselyte, he is addressed as follows: "What reason have you for coming [desiring] to become a proselyte; do you not know that Israel at the present time is persecuted and oppressed, despised, harassed and overcome by afflictions"? If he replies, "I know and yet am unworthy," see Rashi–"If only I may be so worthy" [of the privilege to be a member of Israel], he is accepted forthwith and given instruction in some minor and some of the major commandments (*Yevamot* 47b).

This citation demonstrates the necessity for the proselyte to commit himself to share the fate of *K'lal Yisrael* prior to any discussion of *mitzvot*. The implication is that a commitment to observe *mitzvot* is not even considered unless it is preceded by a commitment to share the fate and suffer the plight of *K'lal Yisrael* amongst the nations of the world. HaRav Yitzchok Hutner (*z"l*), former dean, Rabbi Chaim Berlin Rabbinical Academy, makes the following observation: "If recognition of the negative status of Israel is a precondition for conversion to Judaism, how much more is such recognition essential for those already within the fold?" (*Iggeret*, no. 63).

Accordingly, the following theoretical case could emerge. A proselyte could conceivably inform *bet din* that he was more than willing to personally observe all the *mitzvot* of the Torah but simply refused to suffer the terrible plight of *K'lal Yisrael*. He did not wish to share the fate of being, as the Talmud says, "persecuted, . . . oppressed, despised, harassed and overcome by afflictions."

The Talmud and *Shulchan Aruch* (*Yoreh De'ah* 268) repudiate such a position. The detailed description of the low status of Jews is not merely to present the proselyte with an opportunity to change his mind and remain a Gentile. The proselyte is mandated to orally state that he is fully cognizant of Jewish troubles and (*Af Al Pi Ken*) yet, he still wishes the privilege to join this people. Accordingly, the concept of *K'lal Yisrael* and the oneness of Jewry is not a pious, homiletical, altruistic trait but one rooted in the halachic essence of Judaism.

The Rambam rules (Repentance 3:11):

> One who secedes from the path of the Congregation (*Darchei Tzibur*) *although he committed no transgressions*, but remains separated from the Congregation of Israel, observes no commandments together with them, *does not include himself in their troubles*, nor afflicts himself on their fast days, but follows his own path as the rest of the (Gentile) people of the land, acting as if he was not one of them, he has no share in the World to Come.

As such, a Jew who consistently observes *Shabbat* and *kashrut*, prays each day, and scrupulously performs *mitzvot* yet refuses to be involved with any communal activities nor share the fate of Jews is deemed a sinner.

Danger, K'lal Yisrael, *and Prayer*

QUESTION: Is there a special prayer or a specific role for prayer when the totality of the Jewish people is in danger?

RESPONSE: A cursory reading of Torah verses and Rashi's commentary suggest that prayer may not always be the most propitious response to danger.

A case in point is *K'lal Yisrael's* reaction to the dangers faced at the Red Sea. In front of them were the raging, insurmountable waters of the Red Sea; behind them were the advancing, ruthless soldiers of Pharaoh. The Jews were frightened. What were they to do? What was our leader Moshe (Rabbeinu) doing at that period of time? The Torah records that God said to Moshe, "Why are you crying unto Me, speak to the children of Israel that they go forward" (Exodus 14:15 – *Parashat Beshalach*). Simply put, stop praying, take action. Rashi clearly states that Moshe was praying to God. The Almighty's response, according to Rashi, was twofold. (1) When Israel is faced with danger it is not appropriate to prolong prayers (*lehaarich*); (2) "Why pray to Me: The matter depends upon Me, not you." Both interpretations give the impression that prayers are not the best reaction to danger. The first comment of Rashi is that in times of danger, prayer may be necessary but it should be short and to the point. One should not "prolong prayers," but rather provide action or concrete responses. There is no definition as to how much time may be properly devoted to prayer or, better yet, no guide as to when prayer is excessive. What is clear is that prayer solely by itself is not the proper response to danger. Danger necessitates a combination of both prayer and action. The second comment of Rashi goes against the grain of the religious mind-set. It notes that the decision to save Jews is a divine prerogative that is not due to prayer. Of concern accordingly is whether one should pray altogether in times of crisis. If prayer does not accomplish any favorable divine reaction, then perhaps one should not pray. A prayer that is not germane to effecting a divine response seems to be futile endeavor.

HaGaon HaRav Yitzchok Hutner (*z"l*), former *rosh ha-yeshivah*, Rabbi Chaim Berlin Rabbinical Academy, contends that the true meaning of this Rashi may be derived from yet another citation. *K'lal Yisrael*'s reaction to the crisis of the Red Sea was that "they cried out unto God" (Exodus 14:10). Rashi says, "They grasped the occupation of their forefathers." To demonstrate that prayer was, indeed, the profession of the patriarchs, Rashi cites verses to note that Avraham, Yitzchok, and Yaakov all (at one time or another) prayed. At issue is the rationale for Rashi (citing the Mechilta) to inform us that *K'lal Yisrael*'s prayer was simply an observance of the profession of the patriarchs. What purpose is there for Rashi to so inform us of this information? Perhaps, suggests Rav Hutner, that the statement that prayer was the occupation of the patriarchs defines the essential, unique nature of this prayer. For there is yet another problem relating to this prayer of *K'lal Yisrael*. The Torah informs us that "they cried out to God." The response was that "God will fight for you and ye–hold your peace [be silent]" (Exodus 14:14). In other words, the divine reaction to *K'lal Yisrael*'s prayer was that they should stop praying. Thus, the prayer was futile. If so, why pray altogether? To this our sages say that the prayer at the Red Sea was a unique form of prayer. It was a prayer "which *K'lal Yisrael* grasped the occupation of the forefathers." Namely, this was not comparable to other prayers.

The purpose of this prayer was to establish the holy lineage of *K'lal Yisrael* not to make a specific request from God. For example, someone made a request from a king. The king's response was that under normal conditions there was not any valid reason for him to heed the request. But, during the petition, the young man made note of his pedigree. He noted the name of his father and that the father was a friend of the king. Accordingly, the king assured the son that his request would be heeded solely because of the relationship to the father who was his friend. So, too, by *K'lal Yisrael*. When they were told "be silent" the intention was not to imply that their prayers were in vain. No, the prayers manifested their lineage to the patriarchs. Accordingly, no further prayers were needed. Once Jews relate their relationship (*yichus*) to Avraham, Yitzchak, and Yaakov, then God responds favorably. The purpose of this prayer was to crystallize that once the lineage was noted, further prayer was not needed. The response was not due to the inherent good qualities of *K'lal Yisrael* but to their lineage to the patriarchs.

Whenever *K'lal Yisrael* in its entirety is in danger, then a special form of prayer emerges, a prayer based not on the merits of the petitioners but on their lineage to the patriarchs. When *K'lal Yisrael* is in danger then the purpose of the prayer is for God to base his reaction upon his affection for the patriarchs. Such a response results in divine action and a cessation of further human prayers. As Rashi says, "The matter depends on Me, not you." (An elaboration of this theme is noted in *Pachad Yitzchok*, Purim, *Maamar* 19.)

The three major prayers of each day, the Amidah, commence with reference to Avraham, Yitzchak, and Yaakov. Perhaps such prayers are based upon this consideration. Whatever, when *K'lal Yisrael* is in danger, it appears necessary to make note of the patriarchs. The danger to the entirety of *K'lal Yisrael* sets up a special divine reaction when the roles of the patriarchs are mentioned. They are the secret weapon of *K'lal Yisrael*. Mention of our relationship brings about divine salvation.

Jewish Eternity

QUESTION: Custom has a popular refrain that states "*am Yisrael chai*" – "The People of Israel Live Forever." What does this phrase mean?

RESPONSE: Jewish survival is commemorated at several times throughout the year. Indeed, a number of holidays specifically extoll the eternity of Jewish life. *Halachah*, for example, obligates a festive meal to be eaten on Purim. No such obligation is mandated for Chanukah. The distinction, suggest our sages, is that Purim commemorates salvation from a projected physical genocide while Chanukah celebrates a victory over an attempted *kulturkampf* to eliminate Jewish values and ideas (Taz, *Orach Chayyim* 670:3). Accordingly, Purim is not a holiday celebrating the purity of Jewish thought, the excellence of Jewish character, but rather, the sanctity of Jewish lives. Jews were not destroyed. Of concern is the spiritual or theological impact of this survival. Or, better yet, at issue is the halachic impact of present-day Jewish survival from enemies.

HaGaon Rav Hutner, *z"l* (former *rosh hayeshivah* of Rabbi Chaim Berlin Rabbinical Academy) notes that "tradition has it, that the tribes still exist" (*Bava Batra* 115b). Yet how is this so? Except for members of the tribe of Levi, no one knows accurately his tribe. We simply do not know our lineage. Yet, we must presume that Eliyahu the Prophet at one time will pinpoint the exact tribal lineage of every Jew. We will be made aware at some future date of the name of the tribe of every Jew. In other words, tribal lineage exists (even today), but we simply are unaware of this knowledge. This concept has relevance to the understanding of the divine commitment expressed in the Bible, "Even when they (Jews) are in the land of their enemies, I have not despised them nor abhorred them to make an end of them" (*Lo maasti . . . lechalotam*, Leviticus 26:44). Namely, God promises never to destroy Jews. We are guaranteed to be an integral aspect of existence. This is the concept of Jewish eternity (*netzach Yisrael*). We Jews will never be destroyed.

Of concern, however, are the visual contours of such existence. Are Jews to exist as tribes exist? Namely, an existence not known to anyone. Does it mean that there will always be Jews in the world, but the Jews themselves will not even know that they are Jews? The story of Purim, and acts of comparable salvation, says HaRav Hutner, teaches us that Jews will be saved as a visually recognizable unit. Jews themselves will know that they are Jews. So, of course, will Gentiles. This is the spiritual message of the physical salvation of Jews (see HaGaon HaRav Yitzchak Hutner, *Pachad Yitzchok*, Purim, *Kuntres Reshimot* 2).

This is the meaning of *am Yisrael chai*—"The Jewish people lives." We have been promised by God that the Jewish people will always be a visual, recognizable, integral aspect of life itself.

Common Sense and Mitzvot

QUESTION: Do actions mandated through the vehicle of common sense have the same standing as biblical commandments (*mitzvot*)?

RESPONSE: This requires analysis, for insights gleaned via common sense of logical thinking are highly valued by our talmudic sages. The Talmud, for example, has a rule that the onus of proof is the responsibility of the claimant (*hamotzei mechaveiro alav hareiyah*). Accordingly, the responsibility to substantiate claims is placed upon the person who seeks to extract funds from another. In assessing the underlying source for this ruling, one rabbi cited a biblical verse. "But Rav Ashi demurred, saying, 'Do we need Scripture to tell us this? Is it not common sense (*sevarah*) that if a man has a pain he visits the healer?' " (*Bava Kamma* 46b). The implication is that a biblical text is not necessary to teach a concept that may be derived through logic. As such, the necessity for the scriptural verse is to teach a different matter that simply cannot be crystallized through common sense. Yet, the implication is that the rule derived through common sense has the same validity as if it were overtly stipulated in the Bible.

A second example is the case of a woman who tells a *bet din* (a rabbinic court) that she was previously married and then properly divorced. The Talmud states that the woman's testimony is believable and no additional substantive proof is necessary. She has permission to remarry. Why? "For the mouth that prohibited her is the mouth that freed her." Namely, no one had knowledge of her previous marriage. It was brought to light only by the woman's admission of a former marriage. Yet, this woman's testimony also stated that she was subsequently divorced. Accordingly, her whole testimony is to be believed. The Talmud rejects an attempt to derive this principle from the Bible saying, "Why seek a biblical proof? It's a *sevarah* (common sense)." If the woman's testimony is trusted that she was previously married, she should be also trusted when she says she was divorced (*Ketubot* 22a). Again, it appears that common sense provides a legal standing comparable to a biblical mandate.

Yet, there is a major distinction between actions derived from common sense and those stipulated by the Bible itself.

The *Gemara* notes that the primary source for *berachot* prior to eating food is not a biblical or rabbinic *mitzvah* but, rather, the logic of common sense (*sevarah*). Namely, it is forbidden to have pleasure in this world without first reciting a *berachah* (*Berachot* 35a). This common-sense logic is the impetus for all *berachot* (blessings) (relating to food). The P'nei Yehoshua notes that this concept generates a concern that questions a basic principle of *berachot*. The general rule is that *berachot* are obligations mandated by the rabbinic sages. As such, any doubt as to whether a *berachah* is to be recited is traditionally resolved leniently based on the rule that in matters of doubt relating to rabbinic laws, one is lenient (*safek berachot lehakeil*). Now, if the motivation of *berachot* is common sense and logic generates obligations comparable to biblical statutes, then any doubt as to whether a *berachah* is to be recited should be ruled stringently, according to the principle that in matters of doubt on biblical issues stringency is the rule (see P'nei Yehoshua, *Berachot* 35a). (There are a number of responses to this question. Our concern is to cite those answers that finely hone the relationship of common sense to *mitzvot*.)

Rav Yosef Engel suggests that logic has the force of a biblical *mitzvah*, providing the common sense expressed is endemic to all people: It is an inherent aspect of logic or human nature. Should, however, the logic relate only to the religious mind or to believers such is not afforded the status of a biblical *mitzvah*. Thanking God for usage of fruit is an accepted cardinal expression of a believing mind or a religious soul. To the general population, however, it is not an essential human trait. Accordingly, eating without a *berachah* is not a biblical violation (see *Bet HaOtzar, K'lal* 131).

Rav Yechezkel Landau presents a unique theory on the relationship of logic to *mitzvot*. He contends that common sense has the ability to establish principles of human nature. For example, logic may establish which person must seek proof in litigation and what type of testimony is to believed by a court. Logic *does not make mitzvot. Mitzvot* are found only in the Torah and are *not* derived from common sense (*Tzion LaNefesh Chayyah, Tzlach, Berachot* 35a).

This means that the general rule, that in matters of *d'Oraita*–biblical *mitzvot*–stringency is the guideline, relates only to *mitzvot*, not to doubts over the application of common sense. Verses (*pesukim*) are necessary to pinpoint *mitzvot*, not human nature (*metziut*). The latter may be derived from logic. The former must be specifically commanded.

Halachah *and Majority Rule*

QUESTION: Does *halachah* always follow the democratic concept of majority rule?

RESPONSE: It is an axiom of our religion that no majority has
authority to *chas veshalom* (heaven forbid) rule that *mitzvot* are
not to be observed. This would suggest that on communal issues
that do not impinge upon the observance of *mitzvot* majority rule
based on the principle of one vote per person should guide the
decision-making process. Yet, this is not necessarily the case.

The *Mishnah* rules that a resident of a city may be compelled
to contribute to the building of a wall for security purposes
against marauding gangs (*Bava Batra* 7b). The Codes extend this
concept to mandate contribution for residents to build a synagogue or to acquire such religious items as a *sefer* Torah (*Shulchan Aruch, Choshen Mishpat* 163). Of concern was the process
of collecting funds for these endeavors. Assume a wall was
needed. Were funds to be collected as a poll tax or according to
means? According to the first method, the cost would be divided
into the number of inhabitants, and each person would contribute
an equal share. Thus, a nonaffluent husband and wife with five
children would contribute seven equal portions while a wealthy
individual living alone would be required to contribute only one
portion (see Commentary, *Nemukei Yosef*). Or are the affluent to
be assessed in a different manner from others? Namely, the
wealthy are to be taxed according to their means and obliged to
contribute on a qualitatively different basis from the general
population. The Talmud rules that the second option is the
halachic model for action. A second version in the Talmud is a
question as to whether the tax collected is based on the proximity
of a person's house to the city wall or according to means? The
Talmud rules on this case that proximity is the issue. Tosafot
explain this to mean that nonaffluent residents who live close to
the proposed wall of a city required greater security and, therefore, must pay greater amounts than would nonaffluent residents
who live far from the outskirts of the city. At the same time,
affluent residents adjacent to the proposed wall would pay more
than wealthy residents who live in other areas (*Bava Batra* 7b).

Based upon this consideration that the affluent must contribute more to communal needs than others, the following
dilemma may emerge. A difference of opinion may result be-

tween the affluent group and the general population. The group who, for example, gave the most money may wish one form of action while the majority may seek quite a different state of affairs. Should one follow the majority of the contributors or the viewpoint of the affluent who in fact may have provided the majority of the funds? What is the halachic approach on this matter?

This issue is discussed by the *Aruch HaShulchan*, who makes a number of rulings pertaining to a halachic approach to communal affairs.

1. In the event of a dispute on an issue of communal concerns, a meeting should be called wherein all contributors are requested to attend in order to voice their positions. Those who decline to express their viewpoint (or who do not vote) are considered as if they voted with the majority. All who do not attend are deemed as if they transfered their vote to the majority who do so attend. The basis for communal decisions is to be the majority viewpoint of those in attendance. To rule by unanimous consensus is wrong for such a process will withhold communal entities from making decisions and [may] lead to their destruction (*Aruch HaShulchan, Choshen Mishpat* 163:2).

2. When funds are collected for communal endeavors the affluent are taxed according to their means. As such, they (the affluent) may constitute the majority (for they contribute the majority of funds) even though they are a minority in terms of voters. Accordingly, the general majority of voters may not force the affluent group of contributors to observe the majority viewpoint. The *halachah* supports the position that the affluent consist of a bloc that cannot be outvoted by the majority. At the same time, the "affluent bloc" may not impose their viewpoint against the wishes of the majority. In such a situation where both groups have major differences of opinion, it is basically a standstill and mediation and/or compromise must be utilized for the resolution (*Aruch HaShulchan, Choshen Mishpat* 163:7).

This suggests that the affluent members of a communal group may halachically exert their power as a bloc should they so desire.

Unnecessary Martyrdom

QUESTION: In a circumstance where *halachah* does not require a Jew to martyr his life, may he still select death as an act
of piety and extreme faith?

RESPONSE: There are three orientations to this question.
  1. *Rambam*: The Rambam states:

> If an idolator forces a Jew to transgress one of the command-
> ments of the Torah and threatens him with death for disobe-
> dience, it is mandatory that he not be put to death, for it is
> said concerning the commandments "that which a man may do
> and live by it" (Leviticus 18:5), "live by it" but not die for it
> (*Sanhedrin* 74a). Thus if he chooses death and did not trans-
> gress, "his blood shall be upon his head" (*Hilchot Yesodei
> HaTorah*, 5:1).

Thus the Rambam's position is that where martyrdom is not
mandatory (that is, the idolator is threatening the Jew privately
for personal whims), a Jew who submits to death is considered to
be practicing a form of suicide.
  2. *Radbaz*: Rav David ben Zimrah disagrees with this harsh
decision. He notes the view that such an act is a form of extreme
piety and such martyrs are to be labeled as true holy men of our
people (*Lilshonot HaRambam*, no. 3). The theory, perhaps, is as
follows: Martyrdom is always an act of good faith and pious
devotion. *Halachah* does not merely obligate such action in all
circumstances. In the event, however, that one does not wish to
violate a *mitzvah* even when such action is not required and will
lead to death, such a person is a *tzaddik*.
  3. *R. Yehudah Rozanes*: R. Yehudah Rozanes suggests a
middle position between the theories of the Rambam and the
Radbaz. He cites sages who maintain that where martyrdom is
not mandatory, it is permitted, if performed by a great Jewish
leader who martyrs himself to serve as an example of religious

piety and awe (*Parashat Derachim, Drush* 2). According to this position, the average layman who places himself in a position of danger, when it is not mandatory to do so, may be committing a form of religious suicide.

R. Yosef Babad notes an interesting case where martyrdom is not required. He says that the classic requirement to forfeit one's life rather than to kill another is restricted to a circumstance where the only way one's life can be saved is by murdering another. That is prohibited. In a case where one could save one's life without taking an aggressive action against another, however, martyrdom is not required. Thus, *halachah* does not mandate martyrdom to prevent oppressors from throwing one's body upon a child and thus causing the death of the child. To the extent that the individual is passive and initiated no action against another, personal life takes precedence (*Minchat Chinuch, mitzvah* 237).

Accordingly, should a person say, "Kill that one, otherwise, I'll throw you on an infant, which definitely would kill the infant," and the adult says, "No, kill me rather than the child," the following reactions would emerge:

1. Rambam: The adult is a suicide.
2. Radbaz: The man is a *tzaddik*.
3. *Parashat Derachim*: Should the person be a well-known rabbi or leader, such action is meritorious; otherwise, it is wasteful.

Bail for Jewish Prisoners

QUESTION: Is the *mitzvah* of *pidyon shevuim* (ransoming captive Jews) operational in a case where a Jew is imprisoned for allegations of financial improprieties? Accordingly, is it a *mitzvah* to help such a Jew acquire bail?

RESPONSE: The Talmud rules, "Whence do we know that if a man sees his neighbor drowning, mauled by beasts, or attacked by robbers, he is bound to save him? From the verse, 'Thou shall not stand idly by the blood of thy neighbor' " (Leviticus 19:16). Of concern, states the Talmud, is that such a principle may be derived from quite another scriptural verse. The Torah says, "Thou shall restore him to himself" (Deuteronomy 22:2). This latter verse deals primarily with the restoration of a neighbor's property. The talmudic logic is that just as a Jew is required to restore a person's property, he certainly should be obliged to restore the person himself, should he be in danger of being lost (or killed). As such, the rule that one must help another in danger may be derived from not one but two scriptural verses. Accordingly, one of the verses appears extraneous. The Talmud concludes that each verse provides a message of importance and that the verse of "do not stand idly by" (*lo taamod*) teaches us the rule that one is even obliged to *hire personnel* to save another from danger (*Sanhedrin* 73a).

Based on this, Rabbeinu Asher rules that a person rescued from such a danger is obliged to repay all funds spent in his behalf.

MaHaram bar Baruch contends that an obligation exists to save a person from danger regardless of whether the victim requests such aid. To the extent that the request for aid is not material to the scriptural mandate to provide help, all funds must be repaid to the donor even though the victim may subsequently contend that he never requested such aid (*Responsa*, MaHaram bar Baruch, no. 39).

In medieval times, the family of R. Avraham Ezra (Ibn Ezra) was imprisoned. To save the family from such a plight, David Tzetzer provided their freedom by paying a ransom of 110 pieces of gold. Subsequently, however, Ibn Ezra refused to repay to the donor the expenses incurred for delivering his family from such captivity. One of the defenses presented by Ibn Ezra was that the scriptural obligation to repay the donor was reserved only for problems involving life-and-death situations. Since his family was only imprisoned, he felt that the mandate was not applicable.

The consensus ruling of the Torah authorities in that generation was that Ibn Ezra was mandated to repay immediately everything expended for the safety of his family.

R. Yisrael M. Beruna noted that imprisonment in those times portended possible torture and/or attempts to alter basic religious beliefs. As such, it was considered a status comparable to a life-threatening situation. Consequently, anyone released from such a condition was mandated to repay the donor all funds expended for the release (*Responsa*, Mehari Beruna, no. 236).

R. Pinchas Yaer ruled that since the obligation to expend funds to save a person is limited to life-threatening situations, one is not required to spend a small amount of money to save a neighbor from the loss of a large sum of funds (*Responsa*, Chavat Yaer, no. 165).

The above analysis suggests that a person jailed in an American prison due to allegations of financial fraud, embezzlement, or any violation of law that does not entail a capital punishment would *not* mandate the religious obligation of expending funds to relieve him from such circumstances. In other words, *pidyon shevuim*, the *mitzvah* of ransoming Jewish captives, is operational only in life-threatening circumstances. The sources clearly demonstrate that financial problems do not impose such requirements. (This does not mean that Jews who are compassionate people may not volunteer to help other Jews in financial trouble. It merely notes that the biblical and rabbinic obligations are not operational for monetary problems.)

Of interest is that a case may be made that any imprisonment generates a religious obligation upon Jews to seek all resources (including provision of financial bail) to release another Jew from jail.

The *Mishnah* rules that should "A" pursue "B" in order to murder "B," then every effort should be made to save "B," even if the only means available is by killing the pursuer, "A." The *Mishnah* adds that permission to kill the pursuer is not limited to cases wherein the purported crime is murder. Even if "A" pursues "B" for purposes of homosexuality, the same principle is operational, namely, the pursuer may be killed (*Sanhedrin* 73a).

From this it is clear that a probable homosexual rape classifies the proposed victim as being in a life-threatening position, which warrants killing of the pursuer should no other means be available. Accordingly, lacking guarantees that a prisoner would be in solitary confinement, protected against probable rape, the likelihood of such occurring would generate a life-threatening condition that would make the *mitzvah* of *pidyon shevuim* operational. As such, it would be a *mitzvah* to help such a person acquire bail.

Saving a Dying Jew

QUESTION: Is it permissible to violate *Shabbat* to extend the life of a Jew whom physicians judge will not live beyond *Shabbat* itself? Namely, a person is dying. Efforts to save this person will definitely extend his life. But it is recognized that even after life-saving activities, the Jew will not live for more than a few hours. Is it permissible to violate *Shabbat* for such a person?

RESPONSE: Yes.

The *Mishnah* rules that "every danger to human life suspends the [laws of the] Sabbath" (*Yoma* 83a). As such, one is mandated to violate the Sabbath in order to save a human life. The Talmud seeks the rationale for this principle and presents a number of explanations. One such reason is as follows: "R. Shimon ben Menassia said, 'And the children of Israel shall keep the Sabbath' ('*Veshamru . . . laasot*'–Exodus 31:16). The Torah said profane one Sabbath, so that the victim may keep many Sabbaths in the future" (*Yoma* 85b). The implication is that the quantity and quality of future observance outweighs the present state of violating *Shabbat*. Of concern would be an incident wherein physicians might contend that a person will not live to observe yet another *Shabbat*. Indeed, the biblical commentator

Or HaChayyim (Exodus 31:16) specifically contends that the concern is the issue of future observance. He notes that it is prohibited to violate a *Shabbat* for a person who will not be able to observe future Sabbaths.

The rationale must be that the purpose of medicine is to heal. Thus, one may not be mandated to provide an activity that extends life without healing or bettering the quality of the life of the patient in the future.

This position, however, appears contrary to a well-established halachic precedent. The *Mishnah* rules, "If debris fall on someone, and it is doubtful whether or not he is there, or whether he is alive or dead, or whether he is an Israelite or a heathen, one should open [even on the Sabbath] the heap of debris for his sake. If one finds him alive one should remove the debris, and if he be dead, one should leave him there [until the Sabbath is over]" (*Yoma* 83a – Soncino translation). On the phrase "if one finds him alive one should remove the debris," the Talmud comments, "But is that not self-evident? No, the statement is necessary for the case that he has only a short while to live (*chayyei she'ah*)" (*Yoma* 85a). This talmudic principle is recorded in *Shulchan Aruch, Orach Chayyim* (329:3,4). It is obvious that the Talmud does not suggest that the violation of *Shabbat* is dependent upon assurances of a minimum lifespan for the victim. Indeed, there is no discussion of this matter. There is not even a concern for the victim to live beyond the *Shabbat* itself. The Talmud merely rules that any effort to extend life even for a short time necessitates a violation of *Shabbat*. This definitely challenges the *Or HaChayyim's* position previously mentioned.

The *Minchat Chinuch* cites the theory of the *Or Ha-Chayyim* and rules that it is contrary to general halachic principles. The Talmud notes a variety of reasons to explain the rules suspending *Shabbat* in order to save a life. One such explanation was that such a violation sustained future observance. Yet, the Talmud also reports the view of Samuel who cites the verse, "he shall live by them" (Leviticus 18:5). From this he derives the rule, "but he shall not die because of them" (*Yoma* 85b). Indeed, the Talmud rules that all the theories except Samuel's may be

refuted. Accordingly, violating *Shabbat* to save a person is not
dependent on or interrelated to concerns for future observance
(*Melachot Shabbat* 39 – *Minchat Chinuch*; see also *Daat Torah,
Orach Chayyim* 329).

The *Mishnah Berurah* fully discusses the parameters and
implications of the rule that mandates violation of *Shabbat* in
order to extend a person's life even for but a few hours. He rules
that the violation of *Shabbat* is not dependent on the observance
of a future *Shabbat*. He cites, moreover, the commentary of the
Meiri who suggests that the mandate to extend life is provided so
the victim may yet repent sins that he may have committed. This,
too, suggests the *Mishnah Berurah* may lead to the miscalcula-
tion that *mitzvot* are suspended because of the importance of
observing other *mitzvot* in the future. This is simply not so.
Mitzvot are suspended to save the life of the Jew (*chayyim shel
Yisrael*). An infant, for example, certainly cannot repent for sins,
yet one is still required to violate *Shabbat* to save his or her life.
Indeed, even a person afflicted with a mental problem that
impairs observance and repentance must also be saved. Even for
a person whom doctors have determined is in the throes of death
(*gosses*), one must violate *Shabbat* to extend his or her life even
for a short period of time. Hence, concern as to whether a person
will yet observe future Sabbaths should not hinder a person from
attempting all efforts to save his life on *Shabbat* itself.

Saving a Person on Shabbat

QUESTION: A life-threatening condition exists and *Shabbat*
must be violated in order to save a person's life. Who should
preferably violate *Shabbat* in this situation: adults or minors or
Gentiles?

RESPONSE: The *Shulchan Aruch* rules that when *Shabbat* is
violated to save a person's life, one endeavors to have the action

performed by adults (*Yisrael gedolim*) and not children. The Rema, however, modifies this rule. He suggests that when there is no loss of time it is preferable to have the action done by a non-Jew or through an altered mode of action (*Shinui*). Should, however, one believe the Gentile may not be careful or may delay action, then it should be done only by a Jew (*Orach Chayyim* 328:12). The *Mishnah Berurah* notes that the Rema's rule is based on the principle that one does not violate *Shabbat* even for a *sakanah* (a life-threatening condition) when the act may be performed permissively (*Sif Katan* 35). In addition, where Gentiles are to be utilized one may also use minors (*Sif Katan* 36). He cites the Taz, who disagrees with the Rema's position. The Taz contends that a Jew is always to be used, for a Jew will be more zealous in performance. The *Mishnah Berurah* concludes that where the *sakanah* is definite and the mode of help doubtful, then whoever could be more zealous is praiseworthy (*Sif Katan* 37). The implication is that when the action needed to alleviate the danger is definite and that zealousness is not a material issue, then, perhaps, one should preferably use either a Gentile or a minor. In other words, where zealousness could be a factor, then only an adult Jew should be utilized.

The *Aruch HaShulchan* openly disagrees with the Rema's position. He cites two theories as to why *Chazal* mandate that an adult Jew should be used to violate the *Shabbat* rather than a minor to save someone in danger. (1) To offset a potential false impression that people may assume that an adult Jew is not permitted to violate *Shabbat* to help one in *sakanah* (danger) (Ran). (2) A non-Jew or minor may not be as zealous as an adult (Tosafot, *Halachah* 6). Accordingly, one should always use an adult Jew. Indeed, the *Aruch HaShulchan* concludes that in this *halachah* when the phrase *gedolei Yisrael* is used, it means more than just adult Jews. It refers to those who are *"gedolim"* – great in Torah. This teaches us that just as God instructed us to observe *Shabbat*, so too does He command us to violate *Shabbat* to save a person's life (*Orach Chayyim* 326:7).

Of interest is the position of the Eishel Avraham. He notes that common custom is to utilize the services of a Gentile rather than a Jew to violate *Shabbat* to save another Jew from a *sakanah*. Though this custom goes against original sources, it is rational, he suggests, in that perhaps *Shabbat* may be violated only via a Jew in a circumstance wherein there is a clear-cut, definite life-threatening condition. In the event, however, that the *sakanah* is only doubtful (a *safek*), then no adult Jew should be utilized. To the extent that most cases relate to a doubtful *sakanah*, common usage has been to use the services of Gentiles or minors (see Eishel Avraham, *Mahadura Teninah*, 328). The uniqueness of this concept is the position that though *Shabbat* may be violated to save a person from even a doubtful *sakanah*, the process of violating *Shabbat* in such an instance is different from when the *sakanah* is definite.

Holocaust Monuments

QUESTION: In an attempt to generate physical reminders of the terrors of the Holocaust, stone memorial monuments are being established in major areas throughout America. Is it halachically proper for Jews to establish such stone monuments? Does not the Torah prohibit this form of a memorial?

RESPONSE: Scripture says, "And do not erect for thyself a memorial stone (*matzeivah*) which God thy God hates" (Deuteronomy 16:22). Rashi notes that even though the practice of erecting memorial stones was at one time permissible in the era of the patriarchs, it became forbidden because Gentiles subsequently utilized *matzeivot* for purposes of idol worship. Indeed, Rashi also specifically rules that it is forbidden to erect memorial stones even if the purpose is to use them for sacrificial ritual to *HaShem* (God) (ibid.). The *Siftei Chachamim* commentary suggests that the latter ruling is a logical derivation from the former statement. To the extent that the custom of using memorial stones was once permitted (that is, beloved) in the time of the patriarchs overtly indicates that such stones were subsequently prohibited even for service to God. Why? For should the memorial stones be used for idol worship, then such activity would have been outlawed even in the age of the patriarchs. The Rambam notes that the custom developed to build monuments and then to place *avodah zarah* (idols) on them (*Sefer HaMitzvot*, negative prohibition 11). Accordingly, any monument that could (even subsequent to being built) be used for idolatry should be prohibited.

A similar question was posed to HaRav Yehudah Leib Tzirelson, chief rabbi of Keshenov and Besserabia (*Responsa Marchei Lev, Responsa* 42, published 1932). A community cemetery association in Karlsburg wished to erect in their cemetery a monument memorializing the Jewish youth that died in a recent war. The concern was whether such a monument violated the biblical injunction against erecting stone memorials.

HaRav Tzirelson ruled that research discloses three halachic definitions of the biblical prohibition of making a *matzeivah*.

1. Rashi and Ramban contend that the biblically prohibited *matzeivah* must have two integral factors: (a) It must be composed only of one stone and (b) its purpose must be to serve as an altar (Deuteronomy 16:22).

2. HaRatz (cited in the Semak) rules that a *matzeivah* composed even of many stones is prohibited as long as its purpose is to be an altar for the purpose of bringing sacrifices to God (*HaShem) (Siman* 163:5).

3. Rambam believes that any stone memorial, composed of one or many stones, even should its purpose be not for usage as an altar, but rather simply to gather people (in some way) to serve God is prohibited (*laavod HaShem*) (Laws of *Avodah Zarah* 6:6; see also *Sefer HaChinuch, mitzvah* 493).

The author of the *Responsa Marchei Lev* makes the following halachic conclusion.

A war memorial monument composed of many stones would eliminate any prohibition from Rashi's perspective. To the extent that there is no purpose to use the stone memorial as an altar, this would permit usage both according to Rashi and the Semak. Even according to the Rambam's theory, a monument to memorialize dead youthful soldiers is not to be halachically outlawed for its purpose is not as a vehicle to serve *HaShem*. It is set up for national and communal pride, which is not a religious endeavor. Thus, he rules that *halachah* would permit erecting such a monument. He, however, charges the local *rav* to insure that no prohibited figures (statues) be placed on the monument.

It is apparent that a Holocaust monument would be comparable to the memorial for soldiers discussed by the *Marchei Lev*.

What is evident is that such monuments should *not* be *primarily* used for religious purposes. They should not become centers for prayers or religious devotions. For should Holocaust monuments be used regularly only for religious purposes then, according to the Rambam, such monuments may be prohibited to Jews. For this reason, perhaps, it has not been traditional for Jews to erect monuments.

A hasidic *rosh yeshivah* suggested the following distinction. Perhaps a monument that is set up and used primarily for religious worship is prohibited, even if it is utilized to serve *HaShem*. As such, a Holocaust monument set up for a variety of goals other than religion may on occasion be used for religious service. Its primary purpose is social, not religious. Such a monument is not prohibited.

Din Torahs: *Financial Disputes*

QUESTION: Jews are required to seek resolution of controversies via the vehicle of a *Din Torah* (court of arbitration or rabbinic court). Is there any way to guarantee that a litigant in a financial dispute will actually pay the money that the *bet din* rules he is obliged to pay?

RESPONSE: This question goes to the heart of the effectiveness of a *Din Torah*. Indeed, many people utilize the following ruse to delay obligations. First, they have rabbis and/or attorneys plea that as observant Jews the case should be taken out of the American court system and be resolved by a *bet din*. Many judges are amenable to take cases out of the court docket and have them adjudicated privately. Why? The court system is overcrowded. After numerous delays in setting up the formal structure of an acceptable *bet din*, a *Din Torah* takes place and a judgment against one side is rendered. At that time the person who loses simply refuses to pay. What is *bet din* to do? It may use moral suasion. It may publicly condemn the individual. But it has no legal authority to extract funds. It may also – at that time – grant permission to seek redress from the general American court system. This situation generates a spirit of futility. Indeed, as a result many people do not even attempt to utilize the *bet din* alternative. Why use a *Din Torah* when the only effective means of acquiring funds is by subsequently going to court?

Of interest is the halachic decision established by the *Aruch HaShulchan*. He describes a case as follows: One side contends that he will not go to a *Din Torah* unless the other side will put in escrow (or place under the reliable supervision of a third party) the sums he believes he is owed. The other litigant refuses to place anything in escrow. His contention is that should he lose the *Din Torah* and the other side be awarded funds, he will, at that time heed the judgment of the *bet din*. The *Aruch HaShulchan* rules that the *halachah* is as stipulated by the person who wishes the funds to be placed in escrow. Why? For (in his time and certainly in ours) there is no authority to force fulfillment of a rabbinic court, and no one can legally do anything against a person who repudiates the *bet din's* judgment (*Aruch HaShulchan, Choshen Mishpat* 4:5).

Such a procedure would generate more activity, effectiveness, and respect for rabbinical courts. Indeed, without such a safeguard, the rulings of a *bet din* may be disregarded with impunity. Just as we encourage people to seek out the forum of a *bet din* for the resolution of disputes, so too must we set up

procedures to ensure that rabbinic decisions are implemented
without undue delay or hardship or disrespect to rabbis.

Praying at Cemeteries

QUESTION: Is it a proper Jewish custom to visit cemeteries in
order to pray at the grave sites of loved ones or sages?

RESPONSE: A number of talmudic citations coupled with
observations of Chazal indicate that it is definitely a proper
procedure sanctioned by *halachah* to visit cemeteries for purposes of prayer. Some examples:

    1. The Torah delineates the route used by the spies sent by
Mosheh to investigate the land of Israel. It states, "And they
went up on the south side and *he came* to Hebron" (Numbers
13:22). Note the singular term utilized in the latter part of the
verse. Commenting upon this, the Talmud says it should have
read "and they came!" Rava said: It teaches that Calev [ben
Yefunah] held aloof from the plan of the spies and went and
prostrated himself upon the graves of the patriarchs, saying to
them, "My fathers, pray on my behalf that I may be delivered
from the plan of the spies" (*Sotah* 34a).

    2. Tradition has it that at a public fast decreed because of a
lack of rain, the community would visit local cemeteries. "Why,"
asks the Talmud, "do we visit cemeteries? . . . So that the dead
should pray for mercy in our behalf" (*Taanit* 16a). Tosafot note
that this is the source for the custom to visit cemeteries on the
public fast of Tisha B'Av.

    3. Rav Mani was anguished by the household of the Nasi. He
prostrated himself on the grave of his father and said, "Father,
father, they are causing me pain" (*Taanit* 23b).

The preceding talmudic citations disclose not only that prayer at grave sites is proper, but that sages actually prayed to those no longer alive to intercede in behalf of the living. This latter concept is not clear-cut. The Rema rules that on the day before Rosh HaShanah one visits cemeteries for purposes of prayer and to distribute charity (*Orach Chayyim* 582:4). The Be'er Heitiv, in the name of the Maharil, notes that a cemetery is the resting place for *tzaddikim* and is, therefore, a holy place and, accordingly, prayers are more acceptable emanating from such an area. When praying on the grave sites of *tzaddikim*, he adds, one *should not direct prayers to the dead, but to God*, that He shall extend mercy because of the merits of the *tzaddikim* buried there (*Orach Chayyim* 582:17). Though Rav Yechiel Michal Tukachinsky notes the latter concern of the Maharil, he also clearly writes that the previous talmudic citations strongly indicate that it is proper to pray to the dead themselves (see *Gesher HaChayyim*, vol. 11, chap. 2b). He also cites the *Minchat Elazar* (vol. 1, *Yoreh De'ah*, 68) that it is permissible to pray to the souls of *tzaddikim* to intercede in our behalf.

The position of the popular *Kav HaYashar* is most illuminating on this subject. He cites the *midrash* relating to Calev's prayers at the graves of the patriarchs and notes that this incident is the prime source for the custom to visit the grave sites of parents on their *Yahrzeit*. He also suggests that if on a *Yahrzeit* a person is not able to be near the cemetery where a parent is buried, he should visit another Jewish cemetery for purposes of prayer. His rationale is that God has so decreed that the souls of *tzaddikim* are available at grave sites to help the prayers of those who visit cemeteries for prayer. In addition, anyone with a particular problem should visit a cemetery and pour out concerns via prayer. Such prayers are so potent that they are brought directly before the heavenly throne (*Kav HaYashar*, chap. 71).

Indeed, my paternal grandfather, the famed author of internationally acclaimed halachic works (that is, *Minchat Shabbat*, on laws of Shabbat, and *Madanei Shmuel*, on laws of Pesach) notes a unique testimonial concerning the grave site of his maternal

great-great-grandfather, HaRav Tzvi Hirsch of Czortkow. He
reports that HaRav Tzvi Hirsch said prior to his death that
whenever (heaven forbid) trouble (*tzar*) would impact his children, he will intercede in their behalf should they come to his
grave and pray. Some say that such a commitment was made for
five generations; some say for ten generations; others say that
the commitment had no time limit and was for all time. My
grandfather (*z"l*) reports the following incident detailed in the
introduction to the volume, *Semichat Moshe*. The author, Harav
Tzvi Hirsch HaLevi Hurowitz, a descendent from HaGaon R.
Shmuel Shmelke of Nikolsburg and the Czortkover *rebbe*, reports that he was quite ill. Doctors had given up hope to cure his
left leg. Rav Hurowitz visited the *tzaddik* from Rumanov, who
told him to send a God-fearing Jew to the grave site of the
Czortkover *Rebbe*, and to state at the grave that the relative was
too sick to personally visit the cemetery and therefore sent a
surrogate to pray in his behalf. This took place and the ill Rav
Hurowitz was cured. Subsequently, he received a letter from the
person who attended the grave site who detailed the day and
exact period of time that prayers were uttered at the grave. Rav
Hurowitz testified that such a period of time was exactly when
his pains ceased and he felt relieved. In addition, Rav Hurowitz
reported another miraculous incident. A relative, HaRav Pinchas Margrov, related to the Rumanover *Rav* that he once had a
"pistle" (some form of a [cancerous] growth on his cheek). To seek
medical care, he went to the famous Dr. Rappaport from Lublin,
who informed him that there was no known cure. His mother
took her son to visit the Belzer *Rebbe*, Rav Shalom, and reported
to the *rebbe* the family tradition of the final testimony of Rav Tzvi
Hirsch. The Belzer *Rebbe* directed that both mother and son
should immediately visit the grave of the Czortkover *Rebbe* for
prayer. This they did, and the facial sore dried up and her son was
healed. (For reports of this event, see the *sefer* by my grandfather, HaRav Shmuel HaKohen, Introduction, *Minchat Yom
Tov*.)

   [My relationship to the Czortkover *Rebbe* is as follows: my
father, HaRav Meir Cohen; his father, HaRav Shmuel HaKohen;

his mother, Esther; her father, Rav Nahum; his father, Rav Meyril Hasid; his mother, Miriam; her father HaRav Tzvi Hirsh HaLevi Hurowitz, *Av Bet Din*, Czortkow.]

Accordingly, descendants should locate the grave site for purposes of family prayer and salvation. *Kohanim*, of course, should send surrogates.

A Jewish Good-Bye

QUESTION: Does *halachah* mandate a special manner of departing from a friend?

RESPONSE: Yes. The Talmud states, "A person should only take leave from his friend through a matter of *halachah* (*mitoch devar halachah*) so that he should remember him thereby" (*Berachot* 31a). Thus, an exchange of some Torah learning should accompany the departure. The Shem Rokei'ach remarks on the talmudic usage of the singular construct when referring to Torah information. He suggests that remembrance is better jogged by a single statement than by a smatter of a number of Torah thoughts. The multiplicity of Torah thoughts generates a sense of unclarity. One *devar Torah* (especially a good one) is well remembered.

The *Gemara* notes that "the words of two are written down in the book of remembrance, the words of one are not written down in the book of remembrance" (*Berachot* 6a).

As such, suggests the Vilna Gaon, two people discussing Torah generates a more lasting memory, for the discussion is written in the book of remembrance (HaGra, *Berachot* 31a).

Tosafot states that even the Torah of a single Jew is written in a book of remembrance. The uniqueness of Torah relating to two (or more) people is that it is recorded in a special book of others (Tosafot, *Berachot* 6a). In other words, there is a special holy book detailing acts of Torah relating to more than one person. The underlying opinion may be that Torah discussed with even one other person is a form of knowledge that may be transmitted to yet another generation. It's a form of *mesorah*. As such, it demands a special book of remembrance.

HaGaon R. Shneur Kotler (*zt"l*), former Lakewood, New Jersey, *rosh hayeshivah* once commented (in Los Angeles) on the saying that "Whoever escorts a guest on his way (*Ham'lavah et ha'orei'ach*) receives a reward comparable to other services provided to a guest." Namely, escorting a guest on his way is comparable to such acts as feeding, clothing, and providing lodging to a guest. Yet, the comparison seems unfair. Are not such vital services as feeding or lodging a guest more important than merely escorting a guest on his way? The response, Rav Kotler suggested, is as follows:

Many times a guest overstays his welcome. At other times, the host is gracious to a guest yet prays for the moment the guest departs so that tranquillity and privacy may prevail. Accordingly, when a guest leaves, the host may be emotionally overjoyed at the departure. To escort a guest out of one's home as a gesture manifesting the departure is not one of joy but of sadness. The host is sorry that the guest is leaving. It is indicative that the entire previous hospitality was sincere. It's an act detailing the value the host gave to the guest. As such, the escorting of the guest outside with honor, dignity, and *Menshlichkeit* is proof that the feeding, clothing, and lodging were sincere acts of kindness, hospitality, and joy.

A Chazzan *or* Rabbi?

QUESTION: In the event a community needs to engage a rabbi as well as a *chazzan* yet only has sufficient funds to acquire one of them, which takes priority, the *rabbi* or the *chazzan*?

RESPONSE: The *Shulchan Aruch* rules that the community should engage the rabbi providing he is a *rav* who is well versed and quite knowledgeable in rendering halachic decisions. Otherwise the *chazzan* has priority (*Yoreh De'ah* 251:13). The *Shulchan Aruch* does not designate the specific area of expertise that the rabbi was required to master in order to gain priority over the *chazzan*. The implication is that the rabbi's knowledge was to be so broad in scope that he could render decisions in any area of halachic concern. Should the rabbi lack such knowledge or readily admit he cannot render halachic decisions, then the *chazzan* should be granted priority. The *Shulchan Aruch*, moreover, does not state that a *rav* who has the ability to ask another rav *halachot* has priority. It rather specifically rules that the rav himself must be a master of *halachah*. Accordingly, a simple reading of the text may disqualify many rabbis and show preference for the engaging of a *chazzan* over the rabbi.

Of interest is that the *Shulchan Aruch* does not discuss the role of a *chazzan*. It poses the question concerning hiring either a *rav* or a *shaliach tzibur* (community surrogate). Indeed, the *Tur* overtly states that in the event the *rav* was not qualified then priority is granted to the *shaliach tzibur* who may include the community in [his prayers] and help them observe their obligations. The *Aruch HaShulchan* reasons that the law related to a particular time frame in Jewish history wherein the community was so ignorant of basic Jewish knowledge that no one had the ability to pray. In addition, not even one layman was available to lead prayers. In such a circumstance, the *shaliach tzibur* was of utmost importance to the community. Yet, a *rav* (Muvhak) qualified to render halachic decisions was still granted priority. Why? For Torah is deemed more important than prayer (*Aruch HaShulchan, Yoreh De'ah* 251:19).

This suggests that priority is granted to the *shaliach tzibur* only when the community lacks even one person to lead services. Such is rare. Indeed, even communities who have no person to lead services will certainly have numerous people who know how to *daven* themselves. As such, a rabbi, even one who cannot render halachic decisions, has priority over a *chazzan*. Indeed, even a plain, undistinguished *rav* will be able to provide Torah classes. Communities need Torah. No matter the level of knowledge of the congregation, a *rav* can uplift their appreciation of Torah and Judaism.

Apart from such logical inferences, these halachic conclusions are specifically noted by Commentaries in yet a different section of the Codes. The *Biur Halachah* (of the *Mishnah Berurah*) says that the original *halachah* giving priority to the *rav* who renders halachic decisions is even in a situation wherein the hiring of the rabbi would be tantamount to the community not praying at all for they simply lacked the knowledge. Should, however, members of the community know how to pray, then a rabbi definitely has priority over a *shaliach tzibur* (*Orach Chayyim* 53:24). The *Aruch HaShulchan* states that there did not exist in his time such a community whose congregants did not know how to pray. In fact, he concludes that, accordingly, a rabbi always takes priority (*Orach Chayyim* 53:25).

A Rabbi's Kavod

QUESTION: Does custom dictate any special, unique deferential attitudes and/or actions in behalf of rabbis to sustain and enhance the stature of Torah?

RESPONSE: Yes. Note the following concepts of HaGaon HaRav Yitzchok Hutner (*z"l*).

1. The valuation of a rabbi: In many European communities the town clock was placed in a high, distinctly elevated position. There are two basic reasons for this custom. One, the elevation made the clock noticeable to all. Two, it prevented local residents from constantly altering the community clock to synchronize it with the time noted on their personal timepieces. Having the clock placed beyond reach forced residents to utilize the commu-

nity clock as the standard for personal time. Namely, everyone changed their personal clocks in the event personal time differed from the town clock.

So, too, with the role of a *rav*. As long as the rabbi is held high in esteem, his Torah becomes the standard of the community at large (*Pachad Yitzchok, Iggerot* 132). The reverse is obvious.

2. Questioning a rabbi: The Talmud rules that "when *rebbe* is engaged [learning] a [particular] tractate [of the Talmud] do not question him about another" (*Shabbat* 3b).

An initial observation is that such a rule protects the rabbi from embarrassment. The rabbi may not be able to properly respond to a question pertaining to subjects not currently studied. As such, the concept appears to be a precautionary vehicle to shield the potential ignorance of a rabbi (teacher) from the student. This suggests that the more limited the scope or knowledge of the rabbi, the greater the need for this rule.

HaGaon Rav Hutner, however, contends that a review of early sages (*Rishonim*) indicates quite a different emphasis and perspective. He suggests that the aforementioned cited talmudic rule articulates the masterful stature of a Torah teacher rather than his limitation or lack of knowledge.

True Torah study requires total concentration. A scholar learning Torah is involved in this pursuit with every fiber of his essence. Everything and anything not directly associated with his present Torah subject distracts his intense analysis. Any question, therefore, extraneous to his present talmudic learning is a lessening of his power of concentration, a weakening of his total immersion within the fabric of his present talmudic study. This means that the greater the sage, the more brilliant the *rav*, the more total is the power of his concentrated thinking process. Thus, a question to a *rebbe* on a subject matter not presently studied is wrong in that it lessens the total fusion of the *rebbe* with his current study (*Pachad Yitzchok, Shevuot, Maamar* 9). As such, Torah students must recognize that the rabbi's Torah learning and analysis should be bettered through the relationship, not lessened.

3. A rabbi–student relationship: Secular knowledge im-
parted to a student is comparable to food acquired from a master
chef. Torah received from a *rebbe* is like food acquired from a
nursing mother, for a mother gives over part of her life as she
sustains her child. The Netziv (HaRav Naftali Tzvi Hirsch Berlin) utilized this concept when he coined the phrase "*b'nei yeshivah*" (children of the *yeshivah*) to refer to the student body of a
yeshivah because teaching Torah is a form of parenthood. This
means that Torah transmission is a personalized, distinctly individual process. A mother weans a child, not a mass or a multitude. So too, Torah study from a *rebbe* to a disciple must of
necessity reflect the parental component of a personal, dynamic
relationship (*Pachad Yitzchok, Iggerot* 74).

The Chazzan's *Place*

QUESTION: Common practice is for a *chazzan* in a synagogue
to stand upon an elevated area so that congregants may better
see and hear his prayers. Is this traditional? What was the
practice during the talmudic age?

RESPONSE: Talmudic references indicate that the *chazzan*
did not stand upon an elevated platform while serving as the
agent for public prayer. In fact, just the opposite took place.
Sources demonstrate that the synagogue *chazzan* was actually
formally placed in an area physically lower than the congregation
at large.

The talmud reports that R. Yochanan ben Beruka went
down (*yarad*) before the podium to pray. Rashi notes the reason
for such action is that it is a *mitzvah* to pray in a low area (*Rosh
HaShanah* 32a). The rationale, of course, must be the talmudic
statement that "a man should . . . not stand on a high place when
he prays, but he should pray in a lowly place, as it says, 'Out of the

depths have I called Thee, O Lord' (*mi maamakim*)" (Psalm 130 –
Berachot 10b). It portrays a sense of humbleness and humility. It
also demonstrates that height and might are not important when
compared to the Almighty.

Another example of this position of the *chazzan* may be
noted in the talmudic discussion of Shmuel HaKatan's memory
lapse concerning the prayer against apostates. Shmuel HaKatan
instituted the prayer. Subsequently, he himself served as the
chazzan and simply could not remember it. The Talmud records
that he tried for two or three hours to recall it and they (the
sages) did not remove him (*Berachot* 28b–29a). The phrase used
to note that Shmuel HaKatan was not removed as a *shliach
tzibur* are the words "*Velo heh'e'luhu*," which literally mean "and
they did not bring him up." Such a description, says the Rashash,
reflects the actual physical place wherein the *chazzan* would lead
services in a synagogue. A *chazzan* would actually go down to
pray. Namely, the podium for the *chazzan* was specially set up
structurally to be lower than other areas. Accordingly, when the
chazzan completed his communal function he went up to be part
of the congregation. As such, the fact that the sages did not bring
up Shmuel HaKatan indicates that he was not removed from his
position as a *chazzan*.

The talmud records a third example of this principle: "Such
was the custom of R. Akiva when he prayed with the congregation, he would be brief and ascend (*oleh*), but when he prayed by
himself, a man would leave him in one corner and find him later in
another on account of his many prostrations" (*Berachot* 31a).
Some English translations report that R. Akiva "would be brief
and finish" (translation Maurice Simon). The true meaning may
be as follows. When R. Akiva served as *chazzan*, he would be
brief in his prayers. He would also remain in one area. When he
concluded his function as *chazzan*, he would ascend in order to
be part of the congregation, for the *chazzan* prayed in an area
that was lower than others. When, however, he prayed for
himself, then he permitted himself the luxury of ecstatic move-
ment. Indeed, the Ari (*z"l*) synagogue in Sefad shows the *chazzan*'s area to be lower than other areas.

Of interest is that common custom has it that a person called to read in the Torah is designated as having an *aliyah*, which literally means to go up – to ascend. The rationale for such a term is that the Torah reading took place on a platform elevated above other areas of the synagogue. As such, a call to read the Torah was basically an opportunity to ascend the platform in the congregation. Thus, one goes *up* to the Torah and *down* to lead services. This overtly indicates that the *chazzan* who led prayer services did *not* pray in the same area used for reading the Torah. Each pursuit had a distinctly different area: a platform for the Torah, a low area for *davening*.

Kohanim *Facing Congregants*

QUESTION: The Talmud rules that the *kohanim* face the people during the priestly blessings, "like a man who talks to his companion" (*Sotah* 38a). Are there pragmatic halachic ramifications of this concept?

RESPONSE: Yes. 1. *Bowing and/or prostrating oneself before the kohanim.* Traditional sources indicate that no one bowed or prostrated during the priestly blessing. Indeed, the Talmud reports that bowing did take place at a different format. On Yom Kippur, for example, the *kohanim* and the people who overheard the *kohen gadol* (high priest) recite the Holy Name of God prostrated themselves (*Yoma* 66a). This tradition is part of the contemporary Yom Kippur liturgical service. In synagogues, common practice is for the rabbi, the *chazzan*, and the congregants to prostrate themselves when this historical incident is noted in the *machzor* (prayer book).

HaGaon Rav Yitzchok Hutner (*z"l*) (former *rosh hayeshivah* of the Rabbi Chaim Berlin Rabbinical Academy) noted that this communal mandate to prostrate did not take place at *Birchat*

Kohanim. Why? The Talmud specifically states that at *Birchat Kohanim* the *kohanim* faced the people "like a man who talks to his companion" (*Sotah* 38a). Accordingly, any form of bowing or prostration would violate this principle. For this reason, suggests R. Hutner, the Talmud (and *machzor*) overtly note that when the *kohen gadol* recited the Holy Name, the *kohanim* were together with the people in the audience. This implies that when the *kohanim* were separated from the others as during *Birchat Kohanim,* no one bowed, neither *kohanim* nor congregants (*Pachad Yitzchok,* Yom Kippur, *Maamar* 5:27).

2. *Facing the congregation during a sermon.* Of concern is whether a rabbi is permitted to preach facing the congregation with his back to the Holy Ark? Is this not disrespectful to the *Sefer Torah?*

The Taz (*Yoreh De'ah* 282:1) rules that such behavior is permissible for the *Sefer Torah* in the Holy Ark is considered as if it is in a separate domain. The *Aruch HaShulchan* (*Yoreh De'ah* 282:2) notes that the *derashah* of rabbis is basically a form of *kavod HaTorah* for he is teaching the community Torah and its *mitzvot.* Just as *Birchat Kohanim* must be a process whereby the *kohanim* face the congregation, so too should the rabbi preach facing the people. Indeed, the *Midrash* contends that it is a form of *kavod* to the community for the *rav* to face them during the sermon.

3. *Facing the bride and bridegroom during the marriage ceremony.* At a wedding, the *Aruch HaShulchan* contends that whoever chants the *Sheva Berachot* should face the bride and bridegroom; for all blessings should simulate the posture of *Birchat Kohanim,* whereby the *kohanim* face the people (*Even HaEzer* 62:9).

Conversations with Women

QUESTION: Is there a halachic aversion against men having conversations with women?

RESPONSE: The moral codes of *Pirkei Avot* ostensibly suggest that men should refrain from excessive conversations with women. It is written, *"Ve'al tarbeh sichah im ha'ishah"* ("and do not *indulge in excessive conversation* with your wife"). This was said about one's own wife; how much more strongly does it apply to the wife of one's fellow. Hence the sages say, "Whoever indulges in excessive conversation with a woman brings evil upon himself, neglects the study of Torah and in the end will inherit *Gehinnom* [suffer purgatory]" (*Avot* 1:5).

This *Mishnah* appears quite stringent and negative to women. The implication is that any extended conversation with women or even so-called idle talk will generate negative family problems. This citation and attitude has definitely not been lauded by our contemporary educated religious women. It has even been characterized as an example of religious male chauvinism. Is this so? No.

The key to the understanding of the above text is the meaning of the Hebrew word *sichah*. There are many Hebrew words to describe the process of talking and holding conversations; *sichah* has a special meaning. The Talmud (in another tractate) discusses the proper mental and emotional mood necessary for meaningful prayer. It states, "One should not stand up to pray while immersed in sorrow, nor in sadness, nor through frivolity, nor through *sichah*." Rashi says *sichah* means derogatory, mockery (*litzonit*) (*Berachot* 31a).

As such, the statement of *Pirkei Avot* relating to women becomes understandable. The rabbis are protecting the integrity and moral character of women rather than (as some perceive) denigrating them. The meaning is as follows: Do not mock women. Do not put them down. Do not gain joy by belittling them. It is forbidden to poke fun at one's own wife; certainly it is prohibited to mock another's wife. Indeed, whosoever belittles women will himself be subsequently disgraced. Thus, this citation is a model example of morality, not chauvinism.

Part III

Repentance and Rebuke

Rabbinic Adversaries and Controversy

QUESTION: How should rabbis relate to colleagues who disagree with their halachic decisions?

RESPONSE: Our Torah tradition definitely provides model relationships to guide even controversy. Indeed, the high incidence of acrimony that permeates rabbinic disagreements is sad to behold. It is necessary to recall the *Amidah* phrase, *"Mashiv haruach umorid hageshem"* – "all should lift up the spiritual and downgrade the material." The voice of reason should be the standard; personality attacks should be banned.

The Talmud relates that Bet Shammai and Bet Hillel disagreed on a number of family status laws. Bet Hillel contended that Bet Shammai's rulings were erroneously legitimatizing marriage to Jews classified as bastards (*mamzerim*). Bet Shammai considered many of Bet Hillel's decisions as means of validating marriage with persons who have tainted ancestry. Yet, both families (Bet Shammai and Bet Hillel) freely intermarried with each other. But how did they permit this? Each should have refrained from intermarriage because of their radically different decisions. The Talmud states they intermarried, for they made a practice of "informing each other" of problematic families (*Yevamot* 14a). Each group respected the halachic integrity of the other. No one side felt so certain of its position that it was deemed wrong, embarrassing, or extraneous to disclose problematic families. Indeed, it may have been halachically mandated to inform each other of these cases (see Chatam Sofer, *Mitzvot Lifnei Iver*). No side was to assume that since they considered the matter halachically proper, others were required to agree with their position. True honesty mandated full disclosure even though the rabbis may have ruled that no problem existed.

The Talmud further notes that intermarriage between the two groups taught us "that they showed love and friendship towards one another, thus putting into practice the scriptural text (Zechariah 8:19) 'Love ye peace and truth'" (*Yevamot* 14b). Maharsha comments that even though there is but one real truth, for purposes of *shalom*, both interacted with friendship. Consequently, mutual respect mandated that both interact with integrity for full disclosure. Each group, once aware of a family's case history, had the option of refusing marriage without castigating the decision of the *rav* who legitimatized the family.

Should not this be the practice today? Rabbinic scholars who honestly rule to validate certain practices because of a particular perception of halachic parameters should be respected as alternate legal approaches rather than be attacked and denigrated. One may disagree with a halachic decision. One may feel it is totally in error. One may not wish such ruling to be practiced by his community. One may even publicly attempt to refute the halachic basis for the decision. But, if the decision was developed with proper halachic principles and in conformity with Torah guidelines and precedent, then the ruling has validity for those who wish to observe it. That is the basis of halachic scholarship; for at times *halachah is not monolithic*. Nonhalachic positions must be decried. Judaism—its posture and contours—are the result of halachic decisions, not ideological theories. Jewish decency demands that those within the Torah framework respect the decision of honest Torah scholarship. Torah must validate itself in the open marketplace of ideas. The cruel jest used to be that when one could not challenge the logic, arguments, or sources of another, then the good debater would seek to defame character and "just plain holler." That's certainly not the role of a *ben Torah* or a *talmid chacham*.

The Process of Teshuvah

QUESTION: Are there viable methods to help enhance the process of *teshuvah*?

RESPONSE: Yes. A master teacher of mine, HaGaon HaRav Yitzchok Hutner (*z"l*), the former *rosh hayeshivah*, Rabbi Chaim Berlin Rabbinical Academy, and a brilliant analyst of character, once noted the following poignant concept. He said that when we talk about the great sages of yesteryear, we discuss the finished product of their personalities rather than the tortuous inner process that made them into the great people they became (*Pachad Yitzchok, Iggerot* 128). For example, everyone knows some story about the rabbi known as the Chofetz Chaim. We have anecdote after anecdote of how this rabbi never would say *lashon hara*, never would recite an unkind, unjust, or ungracious comment about anyone, even himself. This rabbi is one of the great contemporary heroes of folklore. We admire his saintliness. He is our image of a *tzaddik* – a truly righteous man. What we do not know, however, is the internal struggle that he must have had to make him into the *tzaddik* he later became. He was not born a saint. We know not the inner war he fought to discipline his mind and mold and forge the contours of his actions into a living well of kindness. We hear only the finished product. Yet, how fascinating it would be to learn of the practical steps he took to overcome normal pursuits. You and I know how delicious it is sometimes to hear some *lashon hara*, some gossip about someone, especially a person we dislike or one of renown. And yet, the Chofetz Chaim must have so girded his control over himself that such gossip would never be permitted to be uttered. How did he do it? How did he win his personal war within himself? That, no one knows. But, for sure, there is a method to understand the process itself.

First, let it be known that no change takes place, be it in *mitzvot*, be it in *middot* (character), be it in ethical behavior, unless there is a recognition, an awareness that something is wrong. Perfect people do not do *teshuvah*. An awareness of the need to correct oneself is necessary. This awareness may be derived from the following:

Sometimes, we ourselves were criticized by others. The awareness of something wrong within us was a result of someone telling us that we did wrong and needed to improve ourselves. This is the worst form of criticism. Why? People dislike being told by another of a fault, a wrong, a sin, or a character trait that should be corrected. "Who is she or he to tell me that I'm wrong—that I should correct myself?" we say to ourselves. "Are they so perfect? So immune to sin that they can tell me what I've done wrong?" So, generally, we discount the criticism.

We prefer to correct ourselves because of faults we see in ourselves. In other words, self-criticism. But such criticism is often blinded by ego and corrupted by hubris. An outer-stimulated criticism is more honest and objective but not as accepted as self-criticism and analysis. But somehow one method or another or a combination is necessary prior to change.

There is yet a third method, which our moralists contend is a means of self-understanding and a force for change. God gives us an opportunity to judge someone else, yet, says Rav Dessler, in reality it's a form of judging ourselves. We all know the story of David and Batsheva, how David wanted Batsheva for himself. But Batsheva was married to Uri Hachitti. Uri was a soldier. So David sent him to the front lines, and he was killed. Later the prophet came to David to request the king's decision for a violation of morality. The prophet told this tale. Two men lived next to each other. One was rich, vastly wealthy. He had thousands and thousands of flocks of sheep. The neighbor was poor. He had but one little lamb. The lamb was like a child to the poor family. The lamb slept with them and ate with them. One day a guest came to the wealthy man. To serve him dinner, it was necessary to slaughter a lamb. The wealthy man did not wish to use any of his thousands of sheep but instead crept under the fence and captured and killed the one lamb owned by his neighbor. "So," asked the prophet, "what is the punishment for such a crime? What should we do to the wealthy man who killed his neighbor's single, solitary lamb?" David was full of righteous anger. "Destroy that man," he said. "That crime was terrible." "Ah," said the prophet, "are you not the same as this odious person? You are king of Israel. You could have married anyone. Why was it necessary to seek out Batsheva, the woman of Uri Hachitti?" Says Rav Dessler, the moralist, the message is that God gives us a chance to judge ourselves by providing us with an opportunity to judge someone else with a similar moral dilemma as ours. Our judgment of a stranger will be the means of bringing about a judgment on ourselves. So, let us watch for such opportunities. Let's recognize that our criticism of others may be a vehicle to bring judgment on ourselves. (The source for the aforementioned is *Siftei Chayyim, Mo'adim* 1, p. 12, "Discourses on Ethics and Morality" by HaRav Chayyim Friedlander (*z"l*), *Mashgiach Ruchani*, Ponevez Yeshiva.)

Sin and Repentance

QUESTION: Is there hope for a real sinner to repent?

RESPONSE: Yes. The Talmud tells a tale of a sinner and how he did *teshuvah*. It defines the essence of sin and the process of *teshuvah* itself.

Elazar ben Durdaya was a sinner. He loved women. He would go anywhere in the world and pay anything to find new conquests. He once heard of a most beautiful woman. So he traveled past seven bodies of water to meet her. When he did, a peculiar thing happened. His body made a sound. The woman remarked just as this sound cannot return to the body, so too, Elazar ben Durdaya would never turn to his religion and be observant. When he heard this he felt terrible and started thinking about repenting. He left the woman and did *teshuvah*. He went to the mountains and prayed that they seek compassion for him. The mountains responded they needed compassion themselves. So he said, "From this I see it's up to me alone." So he prayed to God till he died. At his death, a heavenly voice called out. Rabbi Elazar ben Durdava went to heaven (*Yevamot* 17a).

The tale provides the following lessons for understanding sin and repentance: (1) The story teaches the power of passion.

Passion listens to no logic. Look at Elazar ben Durdaya. When he wished to sin, money was no object. Time was no concern. Travel, no issue. He passed over seven bodies of water. He went into danger for passion. Ah, if only people would so behave when it came to *mitzvot*. When he wished to sin, no obstacle stood in his path. It's true. When one is emotionally involved in a sin, logic and rationale are not always meaningful. Just as one is to love God with all one's heart, life, and money, so too, says the Maharal of Prague, these feelings take place when one is emotionally intertwined with sin. People sin with their soul, their heart, and all their funds.

(2) There is a second lesson to learn from this story. His name symbolized the role of *teshuvah*. The Maharal of Prague says that *durdaya* in Aramaic is the refuse of wine. It's a form of garbage. That's what this man was. He had no morals. He was a user. He wished merely to satisfy himself and his appetite. His name described his essence. A nobody. Yet, says the Maharal, his first name suggests hope. Elazar, *El* = God; *Azur* = will help. He may be living with filth, but God will help. Tomorrow will be better. No man or woman is to be renounced as a lost cause. He may be refuse, garbage, but *El* = *Azur*, God yet helps. And so He did. Never give up hope. Never give up on any person.

(3) The story goes on. The woman tells him just as the sounds that emanated from him cannot be returned, so too will he never return to his religion. What happened? Says the Maharal as follows: No matter what we do, even while committing a sin, God gives us an opportunity to repent. He gives us a chance to think about returning. Some people take the bait and do *teshuvah*. Some people allow their hearts to be open to change. They are not hardened. People all of a sudden hear a question, overhear a nasty word said about them, and begin to question themselves. The opening is made by God. Some people hear the call, others simply get angry. Still others feel too perfect to change. That's the third message. The Talmud continues that Elazar goes to the mountains. He calls out, "Mountains, pray for me." The implication is that it is natural to sin, it's a part of nature.

(4) Then he comes to the most human realization of all "*Ein*

hadavar talui ela bi" – "It's up to me." No longer does he blame anyone but himself. It's not his mate's or his parents' fault that he's a failure. There is no one but himself to blame for his problems. You, or I, we are not innocent. As long as we blame someone, somebody else other than ourselves, no *teshuvah* can realistically take place.

We are the masters of our own fate. We should blame only ourselves. We have the power to change.

When Rav Yehudah HaNasi heard that Rav Elazar ben Durdaya went to heaven, he cried and said, "Some people acquire the world to come after a lifetime of effort, and some acquire it after but a short bit of time. Yes, it's true. If a person who lived a lifetime of sin can change his pattern of thinking and action before his death, how much more so is it incumbent upon us to change now while we have the strength (*ko'ach*) to do so much good for ourselves and for others? How many worlds can we acquire by doing good right now? So if a sinner like Durdaya can repent, so can we all. Let's do it now!

The Halachic Contours of Criticism

QUESTION: In the event it is proper to criticize or rebuke someone, does *halachah* mandate specific guidelines to impact the tone of such criticism?

RESPONSE: Yes. Some examples:

1. It is reported that a rabbi taking leave from HaRav Yisrael Salanter noted that Rav Yisrael was also about to leave his home and was taking with him a very large sum of money. Rav Yisrael explained that the funds belonged to a certain Jew. Of concern to the visitor was the necessity for the *rav* to so

burden himself by personally delivering the large bulk of funds. "Could not the *rav* send the money through the auspices of a surrogate?" asked the the visitor. "No," said HaRav Yisrael, "I believe the Talmud mandates me to personally deliver the funds." The visitor was also a talmudic scholar and was perplexed by Rav Yisrael's response. "If the Talmud mandates such a behavior," he said, "wouldn't I have known about it?" To this Rav Yisrael responded (jokingly), "Maybe in your *Shas* such a mandate is not noted, but it is located in my *Shas* [Talmud]."

Explaining himself, Rav Yisrael Salanter substantiated his view from the following talmudic citation: It is written (2 Samuel, chap. 21), "And there was a famine in the days of David three years . . . and David sought the countenance of the Lord. And the Lord said: It is for Saul . . . because he was not mourned in a proper manner; and . . . because he put to death the Givonim." The Talmud asks, "Justice is demanded for Saul because he was not properly mourned and justice is demanded because he put to death the Givonim? Yes, for Resh LaKish stated, What is meant by the scriptural text, Seek ye the Lord – *Basher mishpato sham po'alo* – where there is His judgment [*mishpato*] there is [recalled] his good deeds [*po'alo*]" (Zefaniah 11:3) (*Yevamot* 78b). This talmudic citation teaches us that whenever criticism is to be leveled at a person, then it is proper to recall that person's good deeds. God did not seek to extract punishment from Israel for failing to properly mourn King Saul at the time of his death. Such criticism was held back until such a time when it was proper to recall King Saul's sin in killing the Givonim. Yet, at the moment of criticism, it was proper to recall King Saul's good deeds and the lack of respect paid to him by his people. Rav Yisrael ended by saying that he intended to criticize a certain person for behavior not becoming to a quality Jew. Yet, he must model his life after the moral examples of our God. At a time when he would criticize a person he must recall such a man's Torah knowledge and good deeds. Such a person was once kind enough to loan Rav Yisrael needed funds. Accordingly, it was necessary for Rav Yisrael to personally repay the funds and provide an atmosphere of *kavod* to the person who was to be criticized (see HaRav Yitzchok Hutner, *Pachad Yitzchok, Rosh HaShanah, Maamar* 4:7).

As such, *halachah* mandates that criticism be provided in a dignified atmosphere and that the good qualities of the person rebuked be openly praised and extolled.

2. It is written *"Vayedabeir Elokim el Mosheh vayomer ailav ani HaShem"* – "And God spoke to Mosheh and said unto him: I am *HaShem* [God]" (Exodus 6:2).

Note the usage of somewhat contradictory words. The beginning of the verse uses the verb *"vayedabeir,"* which is more harsh than the latter verb, *"vayomer"* – "and he said." Also, the verse utilizes two different names of God. The former name denotes judgment while the latter relates to mercy and compassion. Commenting upon these inconsistencies HaGaon HaRav Moshe Feinstein notes that Mosheh Rabbeinu used somewhat of a harsh term against God when it is recorded he said, "Lord, for what reason have you allotted misfortune to this people?" (Exodus 5:22). For that, says Rav Feinstein, (*z"l*), Mosheh deserved reproach. Yet, since he voiced the anguish of his people and did not seek personal benefit, God spoke with a soft and gracious manner. From this we derive the lesson that when a person deserves criticism, one should consider the reason why the person so sinned. If the intention was for altruistic purposes, even though the result was not proper, the person should be treated kindly for such good intentions (*Kol Ram*, vol. 1, p. 62). Namely, one should speak with both kind and hard terms. Or better yet, the harshness should be tempered due to the person's good intentions (*Kol Ram*, vol. 3, p. 92).

Thus, any criticism must take into account the intention of the sinner. If the intention was altruistic, then one may not be harsh. The criticism must be mild.

Shabbat Teshuvah

QUESTION: The *Shabbat* between Rosh HaShanah and Yom Kippur is called *Shabbat Teshuvah*. It is so designated for on this *Shabbat* the prophetic section of Hosea (14) commencing with the

words, *Shuvah Yisrael* ("Return–do *teshuvah*–Israel") is recited in the synagogue (see *Mateh Moshe, Siman* 893). This
suggests that *Shabbat* has no relevance to *teshuvah* itself but is
merely given the name *Shabbat teshuvah* because of its *haftorah*
or preparation for Yom Kippur. Is this so?

RESPONSE: No. It may be demonstrated that the observance
of *Shabbat* plays an integral role within the framework of repentance itself. The Talmud cites Rav Yochanan, who said, "Whosoever observes *Shabbat* according to all its *halachot*, even should
he be guilty of serving *Avodah Zarah* comparable to the generation of Enosh, his sins are forgiven" (*Shabbat* 118b). This talmudic statement puzzled the famed halachic commentator, the
Taz. Somehow this citation does not harmonize with our understanding of the process of *teshuvah*. The Talmud reports that the
act of observing *Shabbat* generates repentance. But why should
this be so? Did the person who observed *Shabbat* do *Teshuvah* or
not? If he did *teshuvah*, then his sins should have been forgiven
even without *Shabbat*. If, however, on the other hand, this
person did not do *teshuvah*, then it is incredulous that he be
granted repentance. How is it possible to be forgiven from sins
without *teshuvah*?

The response of the Taz crystallizes a unique role for
Shabbat as a vehicle to effectuate repentance. It is well known
that *teshuvah*, by itself, does not always brings about repentance. There are certain sins that are deemed to be so terrible
that *teshuvah* cannot undo. Indeed, the Talmud rules, "If he has
committed [a sin to be punished with] extirpation [*keritut*] or
death through *bet din*, and repented, then repentance and Yom
Kippur suspend [the punishment] and suffering finishes the
atonement (*Yoma* 86a). In other words, for certain types of sins,
teshuvah is not potent enough to provide atonement. The former
sinner must personally suffer, feel pain, before forgiveness is
granted. Perhaps, suggests the Taz, that the talmudic statement
of Rav Yochanan (*Shabbat* 118b) teaches us that the spiritual
impact of *Shabbat* observance is so powerfully unique that a

former sinner need not suffer before he acquires atonement. *Shabbat* together with *teshuvah* have the ability to grant repentance (Taz, *Orach Chayyim* 242:1).

This theory of the Taz aptly demonstrates that *Shabbat* observance enhances *teshuvah*. In fact, it provides a means of atonement that Yom Kippur itself does not have the ability to effectuate. The talmudic citation in *Yoma* specifically rules that Yom Kippur together with *teshuvah* cannot provide atonement without suffering for certain types of sins. Yet, it appears that *Shabbat* does have the ability together with *teshuvah* to atone for the same types of sins that Yom Kippur and *teshuvah* do not. This suggests that *Shabbat Teshuvah* is more than just a period of time to address Jews about the forthcoming day of *teshuvah*, Yom Kippur. *Shabbat Teshuvah* is the last *Shabbat* prior to Yom Kippur to acquire atonement for sins even without the divine punishment of anguish and suffering. *Shabbat Teshuvah* is an opportunity for *teshuvah* itself. Jews must be informed that an unusual choice is available to all who wish to do *teshuvah*. Should Jews repent on *Shabbat* itself, by not only doing *teshuvah* but by making certain that all laws of *Shabbat* are properly and scrupulously observed, then atonement may take place even for sins that normally require the punishment of suffering. Should Jews wish to wait to do *teshuvah* till Yom Kippur, then the opportunity to be absolved from sin for certain violations even without suffering will no longer be available. Knowing such a choice, I'm positive that *Shabbat Teshuvah* will become a day of *teshuvah* itself and not just a preparation for another period of time. The *haftorah* is in reality a call to Jews to utilize *Shabbat* itself for *teshuvah*.

The Baal Teshuvah *and the* Tzaddik

QUESTION: Who is greater, the *baal teshuvah* (the penitent) or the *tzaddik* (the consistently righteous)?

RESPONSE: A general reaction to this problem is to cite R. Abbahu, who noted: "In the place where penitents [*baalei teshuvah*] stand, even the wholly righteous cannot stand" (*Berachot* 34b). The overt inference is that a *baal teshuvah* is on a higher religious or spiritual plateau than the *tzaddik*. Of concern is that this citation is not the unanimous or even consensus position of the Talmud. Indeed, to cite R. Abbahu's position without noting the entire discussion is simply to provide a quote out of context.

The Talmud says as follows: "R. Chiyya b. Abba said in the name of R. Yochanan, all the prophets prophesized only on behalf of penitents; but as for the wholly righteous, Eye hath not seen, Oh God, beside Thee what He will do for him that waiteth for Him" (Isaiah 64:3).

He (R. Yochanan) differs in this from R. Abbahu. For R. Abbahu said: "In the place where penitents stand even the wholly righteous cannot stand" (*Berachot* 34b). Accordingly, there is a debate between R. Yochanan and R. Abbahu as to whether a *tzaddik* or a *baal teshuvah* has greater merit. Since the Talmud does not make a determination, the issue should be moot.

Talmudic logic (*pilpul*) may suggest a preference for the *baal teshuvah* while *halachah* indicates a contrary view. The Talmud rules that if a man betrothes a woman saying "On the condition that I am a *tzaddik*," even if he is absolutely wicked (*rasha gamur*), she is betrothed, for he may have meditated repentance in his thoughts (*Kiddushin* 49b). This teaches us that a *baal teshuvah* is on a higher level than a *tzaddik*. Why? For if otherwise then even should we assume that the *rasha* repented, he still would be a *baal teshuvah*, not a complete *tzaddik*. Now if a *tzaddik* is on a higher level than the *baal teshuvah*, then the condition set for the marriage was not fulfilled. He's only a *baal teshuvah*, not a *tzaddik*. On the other hand, should a *baal teshuvah* be greater than a *tzaddik*, then the marriage condition was certainly fulfilled to his bride. (Such logic is orally cited in the name of HaGaon R. Yosef Rosen the Rogachover Gaon.)

This deduction, however, may be somewhat defused. Indeed, the preceding *halachah* of the penitence of a bridegroom is not a simple matter. Scholars detail the difficulty in attaining the status of a *baal teshuvah*. The Rambam has an entire halachic section dealing with the intricate laws of penitence. Rabbeinu Yona has a book on the subject entitled *Gates of Repentance*. Repentance is not a process that is effectuated by a mere change of mind or will. As such, the ease by which the bridegroom is granted *teshuvah* seems somewhat bizarre and contrary to all the accepted prescribed rules of *teshuvah*.

It is reputed that the *Avnei Nezer* deflected this question by noting that a bridegroom is in a status separate and distinct from others. A bridegroom is prone to repentance since his sins are forgiven (*Yerushalmi, Bikurim*).

For this reason a mere change of mind may effect a change of status. Based upon the foregoing, an argument may also be advanced that the status of a repentant bridegroom may be distinctly different from that of a regular *baal teshuvah*. Accordingly, a bridegroom *baal teshuvah* may be even greater than a *tzaddik*, but not other types of *baalei teshuvah*.

The accepted *halachah* is that one should not bury a wicked person adjacent to a *tzaddik*. Commenting on this rule, the Bach says: "A *tzaddik* is one who scrupulously observes [Torah] laws. A *hasid* is one who sanctifies himself [by prohibiting to himself] even that which is permissible. [Namely, the *hasid* behaves above and beyond even the requirement of law.] To the extent that a *baal teshuvah* may be buried next to a *tzaddik*, the implication is that a *baal teshuvah* may not be buried adjacent to a *hasid*" (Bach, *Yoreh De'ah* 362). The Rema rules that a *baal teshuvah* may be buried next to a *hasid* (Rema, *Yoreh De'ah* 362:5; Shach, *Yoreh De'ah* 362:6). Thus, religious Jews are divided into three categories: *hasid, tzaddik,* and *baal teshuvah*, with only the former being granted superiority. This may be R. Yochanan's view that there is a higher religious level than a *baal teshuvah*. The Codes call such a person a *hasid* while the Talmud deems him a *tzaddik*. Yet, one may conjecture that even R. Abbahu may accept the view that a *hasid* is greater than a *baal teshuvah*. Why? The *hasid* must daily overcome the temptation of withholding himself from items even permissible according to law. R. Abbahu merely felt that a *baal teshuvah* was greater than a *tzaddik*, not than a *hasid*.

An analysis by the Radbaz suggests a uniquely different perspective of the debate between R. Yochanan and R. Abbahu. He contends that R. Yochanan deals with *tzaddikim* versus Jewish wicked sinners who repent. R. Yochanan's view is that such *tzaddikim* are on higher plateau than such *baalai teshuvah*. R. Abbahu relates to a different type of a *baal teshuvah*. He deals with righteous Jews who on occasion falter or sin and repent immediately after their error. Such Jews are considered greater than *tzaddikim* for they manifest the piety of *tzaddikim* and the remorse of *baalei teshuvah*.

The Talmud states R. Yochanan's position and contends that he disagrees with R. Abbahu. The reason was that it is difficult to project the view that the prophets who preached repentance related only to certain types of *baalei teshuvah* rather than to all-inclusive situations.

Thus R. Yochanan would maintain that any *tzaddik* is better than any type of a *baal teshuvah*. R. Abbahu, however, does not have to disagree with R. Yochanan. R. Abbahu's position is that a righteous person who occasionally sins and repents is better than a *tzaddik*; but a true *tzaddik* is certainly better than one who was wicked and subsequently repented (*Responsa*, Radbaz, Book 2, no. 832).

Eli's Accusation

QUESTION: The Bible reports that Eli, the *kohen gadol*, falsely accused Hannah of being a drunkard. What action of Hannah misled Eli into making such an error?

RESPONSE: *Tanach* states that Hannah entered the sanctuary (at Shilo) and began to cry (1 Samuel 1:10). Scripture adds,

"And it came to pass, as she continued [excessively] to pray . . . that Eli watched her mouth. Now as for Hannah, she spoke in her heart; only her lips moved, but her voice could not be heard, wherefore Eli regarded her as a drunken woman" (1 Samuel 1:12, 13).

Rashi (1:13) contends that common custom was not to pray silently. As such, Hannah's silent prayer was so strange that Eli assumed she was drunk.

This position appears contrary to *halachah*. Indeed, the Talmud derives from Hannah's silent prayer the rule that all prayer must be silent (*Berachot* 31a). In other words, Hannah's action serves as a model for the proper procedure during prayer. As such, it would seem highly irregular that common custom (in that time) would be to pray in a mode (aloud) contrary to halachic principles. Based upon this question, the Maharsha suggests an alternative reason for Eli's error. He contends that Hannah simply prayed too long. It was the (excessive) duration of her prayer that disturbed Eli (*Berachot* 31a).

Yet, even this theory has difficulty. The Talmud notes "such was the custom of R. Akivah; when he prayed with the congregation, he used to cut it short . . . in order not to inconvenience the congregation, but when he prayed by himself, a man would leave him in one corner and find him later in another on account of his . . . prostrations" (*Berachot* 31a). In other words, when a person prays alone, he can pray longer than when praying in a congregation. Alone, a person can pray as long as he or she so desires. There certainly wasn't a time limit on R. Akiva's prayers. Hannah was praying by herself. It appears that except for Eli, she was alone in the sanctuary. So what sin did she commit by praying longer than most others?

HaGaon R. Yechezkel Landau (the former chief rabbi of Prague) developed a theory to harmonize both Rashi and the Maharsha's positions.

He notes that there is a halachic distinction between personal prayer and prayer with a *minyan* pertaining to the requirement to *daven* silently. The *Shulchan Aruch* rules that the prohibition against audible prayer relates to prayer with a *min-*

yan. By oneself, one may recite even the *Shemoneh Esrei* aloud (*Orach Chayyim* 101:2).

One may assume that Hannah entered the sanctuary to pray in an area dedicated to prayer by all who so desired. In other words, many others may have been praying together with Hannah. But Hannah prayed longer than others. She continued to pray while others departed. As such, she remained alone in the sanctuary. Common custom in those times was to pray silently when praying with others and to pray aloud when praying alone. Eli noted that Hannah was all alone yet was praying silently. This was quite bizarre. (He didn't realize that Hannah started out with others and therefore continued silently even though she was alone.) Hence, it was the excessive length of the prayer that generated the error (Tzlach, *Berachot* 31a).

The Vilna Gaon provides a unique explanation for Eli's error. He suggests that the confusion was a result of the usage of the *efod* carried by the *kohen gadol*. The *efod* had twelve stones with the letters of the twelve tribes. Questions posed to the *Urim veTumin* would receive a response by certain letters (miraculously) being lit. It was the role of the *kohen gadol* to make sense out of the letters. Eli was concerned about Hannah and used the *Urim veTumim*. The following letters were lit: *Kaf, Sin* (*Shin*), *Reish, Heh*. Eli juggled them and came up with the word *shikora* (*Shin, Kaf, Reish, Heh*), which means drunkard. He missed the true meaning, which was *keSarah*, meaning that just as the barren matriarch Sarah gave birth, so too would Hannah (Devrei Eliyahu, 1 Samuel).

Denial

QUESTION: Is denial of pleasure a halachic obligation of the observant Jew? Namely, must a religious Jew seek out an ascetic lifestyle?

RESPONSE: No, not if he learns Torah.

Note the following talmudic citation, "Torah is comparable to a perfect elixir of life. For example, a man struck his son a strong blow, and then put a plaster on his wound, saying to him, 'My son! As long as this plaster is on your wound, you can *eat and drink at will*, and bathe in hot or cold water, without fear; but if you remove it, it will break into sores.' Even so did the Holy One, Blessed be He, speak unto Israel: My children, I created the Evil Desire but I also created Torah as its antidote; if you occupy yourselves with the Torah, you will not be delivered in his hand. . . . But if you do not occupy yourselves with Torah, you shall be delivered in his hand" (*Kiddushin* 30b).

R. Yaakov Raisher (author of the famed halachic classics *Shevut Yaakov* and *Chok Yaakov*) derives from this statement the principle that one who learns Torah need not afflict himself with fasting to curb the power of the evil impulse (the *yetzer hara*). The aforementioned talmudic statement shows that Torah has the power to provide a protective armor against temptation. Indeed, in *Taanit* 11a (another tractate), R. Shaishet contends that a *Ben Torah* who afflicts himself with fasting is deemed as if a dog devoured his meal. Notes Rashi that the meaning is that such a case is deemed as if the fast took place not due to religious motivation but because a dog devoured his food. As such, the person simply had nothing to eat and, therefore, fasted (see Iyun Yaakov – Commentary on *Ein Yaakov, Kiddushin* 30b).

From this we see that, a *Ben Torah* may enjoy life. It is the Jew ignorant of Torah who must perhaps utilize self-denial to control and impede the influence of the evil impulse. Not so the Torah Jew.

Tradition has it that the Brisker *rabbonim* were not enamored with the study of *Musar*, religious ethics. They believed that the study of Torah, by itself, was sufficient to mold character and impact positively moral behavior. When informed that *Musar* is medicine for the mind and spirit, the Brisker retort was "Our students are not sick, they need no extra medicine." Torah itself is the elixir of life.

Though denial may not be an obligatory function of the *Ben Torah*, it does serve as a form of atonement for sin.

The Talmud states, "If one fasts on *Shabbat*, a degree of seventy years standing may be annulled, yet all the same he is punished for neglecting to make the *Shabbat* a delight. What is his remedy? . . . Let him keep another fast to atone for this one" (*Berachot* 31b). Says Rashi, to fast while all are enjoying *Shabbat* is extremely difficult to observe. Accordingly, even if such a person had an evil decree set up over seventy years ago, it would be annulled.

Tosafot contend this is a fast to avert the omen of a dream. The Shita Mekubetzet, however, suggests that the person selected *Shabbat* to fast as a form of repentance (*teshuvah*) for sin. Of interest is that the fact of denial by itself is not granted the potency to annul sin. It is, rather, the fast on a *Shabbat* that is considered a unique atonement. On *Shabbat* Jews are happily enjoying festive meals. It's even a *mitzvah* to treat *Shabbat* with an increase of food and drink.

In the midst of such communal Jewish mirth and festivity, one Jew tortures himself by self-denial of food and drink. He thus compounds his denial by doing it on a day of feasting. The action, therefore, has the power of atonement. It is an unusually difficult task to accomplish. Such a fast requires a super effort of denial. But, it still is a sin. *Shabbat* is a day for joy, not fasting.

The process is comparable to the *nazir*, who vows not to drink wine. The process is a holy experience of denial. But, the Talmud rules, once the *nazir* concludes his period of abstinence a sacrifice (*korban*) must be brought, for the act of denial is classified as a *sin* (see *Taanit* 11a).

It should be noted that denial is not always a voluntary commitment. Indeed, there is a period wherein denial is obligatory, namely, at times when the community is in danger. When communal trouble prevails no one is permitted to say, "I will go to my house and I will eat and drink and all is well with me" (*Taanit* 11a). *In a crisis all must join together* for mutual support, strength, growth, and *even denial.*

Disclosing Tainted Backgrounds

QUESTION: In the event one knows that the wife of a young man is illegitimate (a *mamzeret*, bastard) is there any halachic imperative to inform either mate (or both) of such a tainted status problem?

RESPONSE: The Torah overtly states that a *mamzer* (bastard) is not "to enter the assembly of God." Rashi notes this to mean that a *mamzer* may not marry a legitimate Jewish mate (Deuteronomy 23:3). The Talmud and Codes define a *mamzer* (*mamzeret*, female) to be the offspring of an incestuous or adulterous relationship (*Yevamot* 49a; *Aruch HaShulchan*, *Even HaEzer* 4:4). Many children are unaware that they are classified as *mamzerim*. The most common cases are generated when a woman dissolves a marriage without going through the process of acquiring a *get*. Subsequently, she remarries and has children. These children are halachic *mamzerim*, for the second marriage is deemed comparable to an adulterous relationship since the woman remarried without a *get* (Jewish divorce).

A rabbi aware of such children would definitely not perform a wedding should they attempt to marry legitimate Jewish mates. At issue is a situation wherein it is known that a spouse is an halachic bastard. The question is whether it is obligatory to inform the mates of the family blemish. Should one inform the couple that their marriage was not sanctioned by the Torah or *halachah*? Is one mandated to tell the rabbi who performed the ceremony that he was not permitted to sanctify such a marriage?

Coupled to this may be an apprehension that the parents of the stigmatized family might mercilessly attempt to destroy the creditability of the person who stated that their child is a *mamzer*. Is it still necessary to get the record straight under these conditions?

HaRav HaGaon R. Yechezkiel Landau, famed chief rabbi of Prague, discussed a comparable problem in his *responsa* entitled *Noda B'Yehudah* (vol. 1, *Orach Chayyim* 35). This was the case.

A young man had sex for several years with a married woman. Subsequently, he married and was ashamed of his previous immoral activity. He wished to atone for his sins. Of concern was whether he was mandated to inform the husband of his former lover that his wife was an adulteress. The young man was prepared to commit himself to do any form of atonement suggested. Of major concern was the apprehension that revelation of such an immoral incident would negatively stigmatize the family, which was noted to have a prominent and distinguished lineage. The following represents a summary of the Noda B'Yehudah's key arguments.

The Talmud states, "If one finds *kelayim* (linen and wool) in his garment, he takes it off, even in the street. What is the reason? [It says]: There is no wisdom, nor understanding nor counsel against the Lord (Proverbs 2:30). Wherever a profanation of God's name is involved (*Chilul HaShem*) no respect is paid to a teacher. . . . [A]n objection was raised from the law that permits a *talmid chacham* to pass by a lost object and not return it in the event such involvement was not befitting his dignity. Is this not a case where human dignity of the *rav* takes precedence over the *mitzvah* of returning lost objects?" To this the Talmud replies that there is a special biblical commandment permitting such inaction. One, moreover, cannot generalize from this case "for we do not derive a ritual ruling from a case dealing with property." The Talmud notes another objection. The law is that should a person find a *met mitzvah*, a body, found in an area wherein no one is involved with the burial, then even if the finder is going to bring a *korban Pesach* (a Paschal sacrifice) and involvement with the burial would make him unfit to bring the sacrifice, it is still incumbent upon the person to bury the *met mitzvah*. But why should this be so? Is not the *mitzvah* of bringing the Passover sacrifice more important than caring for the burial needs of a Jewish body? To this again the Talmud retorts that this case is permitted because the Bible so mandated. If so, the Talmud poses the question, "Let us derive a ruling from this?" (namely, that human dignity takes priority over *mitzvot*, so that it would be wrong to remove linen and wool garments in the street—it would be an act against decency and propriety). To this the Talmud responds, "Where it is a case of sit still and do nothing (*shev v'al taaseh*), it is different" (*Berachot* 19b–20a). In other words, when faced with a choice of impropriety versus passive violation of Jewish law, the Jew may be concerned with eliminating the impropriety. However, when the same concern relates to a situation where one is violating Jewish law by an action, then the apprehension against the active violation is more important than are qualms over modesty or indecent behavior. Accordingly, wearing *kelayim* is deemed as if the person is constantly engaged in the action of putting on a forbidden garment. As such, the garment is to be removed even in the street. In such a circumstance, one cares not about personal feelings of modesty.

The Rambam and the Rosh debate the parameters of the above rule. The Rosh contends that the case of *kelayim* relates to a situation wherein a person, himself, becomes aware that he was wearing *kelayim*. In the event, however, where someone notes that another person is wearing *kelayim*, the Rosh does not require the person aware of the sin to remove the garment from his friend. Why? Since the wearer is violating a law unintentionally, it is comparable to a passive violation, and the Talmud rules that propriety and modesty take precedence over passive sins. The Rambam disagrees. His position is that anyone knowing of a sin committed by another is obliged to stop the sin itself, even if the person will be embarrassed by standing naked in the street. The Rambam, moreover, does not believe that an unintentional act is comparable to a passive position (Rambam, *Hilchot Kelayim* 6:29).

The Noda B'Yehudah contends that the issue of informing a husband that his wife is an adulteress may relate to the debate of the Rambam and Rosh. A man is not permitted to live as husband and wife with a women who is a prostitute or adulteress. Indeed, every time the husband has sex with his adulteress wife he is committing a sin. The fact that he is unaware that he is committing a sin is the same as a person unintentionally wearing *kela-*

yim. According to the Rambam, just as one is obliged to stop another from an unintentional sin, one is probably mandated to tell the husband, so that the husband may be averted from future sin. The Rosh's position would be that since the husband is unaware of any sin, it is comparable to a passive violation, which does not take priority over common decency and sensitivity. According to the Rosh, it is preferable to keep silent and not disturb the dignity of the family reputation.

The Noda B'Yehudah finely hones this debate. Perhaps, he suggests, even the Rambam would admit that one should not disturb family tranquillity by informing a husband of his wife's misdeeds against him. Maybe the Rambam requires drastic action only because the case of *kelayim* deals with *Chilul HaShem*, the public profanation of God's name. It's publicly noticeable that the person is wearing *kelayim*. Since *Chilul HaShem* is involved, every Jew is responsible to root out this drastic sin and cast away any violation. For this reason one is obliged (according to the Rambam) to take off another person's garment even in the street. In the event, however, where the violation is totally discreet and private perhaps even the Rambam would admit that "discretion is the better part of valor" and silence or inaction the best mode of behavior. Indeed, in the case at hand, no one but the adulterers are aware of the sin. The wife certainly is not telling of her indiscreet behavior. She, moreover, may not even know that it is sinful to remain as husband and wife after an adulterous union. In such a case, perhaps, even the Rambam would agree with the Rosh that silence is the best reaction to this situation. Namely, only *Chilul HaShem* demands action, even should it generate public embarrassment.

Of interest is that the Noda B'Yehudah rejects this hypothesis. The Talmud noted that a *talmid chacham* need not bother with returning a lost object should this not befit his dignity. This case certainly does not relate to *Chilul HaShem*. How is anyone to know whether the scholar actually saw the lost object and refused to pick it up or simply did not notice it at all? This case is private and does not relate to *Chilul HaShem*. Indeed, the second talmudic objection related to a person who accidently came across a *met mitzvah*. By its very nature a *met mitzvah* is not known to others. When one finds a *met mitzvah* one is required to bury it immediately. If others know about it, it is not a *met mitzvah*. Again, there is no relationship to *Chilul HaShem*. Indeed, the Talmud could have diffused both questions by noting that these above two cases did not relate to *Chilul HaShem* and, therefore, propriety took precedence. But the Talmud did not make this distinction. This implies that the sin itself is an act of *Chilul HaShem* regardless of whether it was a public or a private sin. The Rambam's insistence that one must simply remove a *kelayim* garment off another person has therefore nothing, to do with *Chilul HaShem*.

To the extent that the Rema rules like the Rosh in the matter of *kelayim*, one might assume that such is the final *halachah* (see *Yoreh De'ah* 303). To this the Noda B'Yehudah counsels, it is simply not so. The Rosh does not explicitly permit total passive silence in the face of someone committing a sin. The Rosh notes that should someone wear *kelayim* it is not obligatory to take it off in a public thoroughfare. It is, rather, permitted to return home and therein remove the forbidden garment. In other words, since the sin is only temporary (that is, until one returns home), the Rosh feels it is not necessary to publicly embarrass the sinner. In the event, however, wherein the violation is constant or on a regular permanent basis, then, perhaps, even the Rosh would agree that it is a religious obligation to stop the sin even should an embarrassment take place. Since living with an adulterous wife or a halachic bastard is a constant sinful action, then, suggests the Noda B'Yehudah, even the Rosh would mandate informing the sinner.

One may theoretically counter the preceding by arguing that perhaps temporary permission to wear *kelayim* relates to a situation where the person wearing *kelayim* himself is conscious of his sin. He realizes he, himself, is wearing *kelayim*. Even under such conscious awareness he is granted halachic sanction to temporarily wear the forbidden garment in the street. *Kavod habriyut*, concern for propriety, is so valued that according to the

Rosh it takes priority over even a conscious sin, providing the sin is temporary. However, where the sinner is totally unaware of any wrongdoing, then perhaps, the Rosh would mandate silence or inaction even if the so-called act of unconscious sin were a constant process.

The Noda B'Yehudah rules that such logic is not appropriate. Why? He feels that logically no sense of propriety should in any way impact *mitzvot*. The latter should normally take propriety over even public humiliation. The fact that any consideration is granted to a concern for propriety is by itself a unique concept.

This suggests that, perhaps, one should not derive fine distinctions from this law. Since permission to wear *kelayim* is extended only on a temporary basis (till one comes home), perhaps such should be the guiding principle. Namely, propriety may take precedence over a violation of Jewish law only when the act is of a temporary nature.

A further concern may relate to the pragmatic impact of an action. Perhaps it is mandatory to inform a person of a sinful act only when such information or action may avert a sin. Namely, one may simply remove the garment of *kelayim*. Thus, the public embarrassment of a person at least accomplished the goal of stopping a person from committing a sin. In a case, however, where a person will continue to sin regardless of another's interference, words, or actions, then perhaps, silence or passive inaction may be the best guide.

Testimony stating that a woman committed adultery requires two witnesses to outlaw her husband from living together with his wife. In fact, a husband need not believe the testimony of a single witness. He may but he may not. Should he believe the testimony of the single witness, then he is forbidden to live with his wife. Should he not believe such testimony, then he may remain living together with his wife. Accordingly, perhaps in such a situation one is not to inform a husband of an adulterous wife. To this the Noda B'Yehudah says that one must still inform the husband. His reason is that lack of knowledge as to how the husband may react has nothing to do with the *mitzvah* of providing him with such knowledge. Indeed, should we be certain that the husband would rid himself of his wife the moment he heard of her adulterous past, then no one would question the merit of informing him. Since we do not know his reaction, the doubt shouldn't hinder the *mitzvah* of rebuking him.

Thus, the Noda B'Yehudah concludes that it is imperative to inform the husband of his wife's adulterous affair regardless of the ramifications that may emerge (see *Responsa, Noda B'Yehudah*, vol. 1, *Orach Chayyim*, no. 35). Initial reaction is that the same line of reasoning should apply to knowledge pertaining to someone's tainted lineage. It is a *mitzvah* to withhold people from committing sins. It should, therefore, be a *mitzvah* to inform a couple that a mate is a halachic bastard. This rule should apply regardless of repercussions.

It may be demonstrated that the Noda B'Yehudah's arguments are not necessarily compelling. Originally, it was suggested that even the Rambam's lack of concern for propriety or public shame in the face of a violation of Jewish law was limited to cases of *Chilul HaShem*. In cases wherein *Chilul HaShem* was not an issue, then even the Rambam might opt for passive silence. The logic was good. The reason this position was refuted was that the text of the talmudic discussion of this law seemed to deal with nonpublic cases that had no manifestation of *Chilul HaShem*. A rabbi who did not pick up a lost object was certainly not a case of *Chilul HaShem*. No one would know whether the rabbi actually saw or did not see the object. The second talmudic case of a man going to bring a Paschal lamb who finds a dead body was also suggested that it was a private situation lacking any vestige of *Chilul HaShem*. No one knows of the body nor that this person may have passed it by.

Both arguments, however, may be refuted. The Talmud in another section asks, "What constitutes profanation of the Holy Name (*Chilul HaShem*)?" Rav said, "If, for example, I take meat from the butcher and do not pay him at once." Says Rashi, "Since I (a rabbi) delay payment he'll contend I'm not honest and will in return diminish the butcher's negative value towards stealing . . . or others may feel the rabbi takes objects without payment" (*Yoma* 86a). Thus any public scene wherein people may even falsely make negative assumptions is classified as a *Chilul HaShem*. Said R. Yochanan, "In any case [it is a profanation if] I walk four cubits without [uttering words of] Torah or [wearing] *tefillin*" (*Yoma* 86a). Again says Rashi, people are unaware that he was ill and not able to perform *mitzvot*, but will [erroneously] assume that if R. Yochanan does not need to talk Torah nor should they. Thus, *Chilul HaShem* may occur even though the act was not necessarily sinful. It may even be an innocent action that people falsely (jump to the conclusion) and disparage Torah or its scholars as a result. Such a definition of *Chilul HaShem* is applicable to the talmudic cases in *Berachot*. (1) A scholar passes a wallet in the street. He is alone. He doesn't pick it up. Others subsequently pass by the same object. They learn that a *rav* passed it over. Would not this generate a lack of respect for rabbis? Would not people suggest that the rabbi is so impressed with his own *kavod* that he refused to care for another's property? This is definitely *Chilul HaShem*. (2) A man passes a dead body while going to Jerusalem. Others, however, may come later and see the dead body. It would be known that the first person was so concerned with bringing a sacrifice that he cared not for the dignity of the dead body; that too would be a *Chilul HaShem*. Since the talmudic cases now harmonize with the theory of *Chilul HaShem*, maybe when no *Chilul HaShem* is operational, silence is the best halachic position. Awareness of a tainted ancestry is a very private concern. It is not public knowledge. There's no *Chilul HaShem*. Indeed, one may even conjecture that even the Rosh, who granted permission on a temporary basis to wear *kelayim*, also related to an act of *Chilul HaShem*. For this reason even he prohibited wearing the *kelayim* after a short period of time. Otherwise, even the Rosh would mandate passive silence.

There are additional reasons to suggest silence and inaction as the preferred behavioral mode.

The *Shulchan Aruch* rules that should a person on *Shabbat* be, for example, reading a book in the privacy of his home and someone extended his hand from the outside to the inside of the house and took the book out of the house, the person in the house violates a rabbinic law (*Orach Chayyim* 347). The assumption is that the man inside the house contributed somewhat to the sin. He could have moved his book. He could have, perhaps, called out it was *Shabbat* so that the sin could possibly have been averted. His inaction in being part of a *Shabbat* violation is inexcusable.

The *Mishnah Berurah* (in the *Shar HaTzion*, notes 347:8) questions this law. He states that this law does not relate to the biblical injunction of "do not put a stumbling block before the blind" (*lifnei Iver*) for that injunction is only operational when the person cannot (or without great difficulty) acquire the sin without any Jewish involvement. When the person may easily sin without any activity, there is yet another biblical *mitzvah*. It is the commandment of "giving reproof," *hocheiach tocheiach* – rebuke thy neighbor (Leviticus 19:17). This *mitzvah*, according to the Rambam, is operational whenever one notes another violating a *mitzvah* (see *Berachot* 19b). At issue is why in the laws of *Shabbat* is the man in the house violating only a rabbinic decree. It should be a biblical injunction against silent inaction. To this the *Mishnah Berurah* makes the following distinction: The biblical command to reprove another is only when one may avert the sin. In the event one cannot stop the sin from taking place, there is no biblical command to speak out, only a rabbinic mandate.

In such a case, should there be serious doubt as to whether there is a mandate to disclose anything (that is, no *Chilul HaShem*), perhaps the rule to follow would be *safek d'rabbanan l'kula* – that whenever there is a doubt in a rabbinic rule, leniency is the guide.

The debate previously noted between the Rambam and Rosh related to a situation wherein a person noted another violating a biblical command. The Talmud ruled that *kavod habriyut* – concern for propriety or a need to sustain dignity and avert humiliation took priority only when the sin may be transgressed via a passive inaction. Of interest is that this limiting rule does not apply to a scene wherein the sin is only a rabbinic decree. Whenever there is a choice between transgressing the concept of *kavod habriyut* or that of a rabbinic law, then *kavod habriyut* takes priority (*Orach Chayyim* 13:3 – see Magen Avraham).

Of interest is where the sin taking place is biblical. But I, the person to avert the sin, perceive my obligation to be only rabbinic in nature (that is, he'll continue doing it anyway) and coupled to this is a concern for both the *kavod habriyut* of the sinner's family and mine (to be publicly involved in a family broil); perhaps no obligation is operational in this situation. For up to now no moral or halachic discussion related to the *kavod habriyut* of the informer. Yet, his present or future status is an integral part of the final halachic mandate.

Halachah does not dismiss the potential negative ramifications of the informer or individual who seeks to stop the sin of another. The Rema rules, "Even though it is an obligation to protest sin [by attempting to avert the sin] and anyone who has the potential to do so and resists making such a protest is deemed as if he [himself] committed the transgression, yet one is not obligated to expend funds for this matter and therefore common custom is to be lenient and not protest against sinners for one may be apprehensive that they [the sinners] will retaliate against us both physically and monetarily" (*Yoreh De'ah* 334:48). Accordingly, a realistic fear of retaliation halachicly influences the mandate to respond to another's sin. Why should not one Jew attempt to stop another from sin? Yet, if the motivation for the inaction is fear for personal safety, then the biblical mandate may not be operational. The Rema makes no distinction between a violation of a biblical or a rabbinic *mitzvah*. He states a general rule that whenever retaliation is probable, the best course is silent inaction. How much more so should silence be the course of action when: (a) perhaps no obligation to speak out exists; (b) the sin will take place regardless of any action (or inaction); and (c) definite, serious potential physical and/or financial repercussions will emerge.

What is evident, moreover, is that whenever *Chilul HaShem* is present, then all legal lenient positions may not be operational. In the face of *Chilul HaShem* one cares not about personal dignity. *Chilul HaShem* is such a grave sin that any active process of committing such a sin must be stopped.

The Talmud reports the following incident. A person by error invited his enemy Bar Kamtza to a party rather than his friend Kamtza. The host was so annoyed with Bar Kamtza that he expelled him from his party even though Bar Kamtza said he would pay for the cost of the entire party if he were not publicly embarrassed. Bar Kamtza subsequently was so shamed that he incited the emperor to attack the Jews. Bar Kamtza contended that his humiliation was sanctioned by the rabbis. Why? "Since the rabbis were sitting there and did not stop him [the host]. This shows they agreed with him" (*Gittin* 55b, 56a). Were the rabbis guilty of the charge? Were they mandated to protest Bar Kamtza's public humiliation? The Talmud seems to indicate that the rabbis were wrong in their silence. The solution may be that public humiliation may be a form of *Chilul HaShem*; especially when rabbis are present. That's why they should have protested.

This suggests that rabbis may have more of a pavlovian response to protest sin than others. Their silence may be falsely assumed to be acquiescence and support. So, regardless of whether they have the ability to avert the sin, rabbinical protest of public sin may be necessary to forestall erroneous assumptions of rabbinic approval.

IV

Parenthood, Marriage, and Children

Honoring Nonobservant Parents

QUESTION: Is the biblical command to honor parents applicable even to parents who are not observant of *mitzvot?*

RESPONSE: Halachic sages debate this issue. HaRav Yosef Caro in the *Shulchan Aruch* rules that respect for parents is a mandate imposed upon children regardless of the religious behavioral pattern of parents. He notes that one must respect a father even should the father be a *rasha* or a person who commits sin. The Rema, however, demurs. He contends that respect is not obligatory upon such a father unless he has repented (*Yoreh De'ah* 240:18). Note the terminology of the Rema. He does not state that the *mitzvah* of honoring parents is not applicable to irreligious parents. He merely says that a child is not obligated to respect such parents. The implication is that should a child upon his or her own discretion volunteer to honor parents who are not observant then a *mitzvah* indeed takes place. The observance of the parents relates only to the mandatory nature of the *mitzvah.* Indeed, the Shach notes that even according to those who contend that one is not obliged to honor nonobservant parents, one is still prohibited to cause them harm or anguish (*Yoreh De'ah* 240:20; see also 241:4).

Of interest is that the Vilna Gaon cites the following talmudic case to substantiate the Rema's ruling (*Yoreh De'ah* 240:29). The *Gemara* states, "Where the father [a known thief] left them [through inheritance to children] a cow or a garment which could [easily] be identified [as a stolen object] they [the children] are liable to restore [it] in order to uphold the honor of the father. . . . But why should they be liable to return [the items] in order to uphold the honor of the father? Why not apply to them [the verse] nor curse the ruler of thy people (Exodus 22:27), [which is explained to mean] so long as he is acting in the spirit of thy people." (Namely, excluding one who violates Jewish law. Thus one should not be obliged to restore the honor of a father who is a thief.) (To this the Talmud retorts:) "We assume the father made repentance. But if the father had repented why was the misappropriated article still left with him? Should he not have returned it? It might be that he had no time to restore it before he [suddenly] died" (*Bava Kamma* 94b). The Vilna Gaon contends that this citation demonstrates that children have no obligation to honor sinful parents unless they repent.

It may be noted, however, that this citation may not necessarily be used as proof for the Rema's ruling. The P'nei Yehoshua (*Bava Kamma* 94b) suggests that even if a child is mandated to respect nonreligiously observant parents there is a loophole to this concept. It is that a child is not to disregard the sin that the parent actually commits. In other words, in the event a parent is a thief, a child is not obliged to clear the reputation of his father on this matter since his father himself cares not about honesty. On other issues, however, the son may be obliged to be obedient to his father. One, therefore, cannot establish a general rule that since the father sinned in one situation all respect in other cases is to be denied him.

Indeed, it may be demonstrated that there are special, unusual circumstances in talmudic cases wherein parents were not required to be respected. Two further examples.

1. The *Mishnah* rules that a bastard son (a *mamzer*) is punished for striking his father. To this the Talmud states: "But why? One should apply here the scriptural text, '*nor curse the ruler of thy people*' only when he practices the deeds of thy people." (The father caused the son to be a bastard by committing the crime of incest. Accordingly, the father is a sinner and should not be afforded any honor.) To this the Talmud notes "here is a case where the father [subsequently] repented." (Thus, he is presently observing the dictates of *K'lal Yisrael* and must be treated with respect) (*Yevamot* 22b). From this case it is evident that had the father not repented, the son would not have been obliged to respect him. Again, no general rule may be derived from this citation. This case is unique in that the father's sinful act delegitimized his son. It's as if the father did not care whether his son would be born with a blemish of pedigree. The father cared not about the status of his son. In such a circumstance,

perhaps, the son is not obliged to honor his parent unless the parent repents.

2. The Talmud notes that "six things King Hezekiah did and in three they [the sages] agreed with him. . . . He dragged his father's bones [corpse] on a rope bier, and they agreed with him" (*Pesachim* 56a). Rashi notes that this was not a dignified burial. King Hezekiah's action was to atone for the evilness of his father. The implication is that one need not respect a wicked, nonobservant father.

This case also has specific reasons why respect was withheld.

A. The Radbaz suggests that respect for a nonobservant parent is based on the premise that he may repent. Once a parent dies without repenting, no respect is obligatory (Rambam, *Hilchot Mamrim* 5:12).

B. The Tiferet Yisrael suggests that respect for a parent after death is but a rabbinic command. In the event the parent was not observant, the rabbis never applied their requirement (*Pesachim*, chap. 4).

C. Perhaps King Hezekiah wished to generate a general atmosphere of scorn to sinners. As such, his action was a special case to generate *teshuvah*.

Based upon the aforementioned considerations, no conclusive proof exists to substantiate the general principle that nonobservant parents do not mandate honor from their children. Indeed, all agree that children may volunteer respect to such parents. The implication is that when such respect is granted, a *mitzvah* is generated. The Bible promises that respect to parents is repaid by long life. It would appear, therefore, that since the matter deals with a *mitzvah* (*min HaTorah*) the normal scrupulous response would be to assume that stringency should be the deciding guide and respect should be provided.

Mourning a Parent

QUESTION: Why is it that *halachah* mandates a longer period of mourning for a parent than for children?

RESPONSE: It is reported that when the *rosh hayeshivah* of Yeshiva University, HaRav HaGaon Yosef Dov Soloveitchik, was sitting *shivah* for his wife, the following interesting discussion took place. Many rabbis came to pay their respect and to offer condolences. To the extent that it became an assemblage of great Torah scholars, a theoretical question was posed relating to the laws of mourning.

Jewish law requires a mourner for a parent to demonstrate acts of mourning far in excess of that which is required when mourning over the loss of a mate or a child. For example, mourning for a mate or a child is for a period of only thirty days (*shloshim*). Mourning rituals for a parent are for a period of a year. Yet, such mourning patterns appear to be contrary to logic and nature. Parents, by their very existence and nature are older than we, their children, are. It is, therefore, self-evident and normally anticipated that parents will die while their children are yet alive. It's normal; it's natural for such to take place. On the other hand, it is not so normal or natural for children to die in the lifetime of their parents. It is certainly not the anticipated behavior for such to occur. In fact, it's an unusual, shocking, tragic experience when a child dies. So the *halachah* should really reflect this concept. The duration of mourning should depend upon the quality of the trauma. To the extent that the loss of a child galvanizes and crystallizes a more massive unexpected trauma than that of a parent, the mourning period for a child should be greater and longer than that imposed upon the death of a parent. And yet, that is not the case. Everybody knows that Jewish law imposes a longer mourning period for the loss of a parent. Why is this so? Why does *halachah* deem the loss of a parent to be so unique and so traumatic?

Of interest is that two great rabbis were present during this discussion. One was HaRav HaGaon Yitzchok Hutner, the *rosh yeshivah* of the Rabbi Chaim Berlin Rabbinical Academy. The other was the great pulpit rabbi, the chief rabbi of Elizabeth, New Jersey, HaRav HaGaon Pinchas Teitz. Both expressed thoughts as to why Jewish law considers mourning for a parent so much more tragic than any other loss.

Rav Hutner's position was that the tragedy of parental loss is that such a death formally places the children yet another generation further away from the revelation of Mount Sinai. It is a formal recognition that an era has ended. The children are totally on their own, one more generation further removed from the lessons of Sinai. The message of Torah is therefore fainter and less clear than available to the previous generation. We mourn the distance from the source of Torah. Torah is a *mesorah*, a tradition whereby one generation hands down the eternal truths to yet another generation. *Mosheh Kibeil Torah miSinai umesarah leYehoshua*—"Moses accepted the Torah from Sinai and gave it over to Joshua"; and he to the elders and they to the prophets. Each generation learned from the past what to give to the future. The death of parents formally signifies that the past is no longer here to help us. We are the ones to transmit the future. The death of parents signifies that the new transmission will be weaker than the past. We are now on our own. A Judaism based upon tradition and *mesorah* is not overjoyed when a past generation is no longer available to help us. The goal of the Jew is to become closer to Sinai, not further away.

Rav Teitz, however, gave a more concrete, psychological response to our problem. His contention was that the loss of a parent is in a class of its own, for in no way is it comparable or replicated by any other situation. Parents are unique. They are irreplaceable. A person could pragmatically have more than one brother or sister. A person could conceivably remarry at the loss of a mate. Of course, it may not be the same, but the status of a mate could be replaced. A person could, perhaps, have several children. Though each child is unique, it is still clear that a person could have several children and be consoled by that fact. When it comes to parents, however, there is no replacement. A human is born but once. When parents die they are irreplaceable. There is no way to make up this loss. It is for this reason that *halachah* demands greater periods of mourning for a parent than for any other person. The Torah is teaching us that we have to care for with greater appreciation and unusual sensitivity that which cannot ever be replaced. A priceless relationship is one that is unique. It stands alone.

(For a basic report of this incident, see Maged Yosef, Rabbi Yosef Yehudah Leib Sorotzkin [*Parashat Re'eh*, p. 231].)

Celebrating the Sixtieth, Seventieth, and Eightieth Birthdays

QUESTION: Is there any religious significance to the sixtieth, seventieth, and eightieth birthday? Are parties commemorating such events classified as religious celebrations?

RESPONSE: Yes. A careful reading of talmudic citations intimates that these birthdays are religious milestones and that it is halachically proper to commemorate such events by having a festive meal, which definitely may be deemed a *seudat mitzvah*.

Tradition has it that death prior to certain ages is considered a form of divine punishment. Scripture notes a punishment called *kara'it*. The Talmud reports, "*Rabbah* said, [should a person die] from fifty to sixty years [of age], that is death by *kara'it* (cutting off). . . . Rav Yosef, on his attaining the age of sixty, made a festival day (*yoma tova*) for the rabbis saying, 'I have just passed the [limit of] *kara'it* for years'" (*Mo'ed Katan* 28a). What is the definition of the term "a festival day for the rabbis"? Of interest is that a similar phrase is utilized by the same Rav Yosef regarding another type of celebration. The Talmud (*Kiddushin* 31a) discusses Rav Yosef's unique quandary. He was blind and pondered as to whether such a person was yet obligated to observe commandments. Said Rav Yosef, whoever would inform him that a blind person was obligated to observe commandments, [he would be so overjoyed to such a knowledge of commitment] "he would make a festival day (*yoma tova*) for the rabbis." Rashi explains the phrase to mean a festive meal, a banquet. In other words, he would celebrate such information by hosting a party. Commenting on this citation, Rav Shlomo Luria (the Rashal) contends that this is the source for the common custom to celebrate the *bar mitzvah* of a young boy with a festive meal. Rav Yosef was so overjoyed that he (a blind person) was yet obligated to perform commandments that he celebrated it with a party. In other words, the joy at the assumption of religious requirements obligates a festive celebration. Is this not what occurs at a *bar mitzvah*? Is not a child at his thirteenth birthday becoming newly obligated to observe *mitzvot*? Accordingly, such a party is deemed a *seudat mitzvah* (Yom Shel Shlomo, *Kiddushin* 31a).

From the preceding, it is clear that the phrase "a festive day for the rabbis" relating to Rav Yosef's sixtieth birthday, also refers to a festive meal, a party. Such a party definitely may be classified as a *seudat mitzvah*. It takes place to celebrate passing through the ages of *kara'it*. Indeed, we have a general rule. "R. Shimon said, every feast which is not associated with a religious deed (a *mitzvah*), a scholar may not derive any enjoyment thereof" (*Pesachim* 49a). Accordingly, Rav Yosef would not be permitted to participate at his own party, unless it was classified as one that celebrated a *mitzvah*. To the extent that Rav Yosef even limited the guests to rabbis definitely indicates that it was proper and in accordance with *halachah*.

A Seventieth Birthday

In the talmudic section of *Mo'ed Katan* previously cited, there is another definition of *kara'it*. It states that "if one dies under fifty years that is death by *kara'it* . . . at sixty that is (death) by the hand of heaven." Subsequently, Rabbah states that death from fifty to sixty years [of age], is death by *kara'it* (*Mo'ed Katan* 28a). Of concern is Rabbah's lack of concern for the second fateful form of divine punishment, namely, death by the hand of heaven (*Mita*

b'dei Shamayim). Rabbah mentions only *kara'it*. We must logically assume that Rabbah disagrees with the first citation in not
only one but two instances. Rabbah considers the conclusion of
kara'it to be at age sixty and not fifty. In addition, it appears
logical to assume that he extends the conclusion of "death by the
hand of heaven" to age seventy, not sixty. As such, Rabbah would
also hold that *kara'it* is ten years younger than the second-level
punishment of "death by the hand of heaven." Just as age sixty
was celebrated, similar logic would contend that one's seventieth
birthday should also be afforded religious significance in that the
person may no longer be punished by "death by the hand of
heaven."

An Eightieth Birthday

The aforementioned talmudic discussion (*Mo'ed Katan* 28a) notes
that sudden death was not deemed praiseworthy. Yet, "should
one attain the age of strength [eighty], a sudden death is [classi-
fied] as dying by the Kiss." The latter is deemed a blessing.
Accordingly, one who has arrived at such a blissful state certainly should celebrate the status transformation by a party that
definitely seems to be a *seudat mitzvah*, regardless of whether
special Torah addresses are related.

Marrying Prior to Older Siblings

QUESTION: May a younger brother or sister get married
before an older sibling?

RESPONSE: The Torah deals with this issue. It reports that
the patriarch Yaakov was quite perturbed to learn that by some

error he married Leah, the older sister, and not Rachel, the younger sister whom he loved. Indeed, Yaakov so loved Rachel that he openly stipulated that he would serve seven years in order to gain her hand in marriage. He could not comprehend the motivation for the deception (see Genesis 29:18–25). Responding to Yaakov's indignation, Lavan, his father-in-law states, "It is not done so in our place to give the younger before the elder" (Genesis 29:26).

There are a number of interpretations to Lavan's statement. Rav Samson Raphael Hirsch, for example, suggests that the local custom was unique in that should one seek to marry a younger sister, the unmarried older sister was automatically included. Since one may not marry the younger prior to the older sister, the first marriage must of necessity go to the older sister. As such, the first marriage was to Leah. That was Lavan's deceptive ruse to marry off both daughters.

Of concern is whether Lavan's general principle that a younger sibling is not to marry prior to an older sibling has any basis in *halachah*.

Tosafot report a case brought to the attention of Rabbeinu Tam. A man said to the father of several daughters, "Your daughter is betrothed to me." Yet, he did not specifically name the particular daughter he wished to marry. Rabbeinu Tam (at first) ruled that the man was married to the oldest daughter. Why? Because the Torah established a principle, "It is not done so in our place to give the younger before the elder" (Genesis 29:26). Tosafot conclude that due to unique *halachot* relating to doubtful marriages, Rabbeinu Tam changed his mind and did not act on his theory (*Kiddushin* 52a). Of interest is that the concept of marrying off older children prior to younger children is articulated as a basic premise.

Indeed, the Talmud reports that when the Torah states that the daughters of Zelophehad were married, each daughter was listed according to age, namely, the oldest first and the youngest last (Numbers 36:11; *Bava Batra* 120a). Rashbam notes that this is based on the principle that "it is not done so in our place to give the younger before the elder" (Genesis 29:26). The Shach (citing the Bach) rules that when brothers or sisters are to be married, priority should be granted to marry off the elder sibling prior to the younger, regardless of the degree of wisdom of the younger child (*Yoreh De'ah* 244:13).

The implication is that Lavan's rule is backed by *halachah*. Yet, a number of distinctions may be noted.

1. HaRav HaGaon R. Baruch Epstein (author, *Torah Temimah*) suggests that Lavan's rule is an obligation imposed upon a parent but not necessarily upon the children. It is the parent who is not to marry off a younger daughter prior to older siblings. Yet, the prospective bridegroom, for example, has no sin to seek out a younger daughter before her older sister marries. Proof is the fact that Yaakov committed no sin in attempting to marry Rachel even before the older sister Leah was married. As such, it is the parent who must be sensitive to the feelings and respect for older siblings. The suitor is under no obligation to be concerned with the feelings of the older siblings who might be slighted if a younger sister marries first (see Tosefot *Berachah*, Genesis 29:26).

Though this may be the case, the biblical listing of the marriage of the daughters of Zelophehad indicate that even though parents are not alive, they still marry according to age. Indeed perhaps, suggests HaRav Epstein, younger children should be sensitive to the anguish of their older siblings (see Tosafot, *Berachah*, Numbers 36:11).

2. Yet, the case of the daughters of Zelophehad may indicate that it is a nice gesture, should younger children await the marriage of older siblings, but no sin takes place should younger siblings so desire to marry prior to older siblings. In addition, there also may be no obligation for younger siblings to await the marriage of older siblings. It is merely a gesture of graciousness, not a mandate.

3. I suggest that the issue relates to the concern as to whether younger siblings are required to honor older siblings. The *Shulchan Aruch* rules that "one is obligated to honor one's oldest brother" (*Yoreh De'ah* 240:22). The Shevut Yaakov rules that this honor is limited and restricted to the firstborn son. The

firstborn son (the *bechor*) has a unique role in *halachah* not afforded other children. It is the firstborn son who is granted a double portion of inheritance. Accordingly, he and he alone is to be respected by the other siblings. No other child is to receive such respect (*Responsa, Shevut Yaakov*, vol. 1, no. 76). The Mishmeret Shalom (*Yoreh De'ah* 240:19) disagrees. He contends that all older brothers and sisters must be honored. (For a detailed discussion of this subject see my *Timely Jewish Questions, Timeless Rabbinic Answers*, pp. 310–313.)

Now, if younger siblings need not honor older siblings, they may get married prior to older siblings. If, on the other hand, younger siblings must honor older siblings, then the younger ones must, of course, consider the older ones' sensitivities and not marry before them. To the extent that all agree that one must honor the firstborn elder brother, it would appear that he has priority in marriage.

The Marriage Fast

QUESTION: Why must the bride and bridegroom fast on the day of their wedding? Also, may greater leniency be extended to the bride than to the bridegroom?

RESPONSE: There are two basic reasons why a bride and bridegroom fast on the day of their marriage.

1. Such a time is comparable to Yom Kippur in that sins are forgiven.

2. The fast ensures that the couple will not drink any intoxicating beverages that may dissipate their ability to be fully aware of their marriage commitments.

Each theory generates pragmatic distinctions. According to the first theory, the fast should conclude once the day officially ends even though it is prior to the *chuppah* itself. Also, even though the *chuppah* was at mid-day, perhaps the fast should continue until the end of the day. According to the second theory, the fast should conclude at the end of the marriage ceremony regardless of the time of day (or night).

The Chachmot Adam rules that since this (marriage day) fast is not recorded in the Talmud, one may rely upon the first theory to permit breaking the fast once the day concludes, even prior to the *chuppah*. He cautions, however, that the couple should not ingest any intoxicating beverage (*K'lal* 129:2).

Of interest is that HaGaon Rav Aryeh Levin rules that in such a case, the couple should not drink milk. Why? It appears that sources indicate that milk induces the drowsy effect of intoxication. Some examples: (1) The Talmud states that one who drank milk is prohibited to enter the *Bet HaMikdash* just as one who drank wine has a similar prohibition (*Berachot* 45b). (2) The Shach rules that one who drank milk should not rule on halachic issues (*Yoreh De'ah* 242:20). The rationale must be that, just as usage of alcohol dims intellectual perception, so too does milk (probably hot milk). (3) Numerous commentators contend that Yael fed Sissera milk, which induced a sense of intoxication. Accordingly, even should the couple eat prior to the wedding, no milk (probably hot milk) should be ingested (*Responsa, Avnei Cheifetz*, no. 48).

A custom in a number of communities was that the bridegroom fasted, but not the bride. The Sdai Chemed suggests that, since drunkedness was not prevalent by Jewish women, some communities never imposed a fast upon the women (*Maarechet Chatan V'Kallah*, no. 4). Thus, there is precedent to extend greater leniency to the bride than to the bridegroom (see Eishel Avraham, *Orach Chayyim* 573).

The *Aruch HaShulchan* rules that should it be quite difficult for the bride and bridegroom to fast, they are permitted to eat (*Even HaEzer* 61:21). In other words, halachic authorities did not demand stringency for those who had major difficulties with fasting.

(It should be noted that I have *never* observed any bride *or* bridegroom whose marriage took place in the daytime continue fasting until nightfall.)

Insuring a Dowry

QUESTION: Is it halachically feasible for parents of a bride to ensure that the dowry given to a prospective bridegroom be returned in the event of a divorce?

RESPONSE: The following ruling by the medieval sage Ha-Gaon R. Yosef Katz has contemporary relevance.

A bride's family committed themselves to provide a substantial dowry to a prospective bridegroom. They, therefore, requested that the *ketubah* contain a clause obligating the bridegroom to pay his wife in the event of a divorce an amount equal to the dowry. The bridegroom, however, refused to alter the accepted text of the *ketubah*.

R. Yosef Katz posed two halachic questions:

1. In the event a substantial dowry is granted to a bridegroom, does the bride's family have the right to demand repayment in the event of a divorce?

2. Should the bride's family have such a right? Then, what is the proper procedure to obligate such repayment?

HaGaon R. Katz ruled that logic supports the position of the bride's family. Prior to the *takanah* of Rabbeinu Gershon, a man was permitted to divorce his wife even without her consent. Should a man not be obligated to repay a dowry, the following bizarre case could conceivably occur. A man would marry a woman and receive a substantial dowry. The next day he could divorce her and thus profit by the transaction. This, ruled R.

Katz, would be an illogical, would be an illogical, immoral, and
"boorish" custom. Accordingly, a request for repayment of a
dowry in the event of a divorce is a basic obligation sanctioned by
halachah.

Yet R. Katz believed that such an obligation should preferably not be included within the text of the *ketubah.* The standard
text should not be altered so as not to embarrass those brides
who do not provide dowries to their prospective husbands. The
custom in his area (Cracow) was to write a separate document
delineating the requirement to repay the dowry in the event of a
divorce (She'erit Yosef, *Responsum* 45). Such a procedure has
merit in our contemporary society.

Note: HaGoan R. Yosef Katz was the brother-in-law of the
Rema and *rosh hayeshivah* of Cracow for forty years. The author
is a direct descendant of this sage.

The Date of the Ketubah

QUESTION: A wedding occurred on a Sunday night. The *ketubah* recorded the day of the wedding as Sunday, the first day of
the Hebrew week. The actual ceremony occurred on Sunday
night after sunset (*sheki'ah*). Since Jewish Law reckons a calen-
dar-date change in the evening, is the *ketubah* invalid, for it
contained an incorrect date?

RESPONSE: This issue usually generates problems, and a
variety of halachic techniques are utilized to resolve them. A
practical guideline may be noted in the following incident
(*maaseh rav*).

In August 1981, HaGaon R. Shneur Kotler (*z"l*), the renowned Lakewood, New Jersey, *rosh hayeshivah*, was scheduled
to perform a marriage in Los Angeles. The difficulty was that the

rosh hayeshivah had to attend an emergency meeting in New York City the day of the wedding and would arrive in Los Angeles only in the evening. In fact, he would arrive after sunset, after the wedding procession had commenced. Thus, the date of the *ketubah* became a matter of debate. As a means of resolving the difficulty, it was suggested that I call the *rosh hayeshivah* and directly request his halachic ruling on the matter. This I did. The *rosh hayeshivah* was informed of the problem and was asked, "How much time, if any, after *sheki'ah* may one utilize a *ketubah* that records a calendar date prior to sunset?" His response, "Up to seventy-two minutes after *sheki'ah* the old date may be used."

Covering the Face of the Bride

QUESTION: A common custom is to have the bride's face totally covered during the *chuppah* (marriage) ceremony. Is this proper?

RESPONSE: Though this custom is widespread and practiced without the demure of great sages who perform such ceremonies, logic suggests serious halachic problems with this practice.

The traditional marriage ceremony requires the groom to present a ring to his bride and to recite the betrothal in the presence of two witnesses. Great care is made that the witnesses are observant Jews. To eliminate halachic problems, two witnesses are designated to be solely responsible to observe the ring ceremony to the exclusion of others. Now, this is the issue:

The bride is so covered by the veil that the witnesses under the *chuppah* cannot see her face. As such, it is impossible to testify accurately who received the ring. It's truly not certain as to the exact person under the veil. Is it the same bride noted

before at the *badecking*? Were the witnesses at the ring ceremony present at the veil ceremony? Should they have been
there? Even if they were—there are no witnesses able to testify
who actually received the ring at the wedding.

Assume someone borrowed money from another and the
transaction took place in the presence of two witnesses. Yet the
person who received the money had his face hidden by a mask
and was totally silent. Can the witnesses actually testify who
received the money? Of course not. As such, the custom of
covering the face of the bride with a veil that completely hides
her face during the ceremony should invalidate the role of the
witnesses. It is reputed that because of such concerns a noted
rosh yeshivah would refrain from performing a wedding unless
the bride—even under the *chuppah*—revealed her face to the
witnesses.

A suggested rationale may be derived from the custom of
conducting *tenayim* (the engagement) directly prior to the wedding ceremony. Indeed, even this custom is a matter of halachic
confusion pertaining to its purpose and function. HaGaon Rav
Yosef Engel contends that every marriage ceremony portends a
possible violation of taking God's name in vain. For should the
bride (or bridegroom) change his or her mind under the *chuppah*
and not marry the other, then the rabbi's *berachot* prior to the
ring ceremony may have been a nonpurposeful blessing (*berachah levatalah*). He, therefore, suggests that the function of the
tenayim is to guarantee in advance that under the *chuppah* both
bride and bridegroom will actually marry each other. Consequently, the *berachot* may be recited without qualms as to
whether a marriage will take place.

Similar logic may be extended to the case at hand. Since the
bride has formally consented through the vehicle of *tenayim* to
marry the groom at a specific time and place, perhaps one may
assume that the woman dressed as the bride who accepted the
ring from the groom at the ceremony is, in fact, the same person
who consented previously to marry this man. Consequently, the
witnesses testify that a woman was married to a specific bridegroom at a designated time and place. Who that woman actually

was may be verified by the assumption that she was the same person who committed herself to marriage at the *tenayim*. Again, however, there is no verifiable testimony as to which woman actually received the ring. Even this form of testimony would require the bride in the presence of two witnesses to actually commit herself to marriage. This process would definitely invalidate those versions of *tenayim* that do not require the bride to actually sign the document in the presence of two witnesses.

Indeed, apart from simple logic, the final issue is not clear-cut. On the one hand, the Mabit rules that witnesses must specifically know which woman received a ring from a bridegroom. In the event that the bride's face is so covered that witnesses cannot know definitely who is getting married, he rules the wedding is not valid (*Responsa Mabit*, vol. 1, 226). Yet, the Avnei Melui'im disagrees. He sanctions the custom of covering the bride's face to protect a high degree of modesty. His argument is that at a wedding it is public knowledge as to the identity of the bride (see *Avnei Melui'im* 31:4). Accordingly, witnesses know who is getting married without actually seeing the bride's face. Indeed, such is the general practice for many within the *frum* community.

Rav Ovadya Yosef notes a compromise position. He suggests that when the bride sips wine after the *Birchat Erusin*, generally her veil is lifted. At that time, the witnesses may note the identity of the bride. Indeed, he says that there is no prohibition for men to see a bride only to intently gaze at her (*Responsa* Yabia Omer, vol. 4, *Even HaEzer* 5:6). To make such a position practical would require the witnesses to be designated and present at the conclusion of the *Birchat Erusin*. Such is generally not the case. It is only after both bride and bridegroom sip the wine that the witnesses are called to the *chuppah*. Basically a concern for super modesty, which is translated into a complete covering of the bride's face, generates halachic qualms over the testimony of the witnesses. A simple solution would be to permit the witnesses to see what they are designated to observe.

The First Blessing of a Wedding

QUESTION: The first *berachah* recited under a *chuppah* is the blessing of wine. What is the nature of this blessing? Why is it chanted? Is this *berachah* essential to the marriage ceremony? Why is it that a full cup of wine is not drunk?

RESPONSE: The Rambam rules that this *berachah* is not essential to the ceremony. Accordingly, should no wine (or beer) be available, the subsequent marriage blessing may be recited even without this *berachah*. It became part of the wedding ceremony because of the general folk custom to preface rituals with a blessing for wine (*Hilchot Ishot* 3:24).

The *Aruch HaShulchan* suggests that the wine blessing is chanted at the beginning of the marriage ceremony for the same reason that the wine blessing is chanted at a circumcision. In the latter case, the wine *berachah* has no relationship to the *mitzvah* of circumcision. The *berachah* is chanted, says the Bet Yosef (citing the Mordechai), simply because of the principle that "a song of praise is sung over wine" (*Berachot* 35a; see Bet Yosef, *Tur, Yoreh De'ah* 265). This means that praise to *HaShem* requires wine.

In addition, the Talmud declares wine is unique in that it is, itself, a motive for benediction (*Berachot* 42a). Rashi explains this to mean that wine is utilized on numerous occasions even when it is not necessary to drink. The implication is that wine is added to enhance an event even when there is no *mitzvah* or religious imperative to drink (*Aruch HaShulchan, Even HaEzer* 34:9).

To the extent that the wine *berachah* is not relevant to the marriage ceremony but is merely an "add-on" appended to general events, some explanation must be granted as to why it precedes the main marriage *berachah* itself.

A simple response is that the second *berachah* recited at a marriage is called *Birchat Erusin*. The Talmud notes a debate as to whether this (second) *berachah* should also include the final blessing *"Baruch . . . mekadesh amo Yisrael al yedei chuppah v'kiddushin."* Those who rule that this concluding blessing be chanted compare the marriage blessing to the Friday nite *Kiddush* (see *Ketubot* 7b). Accordingly, just as in *Kiddush* the wine blessing precedes the main blessing, so too should this occur at a wedding. This reason begs the question for it is yet necessary to explain why by *Kiddush* itself the wine *berachah* precedes the main blessing. Also, a circumcision is not categorized as a form of *Kiddush*, yet the wine blessing still precedes the main blessing. As such, some reason must be prescribed as to why the wine *berachah* is still granted priority.

The Talmud notes a debate between Bet Shammai and Bet Hillel regarding the proper sequence for *Kiddush* on Friday night. Bet Hillel rules that first the blessing is chanted over wine and subsequently over *Shabbat* (*peri hagafen* and then *mekadesh HaShabbat*). Two reasons are presented for Bet Hillel's position. (1) The wine provides the occasion for the *Kiddush* to be chanted. (2) The blessing over the wine is said regularly, while the blessing over the day (*Shabbat*) is said only at infrequent intervals, and that which is more frequent (*tadir*) has precedence over that which is infrequent (*Berachot* 51b).

It has previously been noted that the wine *berachah* is not essential at the beginning of the wedding nor at a circumcision. According to Bet Hillel's first theory the wine *berachah*, therefore, should not be granted precedence prior to other blessings at a wedding or circumcision. Yet, the second principle of *tadir* definitely is applicable at both these events. Since the blessing for wine is definitely more frequent than the marriage or circumcision blessings, it is granted precedence.

Of further concern is the amount drunk from the cup of wine. Common custom is for the person who chanted the *berachah* to not drink at all but, rather, to have both the bridegroom and bride merely sip some wine. Is this not contrary to *halachah*? Is there not a rule that mandates a minimum amount of wine to be drunk after the recitation of a *berachah*? Indeed, the *Shulchan Aruch* rules that when a goblet of wine is mandated, one must drink a cheekful (that is, *revi'it*) (*Orach Chayyim* 190:3).

Again, comparison may be made to the *berachah* of wine chanted at a circumcision. The Taz rules that the requirement to drink a minimum amount of wine applies only to situations wherein wine is required as an essential component of the ritual. To the extent that wine at a circumcision is an "add-on" (as previously noted) there is no minimum requirement (Taz, *Yoreh De'ah* 265:10). As such, suggests the *Aruch HaShulchan*, so too may be the custom at a wedding ceremony. The fact that the wine *berachah* is not essential to the wedding removes the requirement for a specific minimum to be drunk.

In reality, the person who recited the *berachah* should, perhaps, sip the wine. Is this not the rule with blessings made over food? The person who recites the blessing should drink or eat. The reason this principle is not applicable is that in some fashion it was categorized as a (semi) *Birchat HaMitzvah* wherein one may recite the blessing and another may drink. Should, moreover, the rabbi who recited the *berachah* desire to sip the wine himself, he may certainly do so. Yet, common custom is to limit the process to the bride and bridegroom (*Aruch HaShulchan, Even HaEzer* 34:9).

Apart from the halachic ramifications, there is a significant symbolic message in the custom for the young couple to both sip the wine. The wine represents the color, the sweetness, the rhythm, the joyful meaning of life itself. The sipping of the wine is the symbolic commitment of the bride and bridegroom to such resolutions.

Some have the custom of having the mothers of both the bride and groom participate in the wine-sipping ceremony. After the groom sips the wine, the goblet (*kos* or *becher*) is given to his mother who holds the wine for the bride, whose veil is uncovered by her mother. (This process is repeated for the second cup of wine with the bride's mother being granted the goblet while the groom's mother holds the veil. Others reverse the process, granting the bride's mother the first opportunity to hold the goblet.) Are these customs rooted in *halachah*? No! But, there's nothing wrong with following such a procedure.

The Marriage Berachah

QUESTION: *Berachot* are recited prior to the performance of ritual commandments. Does this rule apply also to marriage? Namely, is there a marriage *berachah*?

RESPONSE: The wedding ceremony begins with the recitation of two *berachot*. The first is the general wine blessing. The second is termed *Birchat Erusin*—the betrothal blessing (see *Ketubot* 7b). In ancient times a bride would remain in her parents' home for a year to prepare for the setting up of her own home. Subsequently (at *Nesu'in*), when she and her husband would move into their own home, seven additional *berachot* would be chanted. This original *berachah*, *Birchat Erusin*, requires analysis as to its proper function. It begins with a replica of the format used prior to the performance of a *mitzvah*. Namely, it starts with the phrase, "*Asher kidshanu bemitzvotav vetzivanu*" ("with which you sanctified us with your *mitzvot* and commanded us . . ."). This suggests that marriage is a *mitzvah*. Yet, the *berachah* does not clearly articulate this matter. It does not conclude—and command us—"*to get married*" (or some other similar wording). Instead, it notes an acknowledgment that *HaShem* commanded us "about illicit relations—prohibiting relations [even] after betrothal and permitting them [only] after *chuppah* and *kiddushin*." Such a language is not clear as to its purpose. It also does not conform to the typical format of *berachot* chanted prior to the observance of *mitzvot*.

Of further concern is the ordering of the recitation of this *berachah*. When does it take place? The Rambam rules that this blessing must precede the actual marriage (the ring ceremony) comparable to the general principle that blessings take place prior to observance. Should, however, the *Kiddushin* take place without (for some reason) the prior recitation of the *berachah*, it cannot be subsequently chanted, for such would be an unwarranted blessing (*berachah levatalah*). The Ravid disagrees with this rule. He notes a common custom in his age (contrary to contemporary usage) wherein this blessing was chanted subsequent to the marriage. His reasoning is that a marriage depends upon the consent of both a groom and a bride. In the event the *berachah* is chanted prior to marriage and the bride, for example, is not willing to get married to this man, then the *berachah* was recited in vain. To offset any qualms about reciting a proper *berachah*, custom (in the Ravid's area) was to recite the blessing after the fact of the marriage itself (Rambam, Laws of Women 3:23).

The Rambam further notes that the *berachah* is generally recited by the groom. The Haga'ot Maimuni discloses that the custom of the groom chanting the blessing was a practice of the western country. In other areas, the groom did not recite this blessing. The honor was granted to others. Accordingly, it was recited after the wedding ceremony. The principle obligating *berachot* to precede the observance of *mitzvot* applies only when the person chanting the blessing (*hamavarech*) personally observes the *mitzvah*. In a situation where, for example, a stranger recites the blessing, there is nothing wrong with reciting the blessing even after the performance of the *mitzvah*. To the extent that the bride might reject marriage, and thus generate a concern that the *berachah* was chanted in vain, therefore, the custom was instituted to recite the *berachah* after the wedding. (This custom is also cited by the Magid Mishnah as well as the Tosafot, Rid; *Ketubot* 7b.)

Several issues must yet be clarified.

1. Why does the Rambam (and such is contemporary practice) permit the blessing to take place prior to the ceremony? Is there not a serious question pertaining to a potential blessing in vain?

2. If the blessing is a form of a *Birchat HaMitzvah*, then why did the custom develop even to permit a stranger to recite the *berachah*?

Rabbeinu Asher (the Rosh) presents a unique analysis of this blessing. He poses the following questions:

1. If the *berachah* is for the *mitzvah* of marriage, then why does it not simply state such. Namely, *V'tzivanu*—and you commanded us to marry (a) woman.

2. This blessing is somewhat bizarre in that it appears to bless *HaShem* for prohibiting certain relations. Yet, there is no blessing acknowledging the prohibition of meat from live animals and permitting us the meat from ritually slaughtered animals.

3. Since the original blessing took place at the betrothal, there is no reason to mention the word *chuppah* in the blessing.

As such, Rabbeinu Asher concludes that this *berachah* does *not* relate to the performance of a *mitzvah*. Indeed, the *mitzvah* of marriage seems to be the biblical commandment, "Be fruitful and multiply (*Peru urevu*) (Genesis 1:22–9:1). Yet, this *mitzvah* may take place even without the sanctification of marriage. Also, a marriage may transpire wherein there is no possibility of any children to emerge as a result of the union, namely, the marriage of old people or one who is sterile. In such cases, the blessings are chanted even though there is no possibility of children. The *mitzvah* of marriage, it should be noted, is different from the concept of *shechitah—kosher* slaughtering. In the latter case, there is no imperative obligating the eating of meat. Yet, should a person seek to eat meat, then it is necessary to go through the process of *shechitah* (*kosher* slaughter). For this reason a blessing is recited. Indeed, *kosher* slaughtering was required for sacrifices in the *Bet HaMikdash*. Concerning the *mitzvah* of procreation, it needs not the sanctity of marriage for observance. This blessing is, therefore, a *Birchat HaShevach*—a blessing of appreciation to God for the entire sanctity of marriage (see Rabbeinu Asher, *Ketubot*, chap. 1).

This theory of Rabbeinu Asher resolves the dilemma of this *berachah*. The concern as to perhaps the bride may change her mind and not agree to marriage in no way challenges the propriety of chanting this *berachah*. This is not the typical *berachah* recited prior to observance. It's, rather, a thanksgiving *berachah* that has pragmatic application apart from the agreement of a specific bride to consent to marriage. Appreciation to God for establishing marriage is not negatively affected by a bride's

refusal to marry a specific man. Since this *berachah*, moreover, is
not the typical *berachah* chanted prior to the observance of a
mitzvah, there is no insistence that the groom, himself, chant
this blessing. Anyone may recite this blessing. Indeed, the custom for an officiating rabbi to chant this *berachah* rather than for
the groom to do so may be to dramatize that the nature of
the *berachah* is appreciation and not the personal observance
of the *mitzvah*. The *Aruch HaShulchan* rules that since the
berachah is not a *Birchat HaMitzvah* but the sanctity of *K'lal
Yisrael*, then it may be recited even subsequent to the marriage
(*Even HaEzer* 34:5). This, of course, is contrary to the decision of
the Rambam, who may rule that all *berachot*—even thanksgiving
blessings—should be chanted prior to the rituals involved.

The Mitzvah *of Marriage*

QUESTION: Is it a *mitzvah* for a woman to get married? If yes,
what is the actual *mitzvah* that is observed at marriage itself?

RESPONSE: The *Mishnah* rules that "a woman may be betrothed through herself or through her agent." Commenting on
this, the Talmud states, "Now, if she can be betrothed via means
of an agent (a *shliach*) is it necessary [to state that she may do so]
through herself?" Said R. Yosef, "[The reason the *Mishnah*
mentions the woman's ability to betroth herself is that] it is a
greater *mitzvah* through herself than through her agent"
(*Mitzvah Ba Yoter Mivshluchah*). Substantiation of this principle
is that Rava (himself) salted a large fish for *Shabbat*. He definitely could have had others perform this task. But again, it is a
greater *mitzvah* to do so oneself (*Kiddushin* 41a).

This talmudic citation not only classifies marriage as a *mitzvah* but designates the woman's role in the marriage ceremony as also a *mitzvah*.

The Ran (*Kiddushin*, chap. 2) attempts to finely hone the exact *mitzvah* performed. Of concern is that the *mitzvah* of propagation (*peru urvu*—be fruitful and multiply) (Genesis 1:28) is *not* considered a biblical *mitzvah* imposed upon women. As such, it is difficult to understand why the Talmud considered the woman's role in marriage as a woman's *mitzvah*. Perhaps, suggests the Ran, the *mitzvah* is that she aids her husband in the performance of the *mitzvah* of having children. In other words, helping someone do a *mitzvah* is also considered a *mitzvah*.

Accordingly, notes the Rashal, should the groom not see his bride prior to the ceremony and thus commit a sin, the bride would be culpable for abetting such a sin. Yet, the Talmud clearly states that failure of the bridegroom to view the bride is a male sin, not a female transgression. The Rashal, therefore, suggests that even though women are not obliged to observe the *mitzvah* of propagation they still acquire some *mitzvah* on their own right at marriage. Indeed, the Talmud notes that in honor of *Shabbat*, "R. Safra [himself] singed an [animal's] head (*Kiddushin* 41a). Are Jews actively mandated to singe the heads of animals for *Shabbat*? Of course not, but the action is still deemed a *mitzvah*. So, too, is the role of women at marriage" (Yam Shel Shlomo, *Kiddushin*, chap. 2, *Mishnah* 1). In other words, the actual *mitzvah* performed is unclear.

Indeed, Rabbeinu Asher rules that one may perform the *mitzvah* of having children even without the sanctification of marriage (*Ketubot*, chap. 1). This ruling questions whether marriage itself is really a *mitzvah* altogether. HaRav Pinchus Hurowitz, the author of the famed "HaMakneh" talmudic commentary, presents a brilliant, unique theory relating to marriage. The Rambam rules that without the sanctification of marriage, sexual activity is biblically prohibited. Indeed, a woman who engages in sexual activity without the proper sanctification of marriage is classified as a *kedeishah*—a promiscuous, immoral woman, and

the Bible specifically commands men and women not to be
sexually immoral (see Deuteronomy 23:18; see Rambam, *Hilchot
Ishot* 1:4).

Thus, marriage provides the religious permission for sexual
activity. It's comparable to the *mitzvah* of *shechitah*. No one is
required to eat meat. Yet, should a person so desire, then it is
necessary to slaughter animals according to the *mitzvah* of
shechitah. As such, the marriage certainly becomes the *mitzvah*
that allows sexual activity to take place between a specific man
and woman.

The Talmud compares the *mitzvah* of marriage to the
mitzvah of preparing food for *Shabbat*. Yet, the comparison is not
clear-cut. Preparations for *Shabbat* are *mitzvot* by themselves
(*v'heichinu et asher yaevieu*). Marriage, however, is generally a
preparation for the *mitzvah* of propagation (a *hechsher mitzvah*).
Should one utilize the theory that marriage is itself a *mitzvah* – in
that it is the religious event that grants permission for sexual
activity with a specific woman – then the comparison to preparations for *Shabbat* is quite proper. Both are *mitzvot* by themselves. Even those who disagree with the Rambam and contend
that one may have a wife without *kiddushin* (a common-law
wife – *pilegesh*) would also rule that such is permitted only should
one intend to live solely with that woman. But, suggests the
HaMakneh, even they would agree that casual sex is prohibited
without a wedding (see HaMakneh, *Kiddushin* 41a).

HaRav E. Henkin, the previous *posek* of our generation,
developed a different perception relating to the *mitzvah* of marriage. He notes that the biblical mandate of *Peru urevu* – "be
fruitful and multiply" is again mentioned to Noah after the deluge
(Genesis 9:1). Why the need to repeat this *mitzvah*? Rav Henkin
suggests that the *mitzvah* commanded to Noah is different from
the *mitzvah* stated during the Creation. The latter *mitzvah* was
to propagate human beings. The *mitzvah* directed to Noah deals
with a different concern. The Bible says that the departure from
the Ark was "according to families" – "*l'mishepechoteihem*" (Genesis 8:19). As such, there was a special mandate to develop the
type of children that could trace lineage to specific families

(*yichus mishpachah*). This *mitzvah* requires the sanctification of marriage to ensure specific knowledge of parents (Lev Ivra, p. 9). Thus, marriage itself is a *mitzvah*.

Designated Witnesses at a Marriage

QUESTION: What is the rationale for the custom to specifically designate two male witnesses to be exclusively responsible to observe the ceremony whereby the groom gives a ring to his bride under the canopy of marriage?

RESPONSE:
I. The *Aruch HaShulchan* contends that such is the preferable custom and presents the following reasons for this observance:

A. At a wedding there are numerous people in attendance. Should no one be designated specifically as a witness then the entire audience serves as a unit of witnesses to the ceremony. Within the assemblage, there are people who are unqualified to serve as witnesses, for example, women, relatives, nonobservant Jews. To the extent that the audience (or even just those under the canopy) testify as a bloc, or unit, the disqualification of but one member automatically disqualifies the entire unit. This is based on the halachic principle that witnesses who testify as a team or unit must all be creditable witnesses. When testifying as a unit, the inclusion of but one person who is not halachically permitted to serve disqualifies the entire unit. To designate two creditable witnesses eliminates this problem.

B. At times, only relatives stand together with the bride and groom under the canopy. Accordingly, it is possible that no *kosher* witness actually sees the action of the groom. The designation of witnesses insures that two reliable witnesses actually observe the marriage.

C. Even in instances wherein numerous reliable witnesses can potentially observe the marriage, most people simply do not pay attention to the process. Each relies on the other. The designation of witnesses imposes a responsibility upon two witnesses to observe the wedding and insure it was performed properly (*Aruch HaShulchan, Even HaEzer* 42:3).

II. There is yet another vehicle to eliminate the preceding halachic concerns regarding the testimony of reliable witnesses. The officiating rabbi may announce that all Jews who are legally permitted to testify should assume the responsibility to witness the wedding. As such, nonreliable witnesses are excluded. Indeed, the Binyon Tzion contends that this procedure is preferable to the designation of two witnesses, for the latter case may generate halachic problems in an instance where one or both of the designated witnesses are subsequently disqualified from testimony (*Responsa, Binyon Tzion* 157, *Choshen Mishpat*).

The halachic retort to this issue is that under such a procedure *perhaps* all creditable witnesses may be obligated to observe the testimony as a unit. Accordingly, any one (even *kosher*) witness who fails to see the testimony may invalidate all the witnesses (see *HaNisuim K'Halachah,* vol. 1, chap. 8:6, cited in name of the Maharam Shik, *Responsa, Choshen Mishpat,* 57). This response may be diffused by making it clear that the testimony is a request for individual *kosher* witnesses, not an obligation to serve as a unit.

Though common custom is to opt for designated witnesses, the Binyon Tzion's theory has halachic validity. It, however, presumes that the assemblage contains reliable witnesses.

III. Who should designate the witnesses, the officiating rabbi or the groom?

Popular usage is that the bridegroom designates the witnesses. Some officiating rabbis announce under the *chuppah* that the witnesses are solely designated by the groom to the exclusion of others. This procedure has limitations for should one of the witnesses be declared invalid, there is a halachic debate as to whether the marriage is yet legal because of the existence of other *kosher* witnesses in the audience. Some sages contend that the witnesses in the audience may be utilized to validate the wedding providing *the groom himself did not designate the witnesses.* In such a case, others are automatically excluded. The groom, by designating two exclusive witnesses, implies that he wishes to marry only through his designated witnesses, not others. Yet, should the officiating rabbi (*Mesader Kiddushin*) designate the witnesses, then the others in the audience may be utilized (see Kerem Shlomo 21, also Chatam Sofer 100).

Accordingly, it would appear preferable to intermingle two customs.

1. The *rav* should designate the witnesses.

2. He should announce that, in addition, all *kosher* witnesses in the audience who may observe the process may also serve as individual witnesses (not as a unit) to validate the marriage.

Yet, such is not common practice.

IV. There is no halachic reason to insist upon only two witnesses. The custom of using only two witnesses is, perhaps, to emphasize the principle that the two witnesses, by themselves, are the smallest unit to testify. Should a larger group be designated, then the invalidation of but one would invalidate the unit.

V. Should the witnesses leave the canopy after the ring ceremony?

Though many do, in fact, there may be halachic reasons for the witnesses to remain.

A. The witnesses should remain to observe whether the bride retains the ring or gives it away (*Responsa*, Maharsham, vol. 3, 50).

B. The custom of HaGaon R. Shneur Kotler (*z"l*) was to insist that the witnesses who observed the ring ceremony should also observe (as a unit) the process whereby the groom gives over the *ketubah* to the bride (*eidei mesirah*).

VI. The role of two witnesses at a wedding is distinct from the role of witnesses at, for example, the loan of funds. In the latter case the loan transaction is a legal process by itself and the

witnesses serve only as proof in the event the borrower subsequently denies the loan. At a wedding, however, the witnesses
are an integral ritual aspect of the marriage ceremony. Absence
of witnesses simply invalidates the halachic legality of the wedding (*Aruch HaShulchan, Even HaEzer* 42:10).

Skipping the Wine Berachah *at a* Chuppah

QUESTION: What is the proper procedure to follow under a
chuppah in the event a person honored to recite the first two
berachot simply skipped over the first *berachah* (*peri hagafen*)
and quickly chanted the second and third *berachot*?

RESPONSE: This case actually happened. At a wedding, I had
just concluded reading the *ketubah* and was still standing under
the *chuppah*. It was publicly announced that someone was honored to recite the first two blessings. Quickly, before any direction could be provided, someone came forward and rapidly
chanted two *berachot*. The difficulty was that it was immediately
apparent that the first *berachah* was (by error) not recited.
Namely, the wine *berachah* was skipped. What was to be done? A
rosh kollel, also under the *chuppah*, immediately directed that
the normal order of *berachot* should be continued and that the
wine *berachah* should be recited last.

I disagreed. My position was that the wine *berachah* should
be immediately recited and afterward the rest of the *berachot*
should be chanted in order. Both of us presented reasons for our
positions. The *rosh kollel* contended that the Talmud in *Ketubot*
(8a) indicated a systematic ordering of the *berachot*.

Thus, there was a reason why each *berachah* followed each other. Accordingly, the chanting of the wine *berachah* in the middle of the other *berachot* would interfere with the normal flow of blessings and serve as an intolerable interruption (a *hefsek* of the *seder*).

My argument was that whenever a mistake occurred at weddings, the normal custom was to recite the missing *berachah* whenever the error was noted and then to continue to proceed in order. Such custom prevailed at weddings at which great rabbinic sages participated. In addition, to chant the wine *berachah* last might give the false impression that this was a valid (alternate) custom. To recite the *berachah* in the middle of the other blessings would signal to all that an error took place and was simply corrected. I felt it was wrong to convey a false impression. Since I was not the *mesader kiddushin* (the *rav* responsible for performing the wedding), the decision was not mine. As such, I stated my views and walked away from the *chuppah*. The *rav* who was the *mesader kiddushin* accepted the *rosh kollel's* viewpoint and had the *borei peri hagafen berachah* chanted last.

At the wedding meal it was noted that a *sefer* entitled *HaNisu'in K'Hilchatam* (R. Binyamin Adler) was available for review of the matter. (This volume is a collection of laws dealing with marriage.) Therein it was noted that at the *Birchat Erusin* (the blessings recited by the *mesader kiddushin* prior to the ring ceremony) the wine blessing may be chanted subsequent to the other *berachah*, should it be forgotten. Why? For the sage, Ravya, does in fact contend that the wine *berachah* for *Birchat Erusin* should always be said last. Accordingly, in the event of an error such should be relied upon (see *ibid.*, vol. 1, p. 268; chap. 10:34, n. 87).

This so-called substantiation (to my mind) had no bearing. The blessing for the *Sheva Berachot* was not to be derived from a rule relating to *Birchat Erusin*. Each case was different.

Sometime afterward I began to research the issue. Two items needed to be clarified. (1) Was the *rosh kollel* correct in that one may not interrupt the normal systematic flow of *berachot*? Was this halachic policy? (2) Why is it that under the *chuppah* the wine blessing is the first of the seven blessings yet at *Sheva Berachot* celebrations, it is the last *berachah* chanted? Or better yet, why is not the wine *berachah* recited last under the *chuppah*?

Concerning the first question, I located a responsum from HaGaon HaRav Ovadia Yosef, who cites the Rambam (*Responsa*) and numerous sages who unequivocally rule that there is no essential order to the blessing under the *chuppah*. Namely, when a blessing is forgotten it is to be recited immediately and then one continues in order (*Responsa* Yabia Omer, vol. 4, *Even HaEzer* 7).

Accordingly, the same should hold true for the wine blessing as for other blessings. There should be no distinction. Just as, for example, should the fourth or fifth blessing be forgotten and when recalled, recited immediately, so too should be the case with the wine blessing.

Regarding the other issue, the *Aruch HaShulchan* provides cogent clarity. He contends that the wine blessing is chanted first under the *chuppah* because of the general rule of *tadir*, which grants priority to an item (or blessing) that has a greater frequency of usage. Since the wine *berachah* manifests a greater frequency of usage than the other blessings, it is recited first under the *chuppah*. At *Sheva Berachot* celebrations, however, the wine *berachah* is chanted last. Why? Should the wine *berachah* be recited first, people might falsely assume that the wine blessing is due to *Birchat HaMazon*, not *Sheva Berachot*. So, to forestall any misinformation, the wine *berachah* is chanted as far away from *Birchat HaMazon* as possible (*Aruch HaShulchan, Even HaEzer* 62:12).

Based upon the above, any error relating to the skipping of the wine *berachah* should be corrected immediately so that at least the principle of *tadir* should be able to take place. Whenever the wine blessing would be recited, prior to the conclusion, it would still be *tadir* over the other *berachot*. Should the wine blessing be stated last, then the concept of *tadir* relating to wine would not be utilized at all.

In addition, *halachah* generates a basic orientation that no activity should occur that may stimulate false or mistaken notions. Again, a wine blessing chanted last may convey mistaken rules of conduct. As such, I feel quite comfortable in ruling that the blessing of wine should be recited as soon as it is noted that a mistake takes place. Three reasons: (1) *tadir*; (2) *seder* not essential; and (3) to eliminate false conceptions.

(As I walked away from the *chuppah* a young doctor called out to me: "Rabbi Cohen, is this going to be the subject of a *sheur* and another article for the media?" "But, of course," I responded, "that's the grist that serves as the catalyst for halachic research. Questions are not just theoretical concerns. It is life itself and our experiences within it that provide the greatest research laboratory and the most valuable halachic problems.")

Hamotzi *at Weddings*

QUESTION: Who should be granted the honor of publicly reciting the *HaMotzi berachah* at a wedding?

RESPONSE: The bridegroom. The Magen Avraham rules that a bridegroom is to be granted priority in making *HaMotzi,* even over guests who may be greater in Torah wisdom and age. *Mishnah Berurah* cites this principle (see Magen Avraham, *Orach Chayyim* 167:29; see also *Mishnah Berurah* 167:8). This suggests that such is pragmatic *halachah.* The source appears to be the following: "Rabbah bar Chanah made a marriage feast for his son in the house of R. Shmuel son of R. Kattina, and he first sat down and taught his son: 'The one who acts as host (recites *HaMotzi*) may not break bread until the guests have finished responding Amen'" (*Berachot* 47a). Rashi comments that Rabbah bar Chanah taught his son the laws relating to meals for *it was customary for the bridegroom to recite Hamotzi* and the father accordingly wished that his bridegroom son should be knowledgeable as to the correct procedures. To the extent that the bridegroom son was given the honor of chanting *HaMotzi* in the presence of his own scholarly father (or other rabbis as noted by Tosafot) demonstrates that a bridegroom always is granted the honor of *HaMotzi* even when more honorable guests are present (see *Einayim L'Mishpat, Berachot* 47a).

At issue is the significance of the aforementioned *halachah.* In general, the host is granted the honor of reciting *HaMotzi.* The rationale is that the host will "be generous" (*Berachot* 46a). In other words, he will grant a goodly portion. When this rationale is not applicable, namely when all assembled at a meal eat from their own bread and do not rely on the host for distribution, then, rules *Mishnah Berurah*, it is preferable to honor the greatest scholar or guest present rather than the host (*Orach Chayyim* 167:74). Of interest is that halachic sages do not suggest that at a wedding the honor of *HaMotzi* may be extended to anyone but the bridegroom even though all eat from their own bread.

In our age hardly anyone waits for the bridegroom to recite *HaMotzi.* Common custom is for all to recite *berachot* for bread by themselves. This suggests that the public action of reciting *HaMotzi* is merely a symbolic act of honor (*kavod*) rather than a process to include the assemblage (be *motzi*) with one blessing. As such, the bridegroom may not give up this honor or relinquish it to another. Why? It is a well-established rule that a king may not forgo his honor; rabbis may, parents may do so, but not a king (*Kiddushin* 32b). Every bridegroom is a king. As such, he is to be given honor whether he wishes it or not. For this reason, perhaps, the practice of granting the bridegroom the honor of publicly reciting the *HaMotzi* is not limited by halachic authorities to be relevant only to specific conditions or customs. A bridegroom is always a king. He, therefore, is always to be granted honor.

Seating of a Bride and Bridegroom

QUESTION: Does *halachah* mandate special seating arrangements for a bride and bridegroom?

RESPONSE: A general concern at weddings is the proper seating arrangement of the bride and groom. Some prefer the formality of a head table located in the front of the banquet hall. (This may or may not include the immediate family members.) Others contend that wherever the bride and groom sit that becomes the "head table" even should it be in the middle of the banquet hall. It is told that the Gerer *Rebbe* (*z"l*) would hold court in the middle of an assemblage (not in front of a hall or *bet midrash*) to manifest involvement with his *hasidim*.

Of interest is that the Talmud specifically delineates the proper seating arrangement of a groom. It says, "How do we know that the bridegroom should be seated in the front [*b'rosh*] for it is written, '*K'chatan yechahein p'eir*' (lit., 'the bridegroom shall be like a *kohen* decked with garlands') (Isaiah 61:10). Just as a *kohen* sits at the head [of the assemblage] so, too, does a bridegroom. And how do we know the [law] about a *kohen*? The house of R. Yishmael said, it is written, '*V'kidashto*'—'and you shall make him (the *kohen*) holy' (Leviticus 21:8). For all matters of holiness (*kedushah*); to open first; bless first and to take a good portion first" (*Mo'ed Katan* 28b).

The implication of this citation is that the groom had to sit in a place that was visibly and distinctively noticeable as the head or front of the assemblage. Should one presume that wherever the groom sat was deemed as the front, then the entire talmudic discussion appears extraneous.

At issue is that the groom's seating arrangement at his wedding is derived from the seating status of the *kohen*. Yet, the Talmud does not stipulate the exact area wherein the *kohen* was to be seated. Rashi, for example, states that the requirement to

"open first" means that the *kohen* was the first to read in the
Torah, and the rule "to bless first" meant that the *kohen* was
granted the honor of leading *Birchat HaMazon*. Neither relates
to any priority for seating. Rabbeinu Asher, however, suggests
that the rule "to open first" means that the *kohen* was to be the
first speaker to be called upon to address all assemblages (*Nedarim* 62b). For this reason, perhaps, the *kohen* was seated in the
front of a banquet hall to enable him to have easy access for his
speech.

From a practical viewpoint, it should be noted that the
requirement to seat a bridegroom (and bride) in the front of the
hall at their wedding is not reported by the decisors of Jewish
law. (Indeed, common practice is also *not* to provide front seats to
kohanim.) At issue is the question as to which seating pattern
provides greater *kavod* (honor) to the bridal couple. For once the
matter is within the realm of *kavod* to a bride and bridegroom,
neither have the authority to forgo the proper *kavod* due them.
Why? A bride and bridegroom are classified as halachic royalty.
Royalty has no permission to forgo *kavod* due them (*Kiddushin*
32b).

Leaving a Wedding Meal before Sheva Berachot

QUESTION: Is a person permitted to leave a wedding meal
before the recitation of *Sheva Berachot* and *Birchat HaMazon*?

RESPONSE: This question was posed to HaGaon HaRav R.
Moshe Feinstein (*z"l*). At issue is the recognition that many
cannot await the late hour when *Birchat HaMazon* is generally
recited. Coupled to this, many do not live in close proximity to the

area of the wedding. To stay till the conclusion would not enable them to return home till the early morning hours. The problem places people in a halachic quandary. To wait for all to say *Birchat HaMazon* and *Sheva Berachot* is difficult and to some, impossible; and yet to gather their own *minyan* for such early recitations would find even the hosts opposed.

HaGaon R. Moshe suggests that the most viable halachic approach is to vocally note prior to the meal that the person has no intention of joining together with others in establishing any form of permanency (*keviut*) to the meal. As such, the individual would have no obligation to join others for *zimun* or *Sheva Berachot*.

This suggests that eating a meal together with other people does not by itself generate an obligation of *zimun* – which is the joining together at *Birchat HaMazon*. It is necessary to have the added intention that the eating together is also for the purpose of reciting *Birchat HaMazon* together.

The following is cited as proof for this concept. The Rema rules that common custom was not to recite *zimun* in the house of an idol worshiper. The reason is that in such a home they could not bless the head of the household (an idol worshiper). To not recite any prayer at all for the head of the house could be a dangerous provocation. As such it's deemed as if they ate on the condition that no *zimun* would take place and each would recite *Birchat HaMazon* by himself (*Shulchan Aruch, Orach Chayyim* 193:3). From this it is evident that intention to join together for *zimun* is essential for its subsequent occurrence. Any indication that each person is to *bensch* (say grace) by himself removes the meal from an obligation of *zimun*. Accordingly, suggests HaGaon R. Moshe, when there is a clear-cut reason to demonstrate that the meal was eaten on the condition that there was to be no later joining for *zimun*, then it is permissible to leave early. Indeed, Rav Moshe concludes that one may rely on this *pesak* when one cannot await the late hour when *Sheva Berachot* are recited (see *Iggerot Mosheh, Orach Chayyim*, vol. 1, *Responsum* 56).

It is necessary to add an important provision. Many who wish to depart early from a wedding feast seek out a few others to recite *Birchat HaMazon* with the *zimun* of three but less than ten. This custom may not be based upon HaGaon Rav Moshe's *pesak*. The theory of HaGaon Rav Moshe (*z"l*) makes no distinction between *zimun* of three or ten or none. The individual relieves his obligation by stipulating that he is not joining other-together for *zimun*. As such, he should (*bedavka*) *bensch* by himself. This way he is not involved with others in any permanency of coming together for *Birchat HaMazon*. Otherwise, it is difficult to free oneself of the obligation of a *minyan* and yet obligate oneself for the *zimun* of three. One either removes oneself from (the *keviut* of) *zimun* altogether, or one is obligated to remain for *Sheva Berachot*. How does one make the fine distinction of inclusion for three but not for a *minyan*?

Accordingly, the preferable mode should be for one to recite *Birchat HaMazon* by himself. An alternate position may be that one is free from any obligation of *zimun* but, perhaps, one may voluntarily do so at the conclusion of a meal.

The Beginning and End of Sheva Berachot

QUESTION: When does the requirement for *Sheva Berachot* commence?

RESPONSE: It starts at the time of the *chuppah*. "After the *berachot* under the *chuppah*, the couple is halachically permitted to live together as husband and wife. Consequently, the seven-day period of feasting commences" (*Responsa* Rabbeinu Asher [Rosh] 26:2). This suggests that should the *chuppah* be at night even though the *ketubah* was dated the prior Hebrew day, *Sheva Berachot* are calculated from the time of the *chuppah* and not the date of the *ketubah*. (So, indeed, was the practice at a *Sheva Berachot* attended by the Munkasher *Rebbe*.)

QUESTION: When do the *Sheva Berachot* conclude?

RESPONSE: Assume the following: The meal commenced on the seventh day of feasting. Yet the party lasted till the night, during which a calendar change occurred. If the commencement of the meal is the determining factor in the recital of *Sheva Berachot*, the end of the last festive meal is still within the seven-day period. If, however, the time of the *Birchat HaMazon* determines when *Sheva Berachot* are recited, it would now be the eighth day and no *Sheva Berachot* should be recited.

R. Shlomo Kluger rules that the requirement for *Sheva Berachot* is calculated from the time of *Birchat HaMazon* and not from the beginning of the meal. As such, in the aforementioned case, no *Sheva Berachot* should be recited. He also rules that should the *panim chadashot* leave (on any day) prior to *Birchat HaMazon*, then no *Sheva Berachot* are chanted (*Responsa HaElef Lecha Shlomo*, *Even HaEzer*, no. 107).

It should be noted that some contend that the seven days of *Sheva Berachot* are calculated not at sunset, as previously suggested, but by a twenty-four-hour span. Thus, the first twenty-four hours of the wedding ceremony are still considered the first day of *Sheva Berachot*. It is of interest that the *Aruch HaShulchan* describes such a position as erroneous (*ta'ut*) and contrary to the consensus of the sages (*Even HaEzer* 62:31).

Eating Bread at Sheva Berachot

QUESTION: How many people must break bread in order for *Sheva Berachot* to be recited?

RESPONSE: To recite the *Sheva Berachot*, the groom must eat bread and a minimum of three people (inclusive of the groom) must also eat bread (R. Shlomo Kluger, *Responsa* HaElef Lecha Shlomo, *Orach Chayyim* 93).

QUESTION: May someone who did not eat bread recite any or all of the *Sheva Berachot*?

RESPONSE: Yes. Indeed, it is reported that the (former) Satmar *rebbe* was honored with the recitation of the *Sheva Berachot* even though he drank only some beer and ate only fish (*Responsa* Be'er Moshe, vol. 2, no. 118). (This, of course, is exclusive of the *berachah* that is granted to the person who leads *Birchat HaMazon*.)

QUESTION: A person attended a wedding. He partook of the smorgasbord, but did not eat from the banquet subsequent to the ceremony. Is such a person assessed as a *panim chadashot* ("new face") for subsequent *Sheva Berachot*?

RESPONSE: Yes. However, if he ate from the meal subsequent to the ceremony, even if he did not eat bread, he loses his status as a *panim chadashot* (*Responsa* Be'er Moshe, vol. 2, no. 119).

Dancing on Shabbat *at* Sheva Berachot

QUESTION: Is dancing permitted during the celebration of an *aufruf* or at *Sheva Berachot* on *Shabbat*?

RESPONSE: The *Shulchan Aruch* rules that dancing is prohibited on *Shabbat*. The Rema notes that many do in fact dance on *Shabbat* and yet no one protests such activity. Two reasons are presented by the Rema. (1) Since people will not heed any prohibitions against dancing, it is better for them to be unaware of the sinful nature of dancing on *Shabbat* rather than to overtly violate the rule once informed dancing is prohibited. (2) The underlying reason to prohibit dancing is because one may become so emotionally aroused that he may make a musical instrument. Since most are unable to construct musical instruments, in reality it appears that the prohibition is not operational (*Orach Chayyim* 339:3).

Accordingly there was a period of time when all forms of dancing on *Shabbat* were prohibited. This prohibition was altered subsequently, due to the two reasons presented by the Rema. Yet, even when the custom was to outlaw dancing on *Shabbat*, it was permitted to dance on Simchat Torah. The *Mishnah Berurah* contends that on Simchat Torah dancing was permitted for the sake of *kavod HaTorah*, honor of the Torah. Yet at the *simchah* of another *mitzvah* wherein *kavod HaTorah* is not operational, such as a wedding, dancing is prohibited (*Mishnah Berurah* 339:8). The latter phrase of the *Mishnah Berurah* is difficult to comprehend. Marriages are not permitted on *Shabbat*. Perhaps, the *Mishnah Berurah* is alluding to an *aufruf* or a *Sheva Berachot* that takes place on *Shabbat*. Thus, dancing is to be permitted only for *kavod HaTorah*, not for other *mitzvot*.

In noting the final ruling of the Rema, which is lenient about dancing on *Shabbat*, the *Mishnah Berurah* adds the comment that it is not proper to permit dancing on *Shabbat* unless one is *observing a mitzvah in the process*; when no *mitzvah* is observed, dancing is permitted only because of the reason that it is better to be an unintentional sinner than an intentional sinner (*Mishnah Berurah* 339:10).

Here the *Mishnah Berurah* alters his language. Dancing needs not only a situation of *Kavod HaTorah*; it is permitted even while performing an ordinary *mitzvah*. Indeed, there is no limitation or definition of the type of *mitzvah* that permits dancing. As such, the following procedure develops. At a time in history dancing was prohibited on *Shabbat* except when it was to sustain the honor of Torah (that is, on Simchat Torah). Subsequently, dancing was permitted on *Shabbat*. Yet no general permission was granted. It was necessary to perform a *mitzvah* in the process (that is *Sheva Berachot, Simchat Chatan V'Kallah*). In the event no *mitzvah* was available, the dancing would still be permitted but only for those who wish to be included in the principle of "better to sin unintentionally than intentionally." A *Ben Torah* would certainly not use such a leniency.

In a discussion of the laws of Rosh Chodesh, the *Mishnah Berurah*, in his compendium of sources, entitled *Shar HaTzion*, discusses why *Kiddush Levanah* (prayer sanctifying the new moon) was not set up to be recited on Friday night. He suggests that many dance while reciting *Kiddush Levanah*, an act prohibited on *Shabbat*. The fact that dancing is permitted on Simchat Torah is not considered a challenge to his position. Why? For *Kiddush Levanah* may be set up before or after *Shabbat*. Simchat Torah has a permanent calendar period of time (*Shar HaTzion, Orach Chayyim* 426:11). Of concern is the apparent question posed by dancing on Simchat Torah. The *Mishnah Berurah* could have simply responded that dancing is permitted only for *kavod HaTorah*; not for other *mitzvot*. This the *Mishnah Berurah* does not say. To the extent that an *aufruf* or *Sheva Berachot* are events set up on *Shabbat* and cannot be relocated to another day, the logical inference is that dancing is permitted on *Shabbat* to make happy a bride and groom.

Reliable sources indicate that HaGaon Rav Shneur Kotler (*z"l*) danced on Shavuot contending that such was the custom of his father, HaGaon Rav Aaron Kotler (*z"l*).

Caveat: At a *seudat mitzvah* of an *aufruf* in my synagogue, a number of men began to dance with the bridegroom. In the audience was a young *rosh hayeshivah* from Israel. He danced, for he saw that I danced. But he made a condition to his participation. It was that I compose a halachic paper demonstrating the legitimacy of dancing with a groom on *Shabbat*. This is the rationale for formulating the aforementioned Torah analysis.

Sheva Berachot *at* Shalosh Seudot

QUESTION: At the conclusion of *Sheva Berachot* three persons customarily drink wine: the person who led *Birchat Ha-Mazon* as well the bride and groom. What is the procedure for drinking wine when *Sheva Berachot* takes place at *shalosh seudot*, late afternoon on *Shabbat*?

RESPONSE: A means of enhancing *Birchat HaMazon* is to hold a cup of wine (*Kos Shel Berachah*) during the *Birchat HaMazon* recitation and upon its conclusion to chant the *berachah* of *HaGafen* prior to drinking of the wine. *Shalosh seudot* generally extends past sunset. Under normal circumstances one may not drink or eat food at such a late period of time on *Shabbat*. At issue is whether the person who held a cup of wine for *Birchat HaMazon* late *Shabbat* afternoon may subsequent to *Birchat HaMazon* recite the *berachah* over the wine and actually drink the wine at that period of time.

The Magen Avraham rules that one may drink the wine of *Kos Shel Berachah* even after *Birchat HaMazon*. Why? For the wine relates to the meal. Just as a person could continue eating or drinking until *Birchat HaMazon* takes place, no matter how late it may be, all food during the meal is permissible. So, too, is the wine of *Kos Shel Berachah*. It is considered part of the meal and therefore also permissible. The limitation, however, says the Magen Avraham is that the person involved normally and customarily drinks wine directly after *Birchat HaMazon*. The wine, then, becomes a part of the meal itself. If, however, the person who led *Birchat HaMazon* generally does not have (a *Kos Shel Berachah* of) wine after *Birchat HaMazon*, then he should not drink the wine on *Shabbat* afternoon after *shalosh seudot* (Magen Avraham, *Orach Chayyim* 299:7).

The Kuntras Acharon of the *Taamei Minhagim* (no. 993) notes that one hasidic *rebbe* drank wine at *Sheva Berachot* on *Shabbat* afternoon and also gave to the bride and groom to drink.

His reason was the belief that the *tzaddik* from Lublin always drank wine on a regular *Shabbat* after *Birchat HaMazon* of each meal. The implication is that if a person does not normally drink wine at *shalosh seudot*, then no wine should be drunk at *Sheva Berachot* occurring at such a period of time. Indeed, the general custom is to hold a cup of wine during regular *shalosh seudot* and not to recite a *berachah* of *HaGafen* over it but to use the wine subsequently at *Havdalah*. Accordingly, maybe no one should drink any wine after the *Shabbat* afternoon *Sheva Berachot* meal.

Common custom, however, is to have the bride and bridegroom drink the wine. My feeling is that this usage is based upon the halachic consideration of Rav Avraham Butchacha who in two different commentaries argues that drinking wine at *Sheva Berachot* is qualitatively different from drinking wine at a regular *shalosh seudah* on *Shabbat*.

The rationale is as follows:

At *Sheva Berachot*, the last *berachah* is chanted over wine. Should this blessing not be recited, then only six, not seven, *berachot* would be recited. Yet, seven blessings are mandated for a bride and groom. Accordingly, the wine should be drunk to mitigate problems with (heaven forbid) reciting a blessing in vain (see Eishel Avraham, Mahdura Tenina, *Orach Chayyim* 22:7). The distinction is that on a regular Saturday afternoon one does not recite the wine blessing after *Birchat HaMazon* should the hour be late. To the extent that the wine blessing is chanted at *Sheva Berachot*, then the wine should be drunk.

The author of the *Minchat Shabbat*, my paternal grandfather, cites (in his additive notes, *Shirurei HaMinchah*, *Siman* 94:4) that Rav Avraham Butchacha expounded in his commentary on *Even HaEzer* (62) a theory supporting drinking wine at *Sheva Berachot* on *Shabbat* afternoon. Why? A person who regularly drinks wine after *Birchat HaMazon* is definitely permitted to drink the *Kos Shel Berachah* after *shalosh seudot*. Since a bride and groom conclude each meal during the first week after marriage with seven blessings that include a blessing for wine, they, the *chatan* and *kallah*, are classified as people who normally drink wine after *Birchat HaMazon*. Accordingly, they are permitted to drink wine even on *Shabbat* afternoon after *Birchat HaMazon.*

It is reputed that HaGaon Rav Moshe Feinstein's position was that it is preferable for only the bride and groom to drink the wine after *shalosh seudot*, not the person who led *Birchat Ha-Mazon*. R. Avraham Butchacha's logic may be the rationale for R. Moshe's practice. Since the bride and groom regularly drank wine after the meal during the first week of marriage, they are certainly permitted to drink the wine on *Shabbat*. The person who leads *Birchat HaMazon*, however, does not have the same custom. He does not generally drink wine after a meal.

Indeed, at a recent *Sheva Berachot* on *Shabbat* afternoon, such was my custom. When I was honored to lead *Birchat HaMazon* I did not drink of the wine but I did give the bride and bridegroom wine to drink. To the extent, moreover, that such wine is deemed potent for good tidings (a *segulah*) it would be wrong to withhold such *mazel tov* from a bride and bridegroom.

(It should be noted that the custom of HaRav Yosef Tzvi Dushinsky, former chief rabbi of Jerusalem, was himself, to sip some wine and then to give it to the bride and groom [*Minhagei Maharitz*, 58].)

Pouring Wine for Sheva Berachot

QUESTION: Halachic guidance is necessary concerning the proper procedure for filling the cups of wine used at *Sheva Berachot*. The general practice is as follows: Prior to *Birchat HaMazon*, two cups of wine are filled. The person leading *zimun* holds one cup of wine until the conclusion of *Birchat HaMazon*. The second cup of wine is used for the subsequent six *berachot* chanted. The seventh *berachah* (for wine) is recited by the person who led *Birchat HaMazon* and he holds the first cup of wine for this *berachah*. Is this process directed by halachic rules?

RESPONSE: Two issues must be clarified. (1) Should one or two cups of wine be used? (2) In the event two cups are to be utilized, when is the second cup to be poured?

The Talmud reports that should a person start a meal before *Shabbat* and conclude it after *Shabbat* commenced, "he recites *Birchat HaMazon* over the first cup and *Kiddush* [for *Shabbat*] over the second cup of wine." Yet why so? Let us recite both over one cup, said R. Huna in R. Sheshet's name: One may not recite two, sanctities over one cup: What is the reason? Said R. Nachman ben Yitzchak: "Because you may not perform religious duties in wholesale fashion" (*Chavilot chavilot* – literally bundles; see Rashbam, for such a process gives the impression that the *mitzvah* is burdensome). The Talmud notes further that one may recite *Havdalah* and *Kiddush* over one cup of wine for both constitute one observance (see Rashbam, for both are recited on account of the sanctity of the festival) (*Pesachim* 102b). Tosafot note that this talmudic citation is the source for the custom to use one cup of wine for *Birchat HaMazon* and another for *Sheva Berachot*. Also, the *hagafen berachah* should be recited on the cup used for *Birchat HaMazon*. Tosafot, however, cites the viewpoint of Rav Meshulam, who rules that only one cup should be utilized at *Sheva Berachot*. Why? Since the *Birchat HaMazon* serves as the impetus for the *Sheva Berachot*, it is really one sanctity.

The *Tur* cites both customs. First, he states, "One brings a cup and blesses over it *Birchat HaMazon*; after the conclusion of *Birchat HaMazon* one leaves [the cup] and another cup is brought over which six blessing are chanted; this then is left and one takes the [first] cup, over which *Birchat HaMazon* was recited and one chants . . . *HaGafen*. Such is the custom in Germany and France. In Spain this is not the custom. There only one cup is used" (*Even HaEzer* 62).

The *Shulchan Aruch* cites both customs, and the Rema rules that common usage was to use two cups of wine (*Even HaEzer*

62:9). Accordingly, it is not considered proper to use the same cup of wine to perform two different *mitzvot*. Each *mitzvah* deserves its own cup of wine. Usage of one cup of wine for two *mitzvot* gives the impression that the person does not value the integrity of each *mitzvah*. This is the rationale for the two-cup custom. Of interest is the procedure of the *Tur*, who ruled that the second cup is filled after *Birchat HaMazon* is completed. Commenting upon this observation the Drishah notes that it is apparent that contrary to common usage it is *not necessary* to fill the second cup of wine until *Birchat HaMazon* is concluded. In addition, he adds that the prayer *D'vei Haseir* is chanted while using the first cup of wine simply because it is not a special *berachah* and is, therefore, not classified as performing *mitzvot* in a wholesale fashion (*Tur, Even HaEzer* 62; see Be'er Heitiv and Bet Shmuel, *Even HaEzer* 62:11, who concur).

The aforementioned discussion does not prohibit pouring of two cups of wine prior to *Birchat HaMazon*. It merely notes that original sources manifest that the second cup was, in fact, filled after *Birchat HaMazon*. The logic may be that there is no reason to fill a cup and then leave it idle while another *mitzvah* is performed.

There is a more cogent reason for altering the common practice of filling two cups of wine before *Birchat HaMazon*. The Magen Avraham rules that when one person is to perform more than one *mitzvah*, it is prohibited to leave one item idle till the other is concluded. This process is deemed "wholesale performance of *mitzvot*" (*chavilot, chavilot*), which is prohibited. Accordingly, two cups of wine are to be used at a wedding, and the second is not to be filled till the first *mitzvah* concludes (*Orach Chayyim* 147:11). As such, it may be wrong even to fill the second cup prior to *Birchat HaMazon*.

Rav Avraham David Butchacha suggests a novel means of harmonizing all theories. He cites the Peri Megadim (*Orach Chayyim* 147), who notes that the Magen Avraham rules it wrong for a person to leave an object of a *mitzvah* idle while performing another. The Peri Megadim adds the principle that this rule applies only to a single person performing two actions.

In the event two people perform the same action, no charge of *chavilot, chavilot* may be leveled. Accordingly, says the Peri Megadim, it is permissible for two different men to take out *Sifrei Torah* and for one Torah to await the conclusion of the first. Since two people hold the *Sifrei Torah* it is permissible (see *Aruch HaShulchan*, who contends that it is permitted to take out two *Sifrei Torah*, for both relate to the same *mitzvah–Orach Chayyim* 147:17). Rav Avraham D. Butchacha concludes that it is therefore recommended that more than one person should fill the cups of wine prior to *Birchat HaMazon*. The fact that two people perform the action would remove the process from being deemed *chavilot, chavilot*. The reason for filling both cups prior to *Birchat HaMazon* is so that no time would be wasted when the six subsequent blessings are recited (Commentary, *Eizer Mekudash, Even HaEzer* 62). From this it is clear that religious procedures are based upon halachic overtones.

Sheva Berachot *for a Mourner on* Shabbat

QUESTION: Is a person within the first year of mourning for a parent permitted to attend a *Sheva Berachot* celebration on *Shabbat?*

RESPONSE: Yes. Even authorities that prohibit a mourner from attending a *Sheva Berachot* party for a relative on a weekday would grant permission for attendance on *Shabbat*.

A mourner is definitely not at peace or manifesting complete harmony.

The *Shulchan Aruch*, therefore, rules that asking *shalom* of a mourner is prohibited (*Yoreh De'ah* 385:1). Of concern is the

definition of the prohibited behavior. The Gilyon Maharsha
(*Yoreh De'ah* 385:1) suggests that this law refers to usage of the
word *shalom*, which signifies the love of God. Prior to prayer one
is not allowed to grant *shalom*. This prohibition refers to usage of
God's name (*Orach Chayyim* 89:2), while it is permissible to say
good morning. As such, contends the Gilyon Maharsha, the same
principle should apply. Namely, the word *shalom* is not to be
used, but a greeting is to be allowed. Indeed, the *Aruch HaShulchan* overtly rules that the word *shalom* should not be utilized at
all in the home of a mourner (*Yoreh De'ah* 385:4).

Based upon the principle that extending *shalom* to a
mourner is prohibited, the Codes note that on *Shabbat* great
authorities, including the Rambam, contend that it is not operational; for on *Shabbat* there is no public observance of mourning.
Since the prohibition against *shalom* falls within the category of
public mourning it is permitted on *Shabbat*. The Rema notes that
those who contend that *shalom* is yet proscribed on *Shabbat*
would also prohibit a mourner from receiving presents on *Shabbat*. Yet, according to those who permit *shalom* on *Shabbat*, the
Rema says a mourner may receive presents (*Yoreh De'ah* 385:4).
The Taz cites the prohibition against presents and adds the
comment (see also Bach) that a mourner also should not invite
guests or attend (a party) at another's home on *Shabbat* (*Yoreh
De'ah* 385:1).

It is evident that a halachic domino process permeates all the
noted prohibitions. Those who hold that *shalom* is prohibited on
Shabbat also contend that a mourner may not receive presents or
visit with friends on *Shabbat*. Should, however, one hold the
generally consensus principle that *shalom* is permitted on *Shabbat*, then accepting presents and attendance at homes of friends
are also permitted. According to this position, a mourner may eat
a *Shabbat* meal outside of his own home.

Now, if it is permitted to extend *shalom* to a mourner on
Shabbat—for otherwise it is deemed an act of public mourning,
which is decried, then refusal to attend *Sheva Berachot* of, for
example, a nephew should certainly be outlawed as a classic example of public mourning that is not tolerated. An uncle who does

not attend *Sheva Berachot* because of mourning is definitely a case of mourning *befarhesyah* (publicly), which authorities note is not in conformity with accepted *halachah* or usage.

Weddings during Sefirot HaOmer

QUESTION: During the counting of the *Omer*, Jews observe a variety of public mourning customs. Some, for example, do not hold weddings until Lag B'Omer; others hold weddings until and including *Rosh Chodesh Iyyar*. Is it permissible for someone who does not hold weddings till Lag B'Omer to attend a wedding held on *Rosh Chodesh Iyyar*?

RESPONSE: HaRav HaGaon R. Moshe Feinstein (*z"l*) rules on this issue. His position is that there is no prohibition for guests to attend a wedding during *Sefirah*. The custom prohibiting weddings is rather an injunction solely imposed upon the bride and bridegroom. They are mandated not to hold a wedding during a period of public mourning. In the event they select to hold their marriage during a time that one or another of the customs permit weddings, then all guests including the marriage performer may attend even should they follow other customs.

HaRav HaGaon R. Feinstein argues as follows: It is common practice to hold weddings on Lag B'Omer, according to one custom, or on *Rosh Chodesh Iyyar*, according to another. At issue is the celebration of *Sheva Berachot* after the day of the wedding. A bride and groom celebrate *Sheva Berachot* for seven days. A wedding is permitted on *Rosh Chodesh Iyyar*. It is not permitted after *Rosh Chodesh* (according to this *minhag*—custom). Yet, no one prohibits the celebration of *Sheva Berachot* after *Rosh Chodesh*. The rationale must be that the first week of one's marriage is classified as a holiday (a *Yom Tov*). As such, during their week of *Yom Tov*, a bride and bridegroom certainly may celebrate. The mourning customs do not apply to them. Such logic, however, does not apply to guests. It's not their *Yom Tov*. Yet, no one prohibits guests from attending *Sheva Berachot*. The reason must be that the prohibition of holding a wedding relates only to the bride and groom. Thus, when they are permitted to get married, all guests are also permitted to attend. Indeed, the *Shulchan Aruch* rules that in the event that a person held a wedding prior to Lag B'Omer, in a period when it is prohibited to do so, then no punishment is to be exacted (*bidi'eved*, the marriage is legal and binding) (*Orach Chayyim* 493:1).

Now, if guests are not to attend a wedding during *Sefirah*, (when customs do not permit weddings), then no greater punishment to a bride and bridegroom could be meted out than to exclude guests from attendance. To the extent that no punishment is exacted, this clearly indicates that guests may attend weddings during *Sefirah* regardless of personal customs (*Iggerot Mosheh, Orach Chayyim* 1:159).

The Mitzvah *of Making a Bride Happy*

QUESTION: Is the *mitzvah* to make a bride happy a public (communal) *mitzvah* or a private commandment?

RESPONSE: The Talmud records that a public *mitzvah* (*mitzvah d'rabim*) has priority over a private *mitzvah*. Rashi defines a public *mitzvah* as a situation where one may include (*motzei*) others in a *mitzvah*. As such, prayer may be designated as a public

mitzvah. Tosafot appear to present an alternate definition. Their
position is that a public *mitzvah* is one in which the public celebrates a *mitzvah* as a communal entity. Namely, everyone performs the *mitzvah* together or performs the same *mitzvah.*

At issue is that Tosafot contend that making a bride (and
bridegroom) happy for seven days is a public *mitzvah,* while
mourning for seven days is not. For this reason a bridegroom who
is a mourner first celebrates seven festive days and then starts
seven days of mourning (*Berachot* 47b). The Maharsha questions
this distinction and expresses a lack of comprehension as to the
rationale to designate one a public *mitzvah* more than another.

The Noda B'Yehudah clarifies the matter by making a finely
honed distinction between the role of mourning and the function
of making happy a bride (and bridegroom).

When a person mourns, he mourns alone. No one is mandated to mourn with him. No one is commanded to actually
mourn the loss. Guests and friends have a function merely to
console the mourner, not to be a mourner too. As such, mourning
is a private, personal *mitzvah.* At a wedding, however, everyone
is involved in the same *mitzvah* of making the bride happy. It's a
mitzvah shared by all. It's a *mitzvah* all perform together.
Accordingly, the basic distinction is as follows: At a wedding we
are all commanded to empathize with the new couple and be
happy; at a funeral only the mourner is required to mourn
(Tzlach, *Berachot* 47b).

Giving Birth, Emotions, and Halachah

QUESTION: Does the psychological status of a mother giving
birth in any way impact halachic ramifications?

RESPONSE: Yes. The Talmud notes a number of acts permitted to be performed in behalf of a mother about to give birth on *Shabbat*. It states, "If she needs a lamp, her neighbor may kindle a lamp for her." To this the Talmud remarks, "That is obvious." Rashi contends that the obvious law is that a mother about to give birth is classified as one with a life-threatening condition. Accordingly, any such status (*pikuach nefesh*) is certainly more important than *Shabbat*. So why is it necessary to formally state that a friend may kindle a light for this woman? Of course, such may be done. The Talmud responds that the uniqueness of this law is that it deals with a blind mother, about to give birth. "You might argue, since she [the mother] cannot see it, it is forbidden; hence he informs us that [we permit the kindling] to tranquilize her mind. [As] she reasons, if there is anything [required] my friend will see it and do it for me" (*Shabbat* 128b). In other words, it is permitted to kindle a light, which is a biblical violation, simply so that a blind woman, about to be a mother, should not be distressed.

Tosafot finely hone this law. They note, for example, that on Yom Kippur a person may eat, providing a medical scholar so ordered that it was necessary to sustain a life (*Yoma* 83a). Yet, the Talmud appears to permit the violation of *Shabbat* merely to soothe the mother's sensitivities. Tosafot conclude that a woman about to give birth is prone to develop a life-threatening condition, should she become frightened that friends (or professionals) are not caring for her needs. Accordingly, to prevent such fears on the part of the mother, *Shabbat* biblical laws may be violated.

Indeed, the Bach rules that once it gets dark one may light candles on behalf of the mother to give birth, even though she did not make such a request. The Biur Halachah notes other considerations. He cites the Rambam, who relates the law to a time frame of occurrence. If, prior to the opening of a woman's uterus, a woman cries out in pain, then lights are kindled only when specifically requested. However, once a woman's uterus is open, lights are kindled whether or not she requests it for she is classified as a *sakanah* case (a danger to life).

The *Aruch HaShulchan* was concerned with an aspect of the law that guides all efforts in behalf of a woman about to give birth. Namely, the Codes rule that all efforts, for example, in her behalf are expressly preferred to be performed in a bizarre or strange fashion (*Orach Chayyim* 330:1). As such, there is no biblical violation. At issue is that in general, when a person's life is in danger the rule is that it is of such importance that even great sages should be involved in the violation. Why is it that when the law treats a woman giving birth it is necessary to alter the normal process? An alteration of process transforms the action from a biblical violation to a rabbinic violation. But if a woman about to give birth is deemed a *sakanah*, then one should violate even biblical laws to save her.

The *Aruch HaShulchan* contends that giving birth is qualitatively different from other forms of imminent danger to life. It is natural to give birth. Such is the process of life. Most women bear the process and pain for they realize that it will pass, that a child will be born and the pain will cease. As such, the act of giving birth is not really a danger to a woman's life. It's normal. It could be, however, life threatening. In the event that one perceives that the mother is anxious and more fearful than others, then one may kindle her light even if she is blind, for the fear itself could harm her (*Aruch HaShulchan, Orach Chayyim* 330:2). Accordingly, a future mother's emotional agitation definitely would impact the halachic reaction to her condition.

Please note that the aforementioned discussion relates to a woman during labor, prior to the actual process of birth itself. When a woman is actually giving birth she is definitely considered a *pikuach nefesh*.

Children's Rights

QUESTION: Must children (even adults) always abide by the dictates of their parents? Does *halachah* provide any exceptions to the principle of parental obedience? Namely, is there any general rule as to when children need not obey parents?

RESPONSE: The *Shulchan Aruch* lists two cases wherein obedience to parental advice need not be heeded. It rules that should parents and a child disagree as to (1) location of the child's school or (2) with whom a child should marry, a "child need not listen to his father" in such matters (*Shulchan Aruch, Yoreh De'ah* 241:25). Of concern is the rationale for these exceptions to the general principle of obedience. The terminology of the Codes is that "a child need not listen to his parent." The implication is that the child certainly may follow the parental dictate should he so desire. The Codes merely free the child from mandatory obedience and grant him freedom of judgment. This suggests that these cases manifest certain guidelines that are exempt from the biblical mandate to heed parents. What are these rules?

Behavior to parents is guided by two biblical verses. One relates to (*kibud*) honor, the other to (*morah*) awe or reverence. The two verses are:

1. "Honor thy father and thy mother" (Exodus 20:12).
2. "Ye shall revere (fear), every man, his mother and his father" (Leviticus 19:3).

Commenting upon these biblical mandates, the Talmud makes the following pragmatic distinctions. "What is fear (*morah*)? What is honor? Fear means that he [the son] must neither stand in his [father's] place, nor sit in his place, nor contradict his words, nor tip the scales against him. Honor means that he [the child] must give him food and drink, clothe and cover him, lead him in and out" (*Kiddushin* 31b).

Based upon the Talmud, honor (*kibud*) thus relates to action that benefits the parent. *Morah* is a passive situation. It's a form of a negative prohibition. The child must refrain from an action that might in some way hurt the feelings or lower respect for the parent.

This definition generates difficulty for the following citation. Commenting on the verse relating to awe, the Talmud says, "Why state man? A man possesses the means to fulfill this [*mitzvah*] but a woman has no means of fulfilling this because she is under the authority of others [namely, her husband]" (*Kiddushin* 30b). In other words, a married woman has primary responsibilities to her husband and children and is not able to serve her parent. Indeed, the Talmud rules that when divorced, she is equal to her brother(s). The difficulty is that the verse of awe (*morah*) does not delineate action on behalf of parents. It specifically deals with a state of passive inaction. As such, being married, single, or divorced should have no bearing on the issue.

R. Pinchas HaLevi Hurowitz (the HaMakna) suggests that the prohibition not to contradict a parent contains both a passive as well as an action-generating component. A request by a parent for service benefiting the parent is a form of (*kibud*) honor. A request by a parent for any activity that does not physically benefit the parent must be heeded by the child as a form of awe (*morah*). For this reason a married woman may find difficulty in complying with parental requests that may require action and service, yet do not necessarily benefit the parent. Hence the verse mandating awe also relates to action.

The exception to the aforementioned rule is that a parental request for a child to do something that does not physically benefit the parent must also be such that does not harm or injure the child in any way. Should the child assess that the parental whim (which did not physically benefit the parent) is in some fashion detrimental to the child, then the child need not listen to parents. For this reason if the child personally judged that the mate selected for him by his parent is not proper, he need not listen to his parent. Such a case certainly does not directly benefit the parent. Accordingly, the child's judgment of personal loss becomes the guiding rule for action. Should the child (even an adult) perceive the action to be *not* injurious to him, then the biblical mandate to in no way contradict the parent will be the principle obligating obedience (HaMakna, *Kiddushin* 31b).

(This discussion does not relate to payment of services requested or provided. Its exclusive concern is the application of service not directly benefiting a parent, yet requested anyway.)

Children and Chanukah

QUESTION: Why is it that in the *Al HaNisim* prayer for Chanukah reference is made to the role of "children" in formulating the holiday, while in the Purim version no role for children is indicated? (For example, see *Al HaNisim* for Chanukah: "Thereafter your children came . . . cleansed your Temple . . . and kindled lights in the courtyards of Your sanctuary.")

RESPONSE: Usage of the role of children in developing Chanukah may pinpoint an essential element of the holiday itself.

Chanukah and Purim are postbiblical holidays. As such, observance of their rituals may not be classified as biblical commandments. Yet, the term commandment is definitely utilized in the *berachot* relating to both Chanukah and Purim observances. The rationale for such usage, says the Talmud, is the biblical command to listen to the words of the sages (see Deuteronomy 17:11, *Shabbat* 23a). Accordingly, it is deemed a *mitzvah* to follow rabbinic laws. The difficulty with this principle is that a *bet din* of a subsequent era may not necessarily agree with the relevance of a decision of a previous *bet din*. Concern, therefore, emerges relating to the continuity of rabbinic edicts. Are all rabbinic decrees of approved religious courts obligatory upon successive generations comparable to biblical statutes, or are there guidelines for religious courts concerning procedure to abrogate certain laws?

Tradition has it that two basic rules govern this process.

1. There is a maxim that "one *bet din* cannot annul the ordinances of another unless it is superior to it in numbers and wisdom" (*Megillah* 2a).

2. Rabbinic edicts or laws accepted by the totality of *K'lal Yisrael* cannot be annulled (see Introduction to *Mishneh Torah*—Maimonides). Thus, in the event that maxim one is not a deterrent, and maxim two did not occur, change may be formulated.

It is a generally accepted precept that prophecy is distinct from the sphere of *halachah*. Indeed, the Talmud notes that

when R. Eliezer lacked a majority to convince the Sanhedrin on
a particular law, he substantiated his view by having a heavenly
(*bat kol*) voice acclaim that the *halachah* is as he so personally
ruled. R. Yehoshua demurred by stating that halachah "is not in
the heaven." One must follow the majority (*Bava Metzia* 59b).
This case overtly demonstrates that a prophet who expounded
through prophecy a particular *halachah* may be discounted by
other members of a Sanhedrin. Why? Because prophecy does not
play a halachic role.

A rabbinic sage, however, noted that even though prophecy
may be separate from *halachah*, the presence of a prophet in the
Sanhedrin as an integral member does elevate the status of the
bet din itself. Namely, when there is a concern as to which *bet din*
has greater "wisdom," the one that has a prophet as a member is
afforded greater legal standing.

Substantiation of this concept may be noted as follows.

The Talmud notes that the *bet din* of the "Men of the Great
Assembly," composed of "a hundred and twenty elders, among
whom were many prophets, drew up eighteen blessings [the
Shemoneh Esrei] in a fixed order" (*Megillah* 17b). The Talmud is
relating the stature of the *bet din* of the Men of the Great
Assembly. So, why is the presence of prophets noted? Mention of
the prophets, perhaps, was to indicate that their presence added
to the luster of the *bet din*. This principle may also shed light on
a talmudic discussion relating to the question as to whether later
sages could amend decisions promulgated by the Men of the
Great Assembly. The Talmud specifically states that it is prohibited to alter such a decision for "one *bet din* cannot annul the
ordinances of another unless it is superior in numbers and wisdom" (*Megillah* 2a). The assumption is that no *bet din* subsequent
to the Men of the Great Assembly could ever match their stature.
But why is this so? Was it such that no Sanhedrin could in any
way equal the sagacity of the Men of the Great Assembly?
Perhaps, the Talmud points us to the reason why the Sanhedrin
of the Great Assembly was greater than all subsequent rabbinic
assemblages. The Men of the Great Assembly had a number of
prophets as members. It was also the last *bet din* in Jewish

history to have prophets as participants. Accordingly, no subsequent *bet din* could even equal its stature. This, therefore, acknowledges that any decree set up for Purim by the Men of the Great Assembly would survive the historicity of the Jewish people. The all-powerful role of the *bet din* that formulated the *mitzvot* of Purim could not be equaled, therefore all laws could not be subsequently altered.

Chanukah was different. The *bet din* of the *Hashmona'im* did not include any prophets. The age of prophecy was over. Accordingly, it was possible for a Sanhedrin to emerge in a succeeding generation that may manifest greater qualities than the *bet din* that established Chanukah. Such a *bet din* would have the authority to amend or annul the Chanukah rituals, providing that the totality of *K'lal Yisrael* did not embrace its observance. For this reason the *Al HaNisim* prayer for Chanukah emphasizes the role of children – a future generation – in the establishment of the holiday. Chanukah's continuity is not because of the stature of its *bet din*, but, rather, the acceptance by the people and future generations. The term "your children" refers to *K'lal Yisrael*. The rationale for mentioning children is to set the record straight that it was the acceptance by *K'lal Yisrael* that assured its survival as a holiday. *K'lal Yisrael* made it into a holiday (see Pachad Yitzchok – *Vezot Chanukah, Maamar* 14:1, 2; the author takes sole responsibility for setting up the format as well as the sources for all concepts).

Leaving an Inheritance

QUESTION: Is it a *mitzvah* to provide an inheritance for children?

RESPONSE: HaGaon HaRav Baruch HaLevi Epstein contends that sources indicate that a Jew is under no obligation to provide an inheritance for children.

The *Midrash* notes that Rav Meir earned three coins a week. One he used for food and drink, one for clothing, and with one coin he sustained the rabbis. His students were concerned with such a spending pattern and asked, "*Rebbe*, what will be for your children?" Rav Meir responded, "If they are righteous, did not David say, 'I never saw a righteous person forsaken' (Psalm 37); and if they are not [pious] why should I leave my [possessions] to the enemies of God?"

HaRav Epstein suggests the following interpretation. The students believed that Jews are mandated to amass sufficient assets to provide an inheritance for children. Since it is a *mitzvah* to observe the laws of inheritance, it must be a *mitzvah* to also leave an inheritance to children.

To this Rav Meir responded that there is no *mitzvah* to provide an inheritance for children. The *mitzvot* of inheritance relates only in the event a parent leaves assets. In such a situation, the Torah mandates the means of allocation and distribution. Should a parent not leave any assets or property to children, no parental sin takes place.

Somewhat of a substantiation to this view is the rabbinic rule ordained at Usha that contributions to charity should not exceed one fifth of available assets. The rationale expressed is that should a person donate more than a fifth and then subsequently have a financial reversal, people simply would not have compassion upon him. They would feel that such a person brought about his own destruction and financial problem by a wasteful undisciplined largess for charity (see *Ketubot* 50a). Now, if it is a special *mitzvah* to provide children with an inheritance, the Talmud need not have developed the aforementioned theory, namely, that expansive charity allocations may turn people against a person who subsequently became poor. The Talmud could have easily stated that one is not permitted to distribute too much charity for such might generate the sinful lack of an inheritance to children. To the extent the Talmud does not make such references it indicates that there is no *mitzvah* to provide an inheritance to children (see Tosefot, *Berachah*, vol. 5, *Devarim*, *Kohelet*, pp. 324–325).

Prayers at the Birth of a Girl

QUESTION: When a boy is born, *mazel tov* is extended plus a prayer to the parents that they should have the privilege to raise the child "to Torah, *chuppah*, and good deeds (*maasim tovim*)." When a girl is born is the above traditional greeting recited or is it altered?

RESPONSE: Many change the basic prayer when it pertains to girls. They simply eliminate the *berachah* for Torah and state that the parents should have the privilege of preparing the daughter for *chuppah* and good deeds. The implication is that since a girl is not mandated to learn Torah, a blessing for Torah is not proper nor in order.

Of interest is that HaGaon HaRav Yitzchok Hutner (*z"l*), the famed former *rosh hayeshivah*, Rabbi Chaim Berlin Yeshivah, personally had the custom of blessing parents of sons *as well as daughters* with the same blessing. His rationale was that since common custom is for women to recite *Birchat HaTorah* (each day) they are, in fact, included in the *berachah* of Torah and consequently there is no valid reason to eliminate a blessing of Torah from them or their lives. In addition, a Torah blessing to a woman has a two-part function. One aspect relates to her personal involvement with Torah while the other may deal with that of her (future) husband and children. Indeed, as part of a blessing to a father, HaRav Hunter wished that he be granted the *zechut* (privilege) to bring into his family via his daughter a Torah scholar who would be able to develop into a Torah sage (see *Pachad Yitzchok, Iggerot Uchetuvim*, no. 229).

From this we learn that the blessing for Torah to a child deals with much more than the pursuit of actual Torah learning itself. It relates to the development of a Torah personality and a desire to have Torah values permeate the social patterns of behavior. A woman imbued with the blessing of Torah will insure that her husband and children will live up to the goals of Torah knowledge. A woman who believes in Torah will marry only someone who sincerely subscribes to the sanctity of Torah life. A Torah woman will help in every way to elevate the religious stature of her family. Jewish women require, therefore, a Torah blessing as much as men.

This custom and its rationale definitely has great merit. Indeed, whenever I publicly announce the birth of a girl in the synagogue, I make note of the sacred role that Torah plays in the life of all, especially that of a female. Living a life of Torah is a goal of every Jew, male as well as female.

Bringing Children to Yeshivah

QUESTION: What is the halachic function and reward of women who bring their children to a *yeshivah* to learn Torah?

RESPONSE: The *Mishnah* (*Sotah* 20a) rules that a *sotah* (a women who was accused of committing adultery by her husband and in fact was found to have done so) was able to postpone her punishment by producing evidence of *zechut*, that is, of having performed some meritorious deed. In a discussion of the type of deed that could postpone punishment, the following concepts are articulated in the Talmud (*Sotah* 21a): If the deed was the act of learning Torah, women who learn Torah are in the category of those who are not commanded, yet (voluntarily) observe (see Rashi – their reward is not comparable to that of those who were commanded), and thus it does not have sufficient standing to suspend punishment. If the deed was the performance of *mitzvot* (tradition has it that) *mitzvot* provide protection from troubles only when being performed, not afterward. Torah (however) provides protection even after the learning concludes. Thus, *mitzvot* do not have the capacity to withhold punishment. Ravina notes that the *sotah* did, indeed, have the merit of Torah. Her involvement with Torah was not her personal Torah learning but the toil and effort of bringing her children to learn Torah and of waiting for her husband, who often went to another city in order to learn Torah.

Based upon this talmudic citation, HaGaon HaRav Yitzchok Hutner, *z"l* (former *rosh hayeshivah*, Rabbi Chaim Berlin Rabbinical Academy) derives the concept that bringing children to learn Torah (or waiting for a husband who is learning Torah) must be an act that is granted a reward comparable to the actual learning of Torah itself. For the Talmud specifically notes that only deeds of Torah and not of *mitzvot* can suspend punishment. To the extent that the process of bringing children to Torah is deemed to contain sufficient merit to withhold punishment, it must be because it is equal to learning Torah itself.

HaRav Hutner (*z"l*) further suggests that this principle equating the reward of the facilitator to the reward of one who learns Torah is an exclusive precept limited to Torah and does not pertain to the performance of *mitzvot*. For example, a person who enables another to observe the *mitzvah* of honoring his parents is not granted the reward of long life, which is granted those who honor their parents. The rationale is that Torah has a unique status. The Talmud contends (*Menachot* 99b; see Rashi) that when Torah learning ceased for such *mitzvot* as a wedding or a funeral, a reward is granted as if one had continued to learn Torah. The reason is that the commitment to perform *mitzvot* is a necessary condition of the *mitzvah* to learn and is an observance of the ultimate goal of Torah itself (*lilmod al minat laasot*). Now, if the reward of Torah is given to one who ceases learning in order to perform *mitzvot*, should it not be granted to one who facilitates Torah learning (see *Pachad Yitzchok, Shevuot, Maamar* 13)?

(This may be the reason why someone who supports and or sustains Torah by enabling scholars to learn Torah may deserve a reward comparable to those who learn Torah.)

Honoring a Minor Kohen

QUESTION: Is a minor *kohen* to be afforded any special respect or privileges?

RESPONSE: The Torah grants special treatment to a *kohen*, as it is written, *"V'kidashto"* – "and you shall keep him holy" (Leviticus 21:8). The Talmud concretizes this command by noting that one observes the *mitzvah* by granting a *kohen* priority in all matters of *kedushah*; he is to be called (up) first to the Torah, and he is to be granted priority to lead *Birchat HaMazon*. Rabbeinu Asher adds that the *kohen* is to be called first to speak at public assemblages (*Nedarim* 62b). Are these rules applicable to a minor *kohen*?

The Magen Avraham says no. He contends that the very verse that mandates special privileges to a *kohen* contains within it the rationale to exclude a minor from the *mitzvah*. The Torah notes *"V'kidashto"* – "and you shall keep him holy," *"for the offering of thy God doth he bring near"* (Leviticus 21:8, Hirsch translation). The latter phrase specifically grants the *kohen* privileges because of his service in bringing a *korban* to God. The overt implication is that should the *kohen* be excluded from involvement with sacrifices, he therefore would be exempt from special treatment. Since a minor did not bring sacrifices (nor oversee such activity), it is self-evident that there is no *mitzvah* to provide him with any special honor (*Orach Chayyim* 282:6).

HaRav Akivah Eiger, however, notes that the Magen Avraham's logic appears to be questionable. Why? Because early authorities rule that a *kohen* with a blemish (a *baal mum*), who certainly could not be involved with *korbonot*, was still to be afforded the respect and privilege granted to any other *kohen*. As such, the fact that a minor did not bring *korbonot* should not exempt him from the *mitzvah* of *V'kidashto* (see *Sefer HaChinuch, mitzvah* 269; also glosses of Rav Akivah Eiger, *Orach Chayyim* 282).

In an attempt to resolve this question, HaRav Tzvi Pesach Frank, former chief rabbi of Jerusalem, suggested a fine halachic distinction between a minor *kohen* and an adult *kohen* who had a blemish. The latter was granted *kodshim* (holy food from the *korbanot*) to eat. Though a minor also had this right, he had no *mitzvah* in the process. A minor was merely granted permission to eat *kodshim*. There was no requirement to give him such food to eat. For indeed, the Malbim rules that an adult *kohen* was commanded to eat *kodshim*. Even a *kohen* with a blemish had such an obligation. Indeed, the blemished *kohen* who ate *kodshim* observed a *mitzvah* in the process (see *Parashat Tzav*). A minor *kohen* had no such *mitzvah*. Accordingly, the *kohen* "*baal mum*" is yet involved in the *mitzvah* of *korbanot* and therefore is also included in the *mitzvah* of *V'kidashto* (Har Tzion, notes on *Minchat Chinuch, mitzvah* 269).

Determining the Date of a Bar Mitzvah

QUESTION: Tradition has it that a boy becomes officially classified as a *bar mitzvah* when he attains the age of thirteen years and a day. How does *halachah* define this period of time? May a boy whose thirteenth birth date comes out on *Shabbat* celebrate his *bar mitzvah* on his birthday?

RESPONSE: Sources indicate two positions. One theory is that a *bar mitzvah* does not take place until thirteen complete years transpire from actual time of birth. This means that should, for example, a boy be born at 3:00 P.M., his status transformation would not occur until 3:00 P.M. on his birth date; talmudic terminology deems this process "*m'eit la'eit*" (*Niddah* 47b).

A second position is that the actual hour or moment of birth is irrelevant for the determination of a *bar mitzvah*. Once a boy enters into the calendar day of his thirteenth birthday, he is legally deemed an adult even if it is several hours before the actual time of birth (Tosafot, *Niddah* 44b). Thus, a boy born at 3:00 P.M. would be a *bar mitzvah* on Friday night, should the date fall on *Shabbat*.

This debate generates a number of both obvious and not so obvious distinctions. A boy born in the afternoon would, according to the first theory, simply not be able to celebrate his *bar mitzvah* on his birth date should it come out on *Shabbat*. HaRav Moshe Ibn Haviv contends that this debate would have serious ramifications upon a boy born on Rosh HaShanah in the late afternoon. According to the requirement to have thirteen years to the hour of birth, all the sounds of *shofar* heard prior to his actual time of birth would be classified as heard by a minor. As such, at the hour of his birth date in the afternoon, he would be obliged to rehear the *shofar* (see *Kapot Temarim, Rosh HaShanah* 28).

This halachic dilemma is resolved by the Shach, who rules that one need not await the accurate hour of a birth date but once the day of the thirteenth birthday takes place, the *bar mitzvah* is official (*Shulchan Aruch, Choshen Mishpat*, no. 35). This means that a boy is officially considered a *bar mitzvah* on the night of his birth date.

Of concern is the ruling of the Rema that a minor who becomes a *bar mitzvah* on *Shabbat* should not serve as the *shliach tzibur* for the Friday night services (*Orach Chayyim* 53:6). Why should this be so? Is not a young boy officially a *bar mitzvah* once it gets dark? The Magen Avraham contends that the ruling of the Rema in no way contradicts the position (of the Shach) that a *bar mitzvah* takes place at the night of the birth date. The concern of the Rema, suggests the Magen Avraham, was that Jews generally prayed Friday evening before it was dark, prior to the time of the emergence of stars. For this reason, a boy who was to be a *bar mitzvah* on *Shabbat* was not to lead services on Friday night. Should, however, Jews pray after dark, then even the Rema would permit a young boy born on *Shabbat* to lead services on the Friday night of his *bar mitzvah* (*Orach Chayyim* 53:13).

This rule requires further clarification. Indeed, it appears to contradict an established principle relating to *mitzvot* on Friday night.

The Talmud notes that one may welcome Shabbat even prior to darkness on Friday and that one may even recite *Kiddush* at such a time (*Berachot* 27b). Now, here's the problem: If, on Friday afternoon when from a biblical view it is not really *Shabbat*, one may *daven Maariv* and make *Kiddush*, and that *Kiddush* frees a person from any and all biblical obligations to subsequently recite *Kiddush*, then the same logic should apply to a young boy who serves as a *shliach tzibur* prior to the night of his thirteenth birthday. There should be no difference between leading services before or after dark. Just as an adult may recite *Kiddush* at a period (of *Tosafot Shabbat*) that is not really *Shabbat* from a biblical standpoint, yet such recitation frees him from any biblical obligation, so too should a young boy be able to lead services during a period directly before he is biblically mandated to observe *mitzvot*. What difference is there between making *Kiddush* early or leading services prior to darkness?

It may be noted that there are a number of responses to this issue:

1. Jews are permitted to extend *Shabbat* by welcoming it prior to its biblical period of time. This is called *Tosafot Shabbat*. It is a means of extending the *kedushah* (sanctity) of *Shabbat* to the sixth day of the week, Friday. *Kiddush* requires *kedushah*, not necessarily the seventh day of the week. Though one may make *Shabbat* early and generate *kedushah*, such does not effect a calendar change. It does not make the sixth day into the seventh day. To legally be an adult, however, requires an actual calendar date change. For this reason a young boy must await darkness before he may lead services. He must await the period when he actually becomes thirteen years of age.

2. Tosafot contend that the rabbinic *mitzvot* of minors are qualitatively distinct from other rabbinic *mitzvot*. The rabbinic

obligation for minors to perform *mitzvot* is not a personal obligation of the minor, rather, a mandate imposed upon the parents
(*Berachot* 48b). Accordingly, a minor whose birth date is on
Shabbat may not lead services during *Tosafot Shabbat*, for prior
to maturity the minor has no *mitzvah* at all, it's the parent who is
obliged to see to it that the child does *mitzvot*. This is why he
differs from an adult who is permitted to recite *Kiddush* during
Tosafot Shabbat.

3. A third distinction is that the rule of a *shliach tzibur* for
Maariv is quite different from simply making *Kiddush* on Friday
night. Leading *Maariv* is a communal function (*tzibur*), which
may be restricted to adults, not minors, because of the general
principle of *kavod hatzibur*.

In conclusion, one may definitely celebrate a *bar mitzvah* on
the *Shabbat* of one's thirteenth birthday. Leading *Maariv* services prior to the emergence of actual nightfall is a completely
different issue.

Part V

Rituals, Shabbat, Holidays, Prayers

Priority for Washing Hands

QUESTION: Prior to the *berachah* for eating bread it is necessary to wash. Of concern is the proper respect for the head of the household or an honored guest in this process. Namely, should the head of the household wash first or last?

RESPONSE: The *Shulchan Aruch* rules that in the event a large number of people are gathered for a meal the most distinguished or senior dignitary washes first. It is noted that, however, Rabbeinu Asher (the Rosh) had the custom of washing last so as to prevent an interruption between washing and (*HaMotzi*) and also to guard against talking (even minimally) (*Orach Chayyim* 165:2).

It is of interest that the Talmud seems to corroborate the position of Rabbeinu Asher. The Talmud asks: "With whom do they commence the washing of the hands before the meal? . . . with the senior one. Is then the senior one to sit and watch his hands until they have all washed? They bring a table before him immediately." Rashi says that the custom was for each to eat at his own table. As such, the senior person washed first and was immediately given a table with food to eat. Accordingly, he did not wait for others to conclude washing (*Berachot* 46b). This implies that the senior person should simply not await others to conclude their washing of hands. Indeed, the Mishneh Berurah specifically rules that in the event a large number of people are present at a meal, it is simply not proper for all to wait for the senior member to wash, but rather, he should wash first and eat, and so too should all the others (*Orach Chayyim* 165:5). In other words, no one should wait for the *HaMotzi* of another. In the commentary Biur Halachah, it is explicitly noted that "since everyone makes a *berachah* on his own piece of bread, the rationale of Rabbeinu Asher is not applicable."

The difficulty with this ruling is that it definitely implies that in the event one person does, indeed, make a *berachah* for others, then the most proper custom is for the head of the household to wash last. He should not wait for others.

Indeed, the *Aruch HaShulchan* overtly states that on *Shabbat*, for example, where only the head of the household is provided with *lechem mishneh* (double portion of *challot*), he should definitely wash last (*Orach Chayyim* 165:3). Thus, the proper order for the washing of the hands of the head of the household depends on whether one person recites a *berachah* for all or whether each person makes a *berachah* on his own piece of bread. Though the *Aruch HaShulchan* notes that common custom is for the head of the household to wash first, on *Shabbat* where generally only one person has *lechem mishneh*, logic supports following Rabbeinu Asher's custom.

From a practical viewpoint, I found Rabbeinu Asher's custom to be most useful when eating together with my children on *Shabbat* or *Yom Tov*. To ensure that no one tarried or disappeared before (or after) washing hands, I supervise the process. By washing last, I am (to this day) able to ensure that my family goes directly to the table. Prior to following the Rosh's custom, I would sit, wait, sing, hope, and pray that no obstacle befell any one of them. Now that I am a devotee of Rabbeinu Asher's custom, I can monitor the process. I recommend Rabbeinu Asher's custom to all.

Salt and Bread

QUESTION: What is the proper method of salting the *challah* eaten on *Shabbat*?

RESPONSE: At a recent *Shabbat simchah*, I sprinkled some salt on the *challah* that I ate. Sitting at the table were a number of learned *hasidim*. One noted that I should have sprinkled the salt on the table and then dipped the *challah* into the salt. I remarked that I was unaware of such a custom but would look into the matter. Subsequently, the *hasid* sent me a letter substantiating his view. He cited the *Kitzur Shulchan Aruch*, who specifically rules that salt should be on the table ". . . and one should 'dip' (*toveil*) the piece of bread into salt" (*Siman* 41:6). He also cited the *Shulchan Aruch* HaRav, who notes the *kabbalah* directs one to dip the piece (of bread) in salt three times (*Orach Chayyim* 167:8).

Initial reaction is that he is right. The fact that they utilize such terminology as "one dips bread (*toveil*) into salt" suggests that the salt is stationary on the table and the bread is dipped into the salt.

Yet, the *Shulchan Aruch* makes no mention of the dipping process altogether. It rules that one should not eat unless salt is brought to enhance the piece of bread. The implication is that the salt is sprinkled on the bread. The Rema notes that "it is a *mitzvah* to have salt on every table even prior to eating, for [our] table is comparable to the altar (*mizbe'ach*) and eating is comparable to [eating] a sacrifice (*korban*) and it is written, on all your sacrifices should be salt, and it protects us from bad events" (*Orach Chayyim* 167:5). The latter is derived from a *midrash* that notes that when people sit around a table without a *mitzvah*, the Satan could create problems, but the covenant of salt protects them (Tosafot, *Berachot* 40a). The Shibolai HaLeket, the first sage who linked salt to the *korbanot*, makes no reference to dipping, nor does the *Tur*. The *Mishnah Berurah* cites the Mekubalim, who note that one should dip the bread three times in salt (*Orach Chayyim* 167:33). The Magen Avraham specifically notes that the piece of bread used for *HaMotzi* should be dipped in salt (167:13). The *Aruch HaShulchan* adds that all who fear God so follow this custom (167:12). Yet neither direct it be done three times. The Kitzur Shela suggests the reason for dipping three times is that God's Holy Name has the *gematria* number of 26: three times 26 equals 78, which is the same *gematria* as salt (*melach*) (see Kitzur Shela, *Netilat Yadayim*).

Yet, many rabbinic sages simply sprinkle the salt on the bread rather than dip the bread into a plate with salt. (Nowhere does it explicitly state that the loose salt should be actually on the table itself.) My feeling is that the issue relates to the comparison of food to a *korban*. In the *Bet HaMikdash* one did not dip the *korban* into the salt. Rather, one sprinkled salt on the *korban*. Accordingly, the salt should be sprinkled onto the bread, which relates to the *korban*. Dipping the bread into the salt would not be a direct comparison to a *korban*.

Indeed, if the mandated usage of salt is solely due to its function during the ancient sacrifices, then logic would dictate following the Chatam Sofer's custom, which did not use salt on Friday night. His argument was that on Friday evening there was no *ketoret* (incense) for the innards and therefore no usage of salt (see *Siddur*, Chatam Sofer, Friday night, *Minhagim*, no. 5). Most, however, do use salt together with *challah*, even on Friday night. This suggest that the custom is not solely due to the comparison to a *korban*. Accordingly, the Mekubalim would be of the opinion that salt at a table may be due to the second reason presented by the Rema, namely, that it mutes the Satan. The salt is a covenant of peace. As such, the bread, which serves the basic substance of food, is dipped into the covenant of peace (three times, to signify, perhaps, that God's Holy Name is synonymous with peace).

Addendum: Someone suggested that the rationale for dipping bread into salt was based upon a concrete, pragmatic problem. European salt did not sprinkle easily. It was hard. It was so hard that it had to be chopped into small pieces. It was America that was able to manufacture salt that poured easily. As such, ancient sages simply were unaware that salt could "pour like rain."

Minimum for Zimun

QUESTION: What is the minimum amount (or type) of food or drink that a third person must ingest in order to join two others who ate bread so that the *zimun* of *Birchat HaMazon* may take place? (*Zimun* is the special introductory prayer added to the Grace After Meals when three or more adults are in attendance.)

RESPONSE: This case happens frequently. Two men eat a meal and a third arrives almost at the conclusion and is requested to eat something so that *Birchat HaMazon* with *Zimun* (of three) may be recited. The *Shulchan Aruch* presents three options. (1) The third person must eat a *zayit* of bread (size of an olive). This means he must wash and eat an amount of bread that would ordinarily mandate the chanting of *Birchat HaMazon*. (2) He may eat the type of food that requires at least a *berachah achronah*, like cake. (3) He may eat a *zayit* of even a vegetable.

Based on these theories the *Shulchan Aruch* develops sort of a compromise situation. It rules that the third person should be openly encouraged to (wash and) eat bread. If he declines, he should not be offered to eat or drink anything else. In the event he does eat even a vegetable, one may recite *Birchat HaMazon* with *Zimun* (*Orach Chayyim* 197:3). The *Mishnah Berurah*, however, notes that such is not the general custom. Common usage is to offer bread to be eaten. Should this be declined one (even *l'chatchilah*) offers any sort of food to be eaten, for the *halachah* is like the third option of the *Shulchan Aruch* (*Mishnah Berurah* 197:22). In other words, once bread is refused to be eaten by the third person, it is not necessary to suggest cake. Any form of food, even a vegetable, may be offered.

Of interest is that the *Shulchan Aruch* specifically rules that the third person need not eat food, but could even drink wine. Water, however, is specifically excluded (*Orach Chayyim* 197:2). Though the *Mishnah Berurah* records the ruling of the Magen Avraham, who contends that all drinking is comparable to food, including water, and notes that prominent halachic authorities so rule (including the *Shulchan Aruch* HaRav and the Chayyei Adam), he lists three major decisors who disagree with the Magen Avraham (*Mishnah Berurah* 197:12). The implication is that it is simply a matter of rabbinic dispute. Accordingly, a

cautious person would probably refrain from involvement in such
a questionable *halachah* and would not offer water to the third
person.

Of interest is that there are numerous types of liquids that
are neither wine nor water. The *Aruch HaShulchan* discusses
this issue and suggests that a liquid drink must be somewhat
more impressive then mere water (which lacks *chashivut*). Accordingly, he rules that seltzer or lemonade should be of sufficient value or importance to permit one to recite *Zimun*. He
concludes that such should be the law (*ikar k'dinah*) (*Aruch
HaShulchan* 197:5). Now if lemonade and/or seltzer is sufficient
it appears to me that one may offer the third person some soda to
drink. Thus a *revi'it* (for example) of Diet Pepsi may set in motion
Zimun.

Birchat HaMazon, *Part 1:*
Text of the Third Berachah

QUESTION: The actual text of the third *berachah* of *Birchat
HaMazon* appears to have more than one accepted version.
Common practice is to state "*Boneh berachamav, Yerushalyim,
Amen*" – we bless God as He who will rebuild Jerusalem with
mercy. Others delete any reference to mercy and, instead, recite
"*Boneh Yerushalayim, Amen.*" Namely, God will build Jerusa-
lem. Why the different versions? What's wrong with rebuilding
our ancient capital with mercy or compassion?

RESPONSE: The custom of the Vilna Gaon was not to add the
phrase relating to mercy (*Maaseh Rav*). The rationale presented
is that the Talmud makes no reference to mercy. Accordingly, it
should not be infused within the *berachah* (*Likutei Dinim*,

Siddur HaGra). Indeed, the *Shulchan Aruch* discusses this *berachah* without mention of the emotion of mercy (see *Orach Chayyim* 188:1). This suggests that ancient reliable sources had no reference to "mercy" in the third *berachah*. Some scholars cite the verse "Zion will be redeemed with judgment" (Isaiah 1:27), which openly demonstrates that redemption will be through the process of law or judgment and not through compassion (*Kol Bo*). Thus, reference to mercy as a component necessary for rebuilding Jerusalem is not accurate. (Many erroneously cite this verse as substantiation for the Vilna Gaon's practice.)

The Ateret Zekeinim commentary cites the tradition of some to add the word "with mercy" (*Berachamav*) in the blessing and notes that "such is the custom." The rationale, he suggests, is that after the conclusion of the second blessing, the *Birchat HaMazon* commences with the word *racheim*, which means "have mercy." As such, the concluding blessing should also contain some reference to mercy so that its beginning and end should be comparable.

The Kol Bo's contention that Jerusalem will be rebuilt with judgment (not compassion) is rejected by the Ateret Z'keinim. Why? It is true that the actual rebuilding will be via the principle of judgment, but its glory, beauty, and distinction to overshadow even the first *Bet HaMikdash* will yet require heavenly mercy (Ateret Zekeinim, *Orach Chayyim* 188:1). Others suggest that the meaning of the phrase "Zion will be rebuilt with judgment" relates to the people themselves. Justice on the part of Jews will generate a heavenly response. But the deeds even of justice will not be sufficient to merit the rebuilding Jerusalem. For this, God's "mercy" will yet be required (see Be'er Yaakov, *Orach Chayyim* 188:1).

Of interest is the wording of the request for mercy. We do not beseech Jerusalem to be rebuilt "with mercy" but rather, "with His mercy." Why such a terminology? The Peri Megadim suggests that mercy is an emotional sensitivity that is somewhat between love and kindness. We therefore request God's special mercy to bring the Messiah even though we may not be worthy (Be'er Yaakov, *Orach Chayyim* 188:1).

Birchat HaMazon, *Part 2: Amen after the Third* Berachah

QUESTION: Generally Amen is recited when one hears a *berachah* chanted by another. As such, why do all respond Amen even when we, ourselves, conclude the third *berachah* of *Birchat HaMazon*? Also, should this Amen be chanted aloud or silently?

RESPONSE: The *Shulchan Aruch* rules that Amen is recited after the conclusion of the third blessing of *Birchat HaMazon* (*Boneh brachamav Yerushalyim, Amen*) to denote that such is the conclusion of the biblical *berachot* and the subsequent *berachah* (*HaTov uMeitiv*) is but rabbinic in nature (*Orach Chayyim* 188:1). The Rema notes that common custom restricts the chanting of Amen after one's own blessing to the third *berachah* of *Birchat HaMazon* (*Orach Chayyim* 215:1).

The Talmud notes that laborers were not obliged to recite the fourth *berachah*, which was only a rabbinic mandate. The rationale was that the rabbis did not impose a mandate to recite the rabbinic fourth blessing in the event it withheld workers from their obligation to their employers. Accordingly, "Abaye responded Amen in a loud voice so that the workmen should hear and rise" (namely, the workmen may go back to work for they did not recite the fourth blessing). "Rav Ashi gave the response in a low voice so that they should not think lightly of the [last] benediction" (*Berachot* 45b). The *Shulchan Aruch* rules (as does Rav Ashi) that the Amen should be recited quietly so as not to denigrate the last blessing. The Rema adds that when there are others who are answering Amen to *berachot*, then the person leading the *Birchat HaMazon* may chant the Amen aloud like the others (*Orach Chayyim* 188:2).

The *Shulchan Aruch HaRav* and *Mishnah Berurah* note that common custom is to recite the Amen aloud (even without *Zimun*). Why? For the original reason for silently saying Amen was that the laborers would generally leave the table (stop

saying *Birchat HaMazon*) whenever they heard the Amen chanted. If the Amen was said aloud, people may generally denigrate
the last blessing by not reciting it, even when they were not work-
ing. Since, however, in our time everyone, even day laborers,
recite the last *berachah*, there is no reason to chant it quietly
(*Orach Chayyim* 188:2). Of interest is that the *Aruch HaShulchan*
suggests that preference should still be granted to the ancient
talmudic dictum to recite Amen quietly (*Orach Chayyim* 188:3).
The *Mishnah Berurah* does not cite a preferance but does note
that common custom is always to recite the Amen aloud. According to the Rema's position, there should be no tradition to respond
with Amen silently when one leads the *Zimun*.

One precaution. One should stop, even for a second, between
reciting the last word of the *berachah* and the word Amen so that
all recognize that Amen is not the end of the *berachah*, but rather
a response to it (*Mishnah Berurah* 188:2).

Welcoming Shabbat

QUESTION: Why is it that *Shabbat* is welcomed with song?
Also, tradition has it that the kabbalists (mystics) would welcome
the *Shabbat* by accompanying the *Lechah Dodi* prayers with
dance. Why was this necessary?

RESPONSE: (The following responses were culled from the
writings of HaGaon, HaRav Yitzchok Hutner, *z"l*.)
The Ohr Zarua contends that a biblical verse serves as the
source for the general custom to sing songs at the conclusion of
Shabbat (*zemirot* at a *melavah malkah*). The *Chumash* relates
that Yaakov did not inform his father-in-law, Lavan, of his desire
to depart with his entire family to return to Israel. Indeed, Lavan
was so perturbed over this insensitivity that he deemed it an
unfair, immoral act. He contended that had he known of Yaakov's

intention to depart, he would not have withheld the exodus. Just
the opposite. As it is written, "Why did you flee so secretly, and
steal from me, and did not tell me that *I would have sent you
away in joy, and with songs, with taberet and with harp*" (Genesis
31:27). From this we learn that it is proper to escort a departing
person with song. Accordingly, one should escort the departing
Shabbat with song (see *Shelah HaKadosh*, Amsterdam Publications, p. 135).

HaRav Hutner adds a nuance of importance. There is a
general rule that the joy of departure cannot be greater than the
kavod of welcome. As such, *Kabbalat Shabbat*, the welcome of
Shabbat, certainly must be accompanied by song (*Pachad Yitzchok, Shar UveYom HaShabbat, Kuntres Reshimot* 5:8).

Why did the mystics dance when they welcomed *Shabbat*?
The ultimate act of acceptance and commitment (*kabbalat mitzvot*) took place at Mount Sinai. That commitment was more than
a verbal statement. It had an action, for the Jews underwent
immersion prior to commitment (see *Yevamot* 46b). This suggests that a form of beautification of *mitzvot* (*hiddur mitzvah*) is
to associate a commitment with an action. As such, *Kabbalat
Shabbat* was accompanied by dance (*Pachad Yitzchok, Shar
UveYom HaShabbat, Kuntres Reshimot* 5:7).

Friday is unique. It serves as the sixth day of creation, a day
important in itself. It also serves as the day that is the eve of
*Shabbat—Erev Shabbat—*a day of preparation for the holy day of
Shabbat. Because of this unusual role it requires its own song.
Lechah Dodi is the song of *Erev Shabbat* (*Pachad Yitzchok, Shar
UveYom HaShabbat, Kuntres Reshimot* 4:12).

Showering on Shabbat *and* Yom Tov

QUESTION: May one shower with hot water on *Shabbat* and
Yom Tov?

RESPONSE: Halachic research indicates that the act of bathing was prohibited on *Shabbat* and *Yom Tov* regardless of whether a violation of *Shabbat* or *Yom Tov* laws took place.

The Talmud states, "At first people used to wash in [pit] water heated on the eve of the *Shabbat*, then the bath attendants began to heat the water on the *Shabbat*, maintaining that it was done on the eve of the *Shabbat*. So the [use of] hot water was forbidden, but sweating (a steam bath) was permitted. Yet still they used to bathe in hot water and maintain we are perspiring (taking a steam bath). So sweating (steam bathing) was forbidden, yet the thermal hot springs of Tiberias were permitted. Yet they bathed in water heated by fire and maintained we bathed in the thermal springs of Tiberias. So they forbade the hot springs but permitted cold water. But when they saw that this [series of restrictions] could not stand, they permitted the hot springs of Tiberias, while sweating (taking a steam bath) remained in status quo (prohibited)" (*Shabbat* 40a).

Clarifying this rule, the Talmud reports that bathing of particular parts of one's body such as one's face and hands were not included in the prohibition. Indeed, the *Shulchan Aruch* specifically notes that the prohibition is applicable to the bathing of *one's entire body*, even if it be done limb by limb. Accordingly, immersion in a bath of hot water heated even on Friday afternoon would be prohibited because of the talmudic rabbinic decree. The Codes add that it is wrong even to pour water over one's body (*Orach Chayyim* 326:1). The *Aruch HaShulchan* notes that this latter process was prohibited even though it was not the normal mode of bathing; for once an injunction was set up, he contends, the sages did not make a distinction between the normal or other modes of bathing (*lo plug, Orach Chayyim* 362:2).

It is apparent that this relates to showering, which is basically water poured over a person's body. Today, showering is as popular a mode of bathing as immersing oneself in a bathtub. The point is that one cannot contend that the original prohibition did not include showering, for it was not at that time an accepted mode of bathing. Indeed, the Talmud specifically states that bathing with the springs of Tiberias was made permissible because without such permission the Jews would not have had any accepted means of bathing with hot water on *Shabbat* (see Rashi). This definitely indicates that use of hot showers was also prohibited. Accordingly, any form of bathing with hot water, even hot water heated prior to *Shabbat* or without any violation of *Shabbat* (automatic heater) would be prohibited. (My feeling is that the *gezeirah* would extend to immersing one's whole body in a heated swimming pool.)

Of interest is that HaRav Akivah Eiger provides a loophole. He contends that a person in pain, even should he not be sick, may bathe on *Shabbat*. Accordingly, the *gezeirah* did not apply to a person who feels pain or anguish by not bathing. Such a person could use water heated without any violation of *Shabbat*.

Concerning *Yom Tov*, the Talmud clearly notes an incident wherein bathing with water heated *erev Yom Tov* was prohibited (see also Tosafot, *Lemotzi*). Indeed, based upon the Talmud itself, without analysis or research, a general approach would be to assume that showering or bathing with hot water on *Yom Tov* was prohibited because of the *gezeirah*. At issue, however, is the rationale for the *Yom Tov* prohibition. On *Shabbat* it is prohibited to heat water. Accordingly, usage of hot water, even water heated prior to *Shabbat*, was prohibited, to prevent heating on *Shabbat* itself. On *Yom Tov*, however, it is permitted to heat water for drinking or cooking purposes. In addition, there is a rule that states that when an item is permitted for purposes of food, it is also permitted for nonfood purposes (*metoch*). Based on this logic, since it is permitted to cook water for a meal it should also be permitted to heat water for a bath.

Two responses: (1) Rabbeinu Asher, citing the Riva, contends that on *Yom Tov* it is permitted to perform only activities that most people do in fact practice (*Shaveh lakol*). Namely, most simply so accustom themselves. In the event, however, that something is performed only by a small group of people, it is prohibited, even on *Yom Tov* (Rosh, *Shabbat*, chap. 1).

Popular daily bathing of one's whole body, says the Rosh, is an activity practiced only by pedantic, sensitive people. Daily bathing of limbs (such as head, face, and legs) is a normal common practice (*Aruch HaShulchan, Orach Chayyim* 511:12). (2) The *Aruch HaShulchan* notes that the Rambam does not list the preceding theory. According to the Rambam, bathing with hot water on *Yom Tov* is prohibited because of the apprehension of violating Shabbat laws. *Yom Tov* was simply included in the ban (*Aruch HaShulchan, Orach Chayyim* 495:19).

The first theory is seriously questioned as to applicability in the contemporary scene. The Shmirot Shabbat Kehilchata notes that today almost everyone has private bathrooms and that daily baths are a common practice. It is not reserved for the chosen few, consequently it should be permitted on *Yom Tov*. Also, it is permissible to heat water on *Yom Tov* to wash one's head. If that action is permissible then one may also bathe in the same hot water; for the same faucet that opened the hot water to wash one's head is the same process utilized to run a bath or shower. The Rambam's position may also be somewhat challenged in that it is not the normal mode to prohibit an activity on *Yom Tov* because of a possible violation on *Shabbat*. (The response to this is that *Yom Tov* may have been prohibited because of its *Yom Tov* prohibition of *sechitah*.)

Common custom is that many religious Jews who smoke also smoke on *Yom Tov*. Smoking is certainly not the general mode. Yet, the rabbinic world does not inveigh against the *Yom Tov* smokers. The halachic position of the smokers is that to them it is necessary to smoke even on *Yom Tov*. So, too, should apply to the people who bathe every day. It is necessary to feel clean (*Shmirot Shabbat Kehilchata*, chap. 14:7, n. 21).

As such, a person who seeks to bathe with hot water on *Yom Tov* should be directed to shower for such appears to be somewhat different from the original *gezeirah* (ban). Also, should the person be very perspired and in great discomfort or pain, then, according to R. Akivah Eiger, that would mute the *gezeirah*. The Eishel Avraham, moreover, suggests that leniency is more readily provided to a private bath than to a public bath house.

(The above discussion does not apply to a *mikveh*, where a *mitzvah* is performed. Usage of warm or hot *mikva'ot* is a separate issue.)

HaNeirot Halalu

QUESTION: Common custom is to recite the prayer *HaNeirot Halalu* during the kindling of the Chanukah *menorah*. When exactly is this prayer to be chanted?

RESPONSE: There are two halachic positions on this matter. (1) The Baal HaTanya rules that *HaNeirot Halalu* should be recited after all the candles are lit. The official commentary on this law notes that otherwise it would be an undue interruption, a *hefsek* (see *Shulchan Aruch* HaRav, *Hosafot Chanukah*, also notes). Thus, on the eighth night of Chanukah, for example, *HaNeirot Halalu* should not be recited until all the eight candles are lit. (2) The *Aruch HaShulchan* suggests a completely different practice. He contends that after the first candle is lit, *HaNeirot Halalu* should be chanted while the additional lights are kindled. The purpose, he contends, is to publicize the miracle, *pirsum hanes* (*Orach Chayyim* 676:8). Accordingly, on the eighth night *HaNeirot Halalu* should be recited while actually kindling the second to the eighth candles. Of interest is that the *Mishnah Berurah* cites the latter custom yet notes that should one follow the previous position, it is also acceptable (*Orach Chayyim* 676:8).
What are the issues of debate? What is the reason for each custom?
HaRav Yaakov B. Zolti, former chief rabbi of Jerusalem, provided a unique rationale to a halachic debate concerning lighting the Chanukah *menorah* from one candle to the other. On Chanukah there is a component of *hiddur mitzvah* (beautifying and enhancing the *mitzvah*). (1) At issue is whether this element of *hiddur mitzvah* is part and parcel of the basic *mitzvah*; namely, the basic *mitzvah* and the *hiddur mitzvah* are so closely intertwined that one is inseparable from the other. (2) Or, is the requirement of *hiddur mitzvah* a separate and distinct *mitzvah* from the basic *mitzvah*? There is a general rule that one must beautify *mitzvot*, *anveihu*, "this is my God and I will adorn Him" (Exodus 15:2). "Adorn thyself before Him in the fulfillment of *mitzvot* [thus] make a beautiful *sukkah* . . . a beautiful *lulav*, and

so forth" (*Shabbat* 133b). This general rule may be separate and distinct from the *mitzvah* of Chanukah. Those who prohibit kindling one candle to another believe that the *hiddur mitzvah* (of all the candles except the first) is a separate *mitzvah* from the basic *mitzvah*. Accordingly, there should be a noticeable distinction between the basic *mitzvah* and the other candles. As such, one cannot light from the basic candle to others, for they represent different *mitzvot*. On the other hand, should one hold that the *hiddur mitzvah* is finely interwoven within the basic *mitzvah* of Chanukah, there would be no problem in lighting one to another, for all are one continuous *mitzvah* (see *Mishnat Yavetz, Orach Chayyim, Mo'adim, Siman* 74:3).

The preceding analysis may shed light on the different customs relating to the proper time for the recitation of *Ha-Neirot Halalu*. The *Aruch HaShulchan* would contend that the *hiddur mitzvah* of Chanukah is a special distinct *mitzvah*. It is part of the general rule that requires the beautification of *mitzvot*. Accordingly, it may be necessary to demonstrate the beautification by overtly indicating a distinction between the basic *mitzvah* and the other candles. For this reason the *HaNeirot Halalu* prayers should be recited after lighting the first candle, thus manifesting a distinction between the basic *mitzvah* and the *hiddur mitzvah*. The Baal HaTanya, however, may hold that the *hiddur mitzvah* of Chanukah is not a special distinct *mitzvah* but an enhanced part of the basic *mitzvah*. Thus, the *hiddur mitzvah* and the basic *mitzvah* are forged together. For this reason *HaNeirot Halalu* may not be recited until all the candles are lit, for there is to be no demarcation between the basic *mitzvah* and the *hiddur mitzvah*. It is all one continuous *mitzvah*

Parashat Zachor

QUESTION: Many authorities consider it a biblical *mitzvah* to hear *Parshat Zachor* (see *Orach Chayyim* 685:7). Of concern is the proper pronouncement of a biblical word essential to the *mitzvah*. The Torah states, *"Timche et zeicher Ameleik"* – "blot out the *remembrance* of Amelek" (Deuteronomy 25:19). The "z" word is not clear-cut. Some pronounce it *zeicher* (*tzeireh, segol*), others *zecher* (*segol, segol*). Accordingly, it is essential to rule on the proper pronounciation in order to fully observe the *mitzvah*. Basically, which word should the *baal koreh* recite?

RESPONSE: There is no definitive decision on this matter. The *Mishnah Berurah*, therefore, rules that both should be chanted to meet the traditions of all authorities (*Orach Chayyim* 685:18).

What is yet unclear is the proper means of carrying out the *Mishnah Berurah's* suggestion to chant both words. Three viable methods may be projected. (1) The word *zeicher* is recited first, then just repeated but pronounced *zecher* (*zeicher, zecher*). (2) The reader pronounces the word *zeicher*, then returns to the beginning of the verse (*vehayah* – "and it shall be, when God, thy God will have given thee rest from all thine enemies . . ."). When the "z" word comes up again, it is recited as *zecher*. (3) The entire verse is not repeated. The concern is simply to repeat the phrase *"timche et zeicher Amelek."* When the phrase is uttered the second time, the "z" word is prounounced *zecher*.

HaGaon R. Moshe Feinstein rules that the third option is the preferred method. He notes that the process of repeating a phrase rather than merely a word or an entire verse has precedent. Indeed, when reading the *Megillah*, there are two instances when words are repeated to reflect divergent traditions of pronounciation. Each time only phrases are repeated (*l'hashmi . . . and v'ish lo yaamod*). HaRav Feinstein (*z"l*), moreover, rules that, post facto (*bidi'eved*), option one meets the obligation even though option three is preferred. Of interest is the additional ruling of HaGaon Rav Moshe that in *Elul* when *Parashat Ki Teitzei* is normally read in the synagogue, the "z" word should be read in the same manner as on *Parashat Zachor*; namely, the *timche* phrase should be repeated with the words *zeicher* and *zecher*. This requirement has relevance even according to those who hold that the *mitzvah* of *Parashat Zachor* is only observed prior to Purim. The concern is, rather, that words of the Torah should be read correctly (see *Am HaTorah, Mahadura* 2, *Choveret* 9, 5745, pp. 10, 11).

The Magen Avraham contends that the *mitzvah* of *Parashat Zachor* is biblically not limited to an add-on *Maftir* at a specific time prior to Purim. Indeed, whenever *Parashat Zachor* is read, including its normal cycle in *Elul*, one observes the *mitzvah*. Accordingly, there is an added significance of repeating the "z" word during the reading of *Ki Teitzei* in the same manner as mandated for the official *Parashat Zachor* (see *Orach Chayyim, Magen Avraham* 685:1).

I had occasion to attend a family *bar mitzvah* celebration that took place on *Parashat Ki Teitzei*. The *rav* reported, prior to *Maftir*, that the Chatam Sofer ruled that as long as one mentions Amelek once every year, it is deemed sufficient to observe the *mitzvah*. Accordingly, a problem would emerge on a leap year wherein the calendar is extended for an additional month over the normal twelve-month period. On such years, the Chatam Sofer noted that one may offset the problem by having special intention (*kavanah*) on *Parashat Ki Teitzei* (see *Siddur Chatam Sofer*, also *Responsa, Even HaEzer*). To the extent that the year was a leap year, the *rav* concluded that all should have special intentions to observe the *mitzvah* during the reading of the Torah.

I was very disturbed over the *rav's* statement. Why? When *Parashat Zachor* was read in the Torah at the *bar mitzvah*, there was no instruction to reread the "z" word, as is done prior to Purim. Initially, I was not perturbed over the absence of such direction. Perhaps the *rav* had either not heard of Rav Moshe's *pesak* to repeat the "z" word on *Parashat Ki Teitzei*, or he may have ruled that such repetition was extraneous on a regular *Shabbat*. But once the *rav* made a point of informing his *kehillah* (congregation) of the necessity of having *kavanah* to observe *Parashat Zachor*, it was illogical that such pronouncement did not include also the custom of repeating the "z" word. Indeed, by having the "z" word repeated during the reading of the Torah, the *rav* would have dramatically demonstrated the concern to observe the biblical *mitzvah* properly. The mode utilized by the *rav* simply lacked consistency, and common custom has it that one does not observe *Parashat Zachor* without repeating the "z" word.

Addendum

When I related the above to my *chavrutah* (learning partner), he astutely noted that my concerns may be diffused as follows: There are two *mitzvot* relating to Amelek, namely, a positive and a negative *mitzvah*. The positive *mitzvah* is the command to remember Amelek (*zachor*, Deuteronomy 25:17). The negative *mitzvah* is the prohibition not to forget Amelek (*Lo tishkach*, Deuteronomy 25:19). Concerning the process of not forgetting the Talmud rules that "the dead are not forgotten till after twelve months (*Berachot* 58b). Accordingly, after twelve months one tends to forget. This citation is the source for the Chatam Sofer's rule that in a leap year one should have intention to perform the *mitzvah* during the reading of *Parashat Ki Teitzei*. It has nothing to do with the *mitzvah* of *zachor*, only with the prohibition of *Lo tishkach*. For this reason there would be no necessity to repeat the "z" word. My response was that both the positive and negative *mitzvot* were intertwined, so much so that both take place at the same time. Thus, any issue about observing the negative *mitzvah* should be accompanied by a concern for fulfilling the positive *mitzvah*. The positive *mitzvah*, reports the Mishnah Berurah, may only be observed via reading in a *Sefer Torah* (*Orach Chayyim* 685:14). As such, any attempt to fulfill the negative *mitzvah* (because of time constraints, i.e., leap year) should seek to observe the entire *mitzvah* (including the positive aspect) properly. The response to this is that *Parashat Zachor* need not be completed within a twelve-month period. It is the negative commandment that must be done within twelve months. This aspect does not need a *Sefer Torah*.

Whatever, it is important to inform a congregation that due to leap year it is the negative commandment that needs to be within the twelve-month limitation. Accordingly, intention should be to observe *Lo tishkach* (not *Zachor*).

The Megillah *and Torah Study*

QUESTION: The Talmud rules that hearing the *Megillah* on Purim is of such importance that *Bet Rebbe*, the rabbis in the household of Rav Yehudah HaNasi, would interrupt their Torah learning in order to hear the public reading of the *Megillah* (*Megillah* 3a). Of concern is that the reading of the *Megillah* is also a form of Torah study. Accordingly, there does not appear to be any interruption of Torah altogether. It's as if someone closed his *Gemara* and opened up a *Tanach* to study. The change of a text or subject matter certainly should not be classified as an interruption (or cessation) of Torah. As such, the talmudic terminology seems somewhat strange.

RESPONSE: It may be demonstrated that the *mitzvah* to learn Torah and the *mitzvah* to hear the *Megillah* are two distinctly different areas of concern.

Torah, for example, is a pursuit that must be understood. The Magen Avraham explicitly rules that a person who does not understand what he is learning does not observe the *mitzvah* of *Talmud Torah* (*Orach Chayyim* 47:17). The *Shulchan Aruch HaRav*, however, contends that the Magen Avraham's rule does not apply to the written Torah, which generates a *mitzvah* even without comprehension (*Hilchot Talmud Torah*, chap. 2:12, 13).

It should be noted that the *Shulchan Aruch HaRav's* limitation is not necessarily held by other scholars. The Peri Megadim, for example, states that comprehension is a requirement

even of the portion of written Torah mandated for Jews to learn
each day (see *Orach Chayyim* 50). This is overtly contrary to the
Shulchan Aruch, HaRav.

The *Mishnah Berurah*, moreover, cites the Magen Avraham
that comprehension is essential to *Talmud Torah* yet brings no
limitations or qualifying factors (see *Orach Chayyim* 50 and 47).
In addition, it may be demonstrated that the Magen Avraham,
himself, does not agree to the limitation presented by the *Shulchan Aruch HaRav*. The Codes rule that *Birchat HaTorah* is
obliged even for one who writes Torah (*Orach Chayyim* 47).
Commenting on this law, the Magen Avraham states that it is
applicable to one who writes Torah (books) as a vehicle of Torah
learning; but a scribe who simply copies and does not attempt to
understand what he writes does not make a *berachah* (*Orach
Chayyim* 47:1). Scribes generally copy Scripture, the written
Torah. Yet, the Magen Avraham still insists that comprehension
should permeate the learning process. This demonstrates that
any and all forms of Torah must be imbued with understanding
for it to be classified as *Talmud Torah*.

The Talmud states, "When a child knows how to talk, his
father teaches him Torah and the *Shema*." *What* [form of] *Torah*
[is taught]? Said Rav Hamnuna, the verse – Torah *Tzivah lanu
Mosheh* – the Torah which Moses commanded us is an inheritance
of the Congregation of Jacob (Deuteronomy 33:4), and what is the
Shema? The first verse [of the *Shema*] (*Sukkah* 42a). The *Aruch
HaShulchan* explains the talmudic question, "What Torah?" to
mean why is it necessary to teach Torah to a very young child
who does not comprehend what he is being taught. As such, the
process cannot be considered Torah. To this the Talmud responds that the obligation refers to the verse, "*Torah tzivah
lanu*." The purpose is to imbue within us the belief that Torah has
a divine aspect to it (see *Aruch HaShulchan, Yoreh De'ah* 245:1).
Thus, the Torah taught to an infant is not the *mitzvah* of *Talmud
Torah*, but basically a vehicle to instill belief in Torah values. The
mitzvah of *Talmud Torah* occurs only when comprehension
takes place.

The *mitzvah* of hearing the *Megillah* is unique in that it does not relate to comprehension. The Talmud rules, "If one who does not understand Hebrew heard [the *Megillah*] read in Hebrew, he has performed his obligation. But he does not know what he is saying . . . Ravina said, and do we know the meaning of *haahash-teranim benei haramachin*? But all the same we perform the precept of reading the *Megillah* and proclaiming the miracle. So, too, they [who do not understand Hebrew] perform the *mitzvah*" (*Megillah* 18a).

Accordingly, the *mitzvah* of observing Torah is different from the *mitzvah* of the *Megillah*. This is what the Talmud means when it states that scholars *interrupt* Torah to hear the *Megillah*. They cease a process wherein comprehension is essential (Torah) and commence a form of study (*Megillah* reading) wherein understanding is not key to the *mitzvah* altogether.

A different response to the original, question is presented by the talmudic commentator, the RaShash. He suggests that the talmudic mandate to cease Torah learning in order to hear the *Megillah* relates to a specific situation wherein the students already heard the *Megillah* while the *rebbe* did not. As such, the public Torah learning of the students is interrupted so that the *rebbe* may fulfill his personal *mitzvah* of hearing the *Megillah* (*Megillah* 3a).

Proper Timing for the Purim Seudah

QUESTION: When is the proper time to celebrate the festive meal required to be eaten on Purim?

RESPONSE: This is an issue where the general practice verges somewhat from halachic principles. The Rema overtly states: "Common custom is to make the festive meal after *Min-chah* . . . [concerning the time for the meal itself, Rema rules] the majority of the [Purim] meal should be eaten while it is yet day and not like those who commence [the Purim *seudah*] in the late afternoon so their main meal is eaten during the evening of the fifteenth [of *Adar*]" (*Shulchan Aruch, Orach Chayyim* 695:2). The *Mishnah Berurah* notes that the meal is generally eaten after an early *Minchah* for most are busy with *mishalo'ach manot* (giving gifts) in the morning and are so engaged until early afternoon wherein the onset of *Minchah* prohibits eating until after prayers (*Orach Chayyim* 695:8). Of concern is a rationale for those whose practice it is to eat the main part of the meal in the evening of the fifteenth, a custom apparently against the *halachah*.

HaRav Tzvi Pesach Frank, former chief rabbi of Jerusalem, cites a scholar who suggests that the common practice at Purim may be derived from the following analysis of the specific periods set up for prayers, namely, *Shacharit, Minchah*, and *Maariv* have allotted times for expression. Accordingly, it is necessary to clarify the status of a person who starts praying during the time, for example of the morning prayers, but extends prayers till way after such a period of time. At issue is the definition of the ruling that sets time frames for prayers. Do such time frames mean that the entire prayer must be within such limited periods? Or is it sufficient for just part of the prayer to be within the specific time alloted to either morning, afternoon, or evening prayers?

The Yehudi HaKodesh notes that the resolution to this issue may be derived from a commentary of Tosafot. The Talmud notes that the wrath of God lasts "one moment." Subsequently, it states that Israel is fortunate in that God has not turned His anger against them. For had He done so, "not one remnant would have remained." Commenting upon this, Tosafot ask, "What could be said in but one second?" They respond, "Once a curse starts in the time of anger, it could continue even afterwards" (*Berachot* 7a). The Yehudi HaKodesh reasons that blessings or good deeds certainly are greater than and have more impact than evil tidings. As such, just as anger starting in the proper time has an impact afterwards, then so should this be said about prayer. Once some phrase is recited in its time period, it may extend afterwards. So, too, perhaps may be said of the Purim meal. Once it begins in the proper time, one should not be concerned with the time of conclusion or whether the main part of the meal was by day or night.

Though HaRav Frank cites this rationalization, he concludes that one should not rely upon it but seek to observe the *halachah* as ruled by the Rema in the *Shulchan Aruch*.

Of interest is that the Rema objects only to those who eat the main part of the meal in the evening of the fifteenth. He does not in any way even intimate that the total meal must be eaten on the fourteenth of *Adar*, Purim itself. This suggests that there is some form of a tradition to have the Purim *seudah* eaten on both the day of the fourteenth and the evening of the fifteenth. The Rema's concern is that the main part of the meal should be on the fourteenth. But why should this be so? Why does not *halachah* demand that the Purim meal must be eaten entirely on Purim itself? Jerusalem Dayan Yosef Cohen, grandson of HaRav Frank, suggests that a theory of HaRav Meir Simcha of Dvinsk may shed light on this matter.

Haman's evil decree was that pogroms should start on the thirteenth day and the following night (which to Jews is the fourteenth of *Adar*). Accordingly, for those who lived in walled cities, the miracle occurred on the fifteenth and the following night. Jews celebrate according to Jewish calculations. Namely, on the fourteenth the war ended. On the night of the fifteenth concludes the regular Purim, and the night of the sixteenth Purim concludes in walled cities like Jerusalem. In general, it is prohibited to extend Purim beyond its normal dates (*lo yaavor*).

Yet, it is possible that the night subsequent to the dates were originally included in Haman's scheme. Citing this principle, Dayan Cohen suggests that it may be the rationalization for why Jews eat the Purim meal at a period of time that is both the fourteenth and the fifteenth of Adar. Perhaps Jews wish to recall the original day of joy. It was on the fourteenth, and by the method by which Gentiles calculate time, it lasted through the following night. To re-create that historical event, Jews, perhaps eat their meal at a period that spans both days. The only precaution is that the main meal be by day (see *Mikrei Kodesh*, Chanukah and Purim, by Rav Tzvi Pesach Frank; see also notes of Dayan Cohen, *Seudat Purim*, *Siman* 43).

The Chidushei HaRim notes common custom to eat the Purim festive meal on the night of the fifteenth. (He does not even mention the amount of the meal that is to be eaten on the day of Purim.) The reason, he says, is that the *Midrash* contends that the destruction of evil (*reshaim*) is comparable to bringing a holy sacrifice in the *Bet HaMikdash* (see *Midrash Rabbah*, *Bamidbar*, chap. 21). Yet, *korbanot* (sacrifices) have a special calendar calculation. One may eat a sacrifice on the day it was offered and on its subsequent night. In other words, sacrifices follow the procedures that the night following the day is interwoven with the past day. The Purim *seudah* celebrates the fall of Haman. Consequently, it is a token *korban*. Thus, the night follows the day. That's why Jews eat the meal at a period of time that transcends both day and night (Chidushei HaRim, *Al HaTorah*, Purim).

Recalling the Exodus at the Pesach Seder

QUESTION: The *mitzvah* to recall the Exodus is not restricted to Pesach. Indeed, each day and night of the year Jews are mandated to make mention of the deliverance from Egypt. As it is written, "Remember the day when you came forth out of the land of Egypt, all the days of your life" (Deuteronomy 16:3; see also Rambam, *Hilchot Keriyat Shema*, chap. 1:3). Of concern, therefore, is the distinctive nature of the *mitzvah* on the night of Pesach itself. Namely, *Mah Nishtanah*—"Why is this night different?" Wherein is the *mitzvah* to recall the Exodus on Pesach itself qualitatively different from that required throughout the year?

RESPONSE: Pesach has a number of unique customs:

1. Pesach requires a *question-and-answer* format. Though common usage is to have children ask questions of parents, the *halachah* is that even if children are not present, the question-and-answer process should take place. A wife should ask her husband, and even if one is all alone, one is required to ask questions of oneself at the *seder* (*Orach Chayyim* 473:7).

Thus, the process of recalling the Exodus on the night of Pesach is an outer-directed function. It simulates the teaching role of question and answers and suggests that it must be aloud, not silent, to symbolize the giving over of information from one generation to another. Indeed, the *pirsum hanes* (the publicizing of the miracle) of the *seder* is exemplified in the necessity to recall the Exodus (*bedavka*)—specifically, by questions and answers.

2. Pesach mandates an *extended report* of the Exodus. Note the phrase in the *Haggadah*, "*Kol HaMarbeh*"—"whoever endeavors to extend the relating of the deliverance is deemed meritorious." There is no such law a whole year. Throughout the year the *mitzvah* is observed by simply stating that God delivered our ancestors from Egypt. Nothing more is required or suggested.

3. Pesach mandates a report of *historical origins*, even negative overtones. As such, the *Haggadah* records the fact that our forefathers at one time were nonbelievers (for example, Avraham's father).

4. On Pesach, it is vital to present the *reasons and motivations* for certain observances. (Rav Gamliel noted that one must know the rationale as to why one eats *matzah* and *maror* [bitter herbs].)

5. The eve of Pesach mandates a *minimum statement*; a whole year there is no such minimum. (Rav Gamliel said that whoever does not say the following three items, does not observe

the *mitzvah*: *Pesach, matzah, maror.*) Accordingly, should a person be tired and/or lack the ability to read the *Haggadah* prior to the meal, it is necessary to direct him to Rav Gamliel's statement so that at least he recites the minimum obligation for the performance of the *mitzvah*.

Why Two Days of Shavuot?

QUESTION: Why is Shavuot celebrated as a two-day holiday? The Bible does not fix the date for the Shavuot holiday as it does for other holidays. It does not state the exact day or month for its occurrence. It, rather, states, "And you shall count for yourselves from the morrow after the Sabbath . . . seven complete Sabbaths shall there be: To the morrow after the seventh Sabbath shall you number fifty days" (Leviticus 23:15, 16). The Talmud rules that the phrase "the morrow after the Sabbath" means the day after the first day of Passover, not the day after Shabbat (see *Menachot* 65b). If so, then Shavuot should always come out on the fiftieth day of the counting of the *Omer*. The second day of Shavuot is the fifty-first day of the *Omer*. As such, it has no relationship to the biblical mandate, for the holiday as noted in the Bible relates to the counting of the *Omer* and not to when revelation (*Matan Torah*) took place.

RESPONSE: It is necessary to clarify the methods by which Jews calculated calendar changes of time. To the Jew, a calendar change occurs not at midnight, nor at sunrise, but rather, with sunset and the onset of the darkness of the night. Accordingly, all Jewish observances of *Shabbat* and Festivals commence at sundown. Birthdays, anniversaries, historical events all follow this procedure.

Some maintain that this custom is derived from the biblical description of creation where, at the conclusion of each day, it states, "and there was evening and there was morning" (Genesis, chap. 1). Thus, the day follows the evening preceding it.

Yet, it has been suggested that this verse is but a description of chronological events rather than a mandate for calculating a day change. The rationale is that Scripture itself implies a day calculation contrary to the preceding formulation; namely, that the night follows the day. Upon conclusion of the deluge, God vows never again to curse the earth because of man's sake. He says, "While the earth remains, seed time and harvest, and cold and heat, and *day and night* shall not cease" (Genesis 8:22). R. Pinchas HaLevi Hurowitz (1730–1805, Frankfurt, author of *Panim Yafot*) notes that the phrase "and day and night shall not cease" lends credence to the view that a full calendar day was the combination of the day and the night subsequent to it.

Jewish time as it practiced today, he suggests, is rather derived from the verse, "From evening to evening shall you celebrate your Sabbath" (Leviticus 23:22). This phrase deals with the observance of Yom Kippur. It is a specific imperative detailing the actual time parameters of the holiday. Accordingly, the day follows the night preceding it. To the extent that this law is an integral part of the statutes given to Moses on Mount Sinai, Jewish time is, therefore, an innovation that occurred at Sinai. Hence, contends the Panim Yafot, prior to Sinai and the Revelation a day change was reckoned differently. Namely, during the era of the patriarchs and the Egyptian bondage, a day was considered the morning and the evening following it. A calendar date change took place at sunrise.

R. Moshe Sofer (Pressberg, 1762–1839), author of the *Chatam Sofer* (see *Derashot Shavuot*), utilized this theory of his *rebbe* (R. Hurowitz) to explain why Shavuot is celebrated as a two-day holiday. Prior to the Revelation, each day began at sunrise and concluded at the following sunrise. The Jews began to count the *Omer* on the second day of Passover at sunrise. Tradition has it that the Revelation at Mount Sinai *transpired in the morning prior to sunrise* at the coming of the dawn (*amud hashachar*). Hence, it was the fiftieth day of the *Omer*. To the extent, however, that Revelation crystallized a new concept of time, namely, that a date change occurred at the evening preceding the day, such a period was the fifty-first day according to the new method of calculating time.

Accordingly, both days are currently celebrated (in the Diaspora) to symbolically record the date change transformation that took place on Mount Sinai.

Kiddush Levanah *after* *Tisha B'Av*

QUESTION: Should *Kiddush Levanah* (prayers sanctifying the new lunar month) be recited on the night after Tisha B'Av upon the conclusion of the *Maariv* services?

RESPONSE: Synagogues generally follow the order of procedure noted in the *lu'ach* published annually by Ezrat Torah and originally formulated and edited by HaGaon Rav Henkin (*z"l*). The *lu'ach* contends that *Kiddush Levanah* is to be chanted directly following *Maariv* services after Tisha B'Av. This rule is presented without any limiting factor or condition.

The difficulty is that the matter is not clear-cut. The Rema, for example, rules that *Kiddush Levanah* should not be recited after Tisha B'Av. His reasoning is that Jews at such a time are not in a framework of *simchah* (happiness) (*Orach Chayyim* 426:2). The *Mishnah Berurah* notes that many sages disagree with the Rema's position and, just the opposite, insist that *Kiddush Levanah* be recited after Tisha B'Av. These authorities, however, recognize that *Kiddush Levanah* should not be recited when one manifests a sense of mourning or a lack of happiness.

Accordingly, prior to *Kiddush Levanah* it is necessary to eat food or drink something as well as to wear regular shoes (that is, change into normal footwear). On the night after Yom Kippur, no such requirement is imposed due to the joy of atonement for sins (*Mishnah Berurah, Orach Chayyim* 426:11). The Chai Adam also notes the requirement to "taste something" prior to *Kiddush Levanah,* saying it should not be recited while fasting. He does not mention any need to change shoes (*K'lal* 118:15).

Based upon the *Mishnah Berurah*'s ruling, it appears that the guidelines specified in the *lu'ach,* namely to recite *Kiddush Levanah* without any mention of changing shoes or breaking the fast, may be somewhat misleading.

Students of the *Mishnah Berurah* are aware of a commentary on the lower level of each page entitled *Shar HaTzion.* This provides footnotes and sources compiled by the *Mishnah Berurah* himself. Therein it is noted that should an opportunity be available to recite *Kiddush Levanah* with a large gathering, then even if one does not break one's fast it is permissible because of the principle of *Berav am hadrat melech*—"In the multitude of people is the King's Glory" (Proverbs 14:28; *Shar HaTzion, Orach Chayyim* 426:9).

This may be the source for the ruling of the *lu'ach,* which is basically a guide for synagogue behavior and not a code for individual observance. Since synagogue *davening* has the element of *berav am,* such a principle supersedes the problem of reciting *Kiddush Levanah* while fasting.

There is yet some difficulty with this position. A synagogue may announce another period of time for *Kiddush Levanah*: a date other than the night after Tisha B'Av. As such, one may observe *Kiddush Levanah berav am* without compromising the principle that requires a degree of happiness for its recitation.

Indeed, one may even question the application of *berav am* in this instance. The Magen Avraham contends that the principle of *berav am* (*davening* with a large number of people) is more important than the concern of saying *Kiddush Levanah* while fasting. His proof is the *halachah* that mandates one person in a *bet midrash* to recite *Havdalah* for all even though such a process may withhold others from learning Torah (see Magen Avraham, *Orach Chayyim* 426:6; also 298:14).

My concern is that these two cases, *Kiddush Levanah* while fasting and *Havdalah* in a *bet midrash*, are not comparable. In the latter situation, no sin or irregularity takes place while *Havdalah* is recited. The *Havdalah* is performed without any deviation of a *Havdalah* practice. In the former situation, *Kiddush Levanah* is recited while fasting, a condition antithetical to the prayer itself. Under normal circumstances such is not permitted. Accordingly, there is no precedent to substantiate the view that *berav am* permits a deviation in the *mitzvah* or ritual performed.

The Netziv makes a similar position regarding prayer. He says that even sinners should be included in a *minyan* for prayer. The limitation is that the prayer itself should be pure and not violate *halachah* (see Merom'ei Sadeh, *Berachot* 22b).

Laws of Mezuzah

QUESTION: When is a person required to have a *mezuzah* placed on the doorposts of his or her home? Also, when should the blessing be recited?

RESPONSE: The *Shulchan Aruch* rules that the rental of a home in the land of Israel, because of the *mitzvah* to settle and inherit the Holy Land of Israel, imposes an immediate mandate to install a *mezuzah*, while the rental of a home in the Diaspora is freed from this obligation for thirty days (*Yoreh De'ah* 286:22). The logic appears to be that in less than thirty days, a place is not deemed a viable dwelling and is therefore not an area that requires a *mezuzah* (Shach, *Yoreh De'ah* 286:28).

Two exceptions: (1) This thirty-day grace period applies only to rented quarters, not to the purchase of a home. Accordingly, should one buy a new home, the obligation to install a *mezuzah* is immediate. (2) Of concern is the status of the first thirty days in a situation where the quarters are rented for more than thirty days. The *Aruch HaShulchan* contends that the thirty-day grace period is extended only to quarters rented for less than thirty days. Lacking any degree of permanency, there is no obligation to place a *mezuzah* in such a home. Should one contract to rent for more than a month, then such a home is not a temporary abode and a *mezuzah* is required from the first day of residence. Though others disagree (see Nachlot Tzvi, *Yoreh De'ah* 256), the *Aruch HaShulchan* concludes that such is the general custom and the obligation is rabbinic, for the biblical *mitzvah* is operational only on a home owned by a Jew (*Yoreh De'ah* 256:49; see also the *siddur* of Rav Yaakov M'Lissa, who concurs).

HaGaon Rav Akivah Eiger further finely hones the onset of the *mezuzah mitzvah*. He contends that the obligation to have a *mezuzah* does not commence simultaneously with the purchase (or permanent rental) of property. Ownership by itself without residence doesn't incur an obligation. The *mitzvah* commences when the owner actually becomes a resident. Accordingly, until such time that one moves into a new home, no obligation is mandated.

Based upon this principle it would appear that the *mitzvah* is operational only while a person actually resides in a home. This suggests that when a person lives alone and is not at home, namely he left his house (empty) for he went to work for the day, perhaps, there is no obligation to have a *mezuzah* at such a period of time. The obligation for a *mezuzah* would be generated once again when such a person would return to his home at night, for at that moment his house would again become a residence.

In other words, the obligation of a *mezuzah* would depend on whether a house was actually used as a residence. As such, Rav Akivah Eiger poses a question as to why a *berachah* for a *mezuzah* is not recited each evening such a person returns home from work. Why, he asks, does this case differ from the laws relating to *berachot* recited upon leaving and reentering a *sukkah*? In the latter case, should a person leave a *sukkah* to go to work and then several hours subsequently return to the *sukkah*, he would be obliged to recite the blessing upon returning to the *sukkah*. So, why should the situation for a *mezuzah* be in any way different? Namely, a *berachah* for the *mezuzah* should be recited after each extended absence from a home. Rav Akivah Eiger cites a Birkei Yosef who rules that the *berachah* for a *mezuzah* was formulated to be a one-time event when placed on a doorpost and not as a daily requirement. Though Rav Akivah Eiger accepted the ruling, he was perturbed over the rationalization and concluded that the issue needed further clarification (*tzarich iyun*) (see *Teshuvot HaRav Akivah Eiger, Siman* 9).

HaGaon HaRav Baruch Mordechai Ezrachi (*shlitah*) the brilliant *rosh hayeshivah* of Ateret Yisrael, Jerusalem, resolves the aforementioned halachic dilemma by delineating a major distinction between the *mitzvah* of *sukkah* and the *mitzvah* of *mezuzah*. *Sukkah*, he notes, is a personal *mitzvah* incumbent upon all Jews to observe. Indeed, whenever a Jew dwells in a *sukkah*, he acquires a *mitzvah*. However, there is no *mitzvah* to own a house. A Jew who does not own his own house commits no sin. The *mitzvah* of *mezuzah* is not a personal obligation upon each Jew. It is, rather, a rule that should one live in a house, then the doorposts must manifest a *mezuzah*.

As such, on each occasion that a person returns to his home he does not generate a new *mitzvah* or an obligation to recite a *berachah*. For this reason, perhaps, the *berachah* for a *mezuzah* was set up only when it was placed on the doorposts and not at later periods of time (see *Vehagita*, vol. 2, pp. 26–31).

Public Torah Learning

QUESTION: Is public Torah learning qualitatively different from private Torah study? Namely, does public Torah learning convey certain halachic ramifications not noted in private Torah study?

RESPONSE: Rabbinic sources indicate that public Torah study may generate diverse halachic considerations. Indeed, there are different levels of public Torah study. The Talmud, for example, states that [a form of] public Torah study is even more important than the offering of the daily sacrifice (*Megillah* 3b). Rabbeinu Channanel says this refers to the Torah study of *K'lal Yisrael* in totality. The implication is that, should a great sage present a public Torah lecture to even thousands of students, such a learning process would not take priority over the daily sacrifices. To the extent that it is difficult to relate to a situation wherein the totality of *K'lal Yisrael* is involved in Torah study, it is self-evident that such is not the issue of pragmatic concern.

The Talmud relates that Rav Yehudah HaNasi recited only the first verse of the *Shema*. Scholars, moreover, testified that *Rebbe* never overtly even chanted this verse. Each day he would commence his public Torah lecture prior to the time to chant the *Shema*. Instead of interrupting his lecture to say the *Shema*, *Rebbe* would put his hands over his eyes (as if he were thinking) and recite the *Shema* at such a period of time. Bar Kappara even contended that when *Rebbe* concluded his *she'ur*, he did not recite the *Shema* (*Berachot* 13b).

Rabbeinu Asher was concerned with the rationale for *Rebbe's* action. It appears contrary to general halachic principles. Indeed, the Talmud rules that even a professional Torah scholar who learns constantly (*torato umanuto*), such as Rav Shimon bar Yochai, must interrupt his Torah for *Shema* (see *Shabbat* 11a). Accordingly, *Rebbe* should have interrupted his Torah lecture. Indeed, once an interruption is mandated, then the entire *Shema* should be recited, not just the first verse. Rabbeinu Asher responds that public Torah is unique in that anyone who teaches Torah publicly need not interrupt his Torah lecture altogether (Rosh, *Berachot*, chap. 11:3). The implication is that public Torah is on a greater plateau than even one who constantly learns

Torah. The latter must interrupt his studies for the *Shema*, while the former should continue the *she'ur* and only symbolically recite the entire *Shema*.

The sages debate the propriety of learning Torah prior to the morning prayers. Rashi's view is that learning Torah prior to *Shacharit* is prohibited. Rabbeinu Yona suggests that Rashi's prohibition applies only to a person learning Torah by himself. Such a person could conceivably *daven* and then return to his studies. A person who publicly teaches Torah, however, is definitely to be permitted to give a *she'ur* prior to *Shacharit*. For (perhaps) should no *she'ur* take place, none of the people involved would learn Torah. It is also possible that subsequent to davening no one would be able to learn Torah. Indeed, Rabbeinu Yehudah HaNasi gave a *she'ur* prior to *Shacharit*. The implication is that he davened after the lecture. Nor was there apprehension that prayer would be forgotten. For since prayer is a daily event, people will remind themselves to pray (see Rif, chap. 1, 3a).

The P'nei Yehoshua, moreover, suggests that those who provide public Torah lectures do not have to interrupt their studies for prayer. His reasoning is that a public *magid she'ur* (a Torah lecturer) has a status comparable to R. Shimon bar Yochai (see P'nei Yehoshua, *Berachot* 30a).

Of interest is that the Bet Yosef notes that the *Tur Shulchan Aruch* does not even mention Rabbeinu Asher's distinction between public and private Torah study. He cites Rabbeinu Yerucham who suggests that, perhaps, public Torah study may not be interrupted only when such an interruption would make it impossible to return to the Torah study. The Bet Yosef concludes that in his period of time, it was not so common to assume that public Torah learning would stop in the event one chanted the *Shema* (or *davened*). The *Tur*, therefore, did not report this *halachah* (*Tur, Bet Yosef, Orach Chayyim* 70).

Of interest is that many scholars, including the *Mishnah Berurah*, do not even mention Rabbeinu Asher's concept. Yet, the Bet Yosef never dismissed this *halachah*. He merely stated that it wasn't likely that the recitation of the *Shema* would be an

obstacle to the continuation of the *she'ur*. Should, however, facts
so emerge to demonstrate that any interruption would force the
she'ur to stop altogether, then it appears there would be halachic
validity to continue learning.

The *Aruch HaShulchan* specifically rules that public Torah
study is considered a special *mitzvah* by itself. Accordingly,
someone giving a *she'ur* to students need not stop to recite the
Shema (*Aruch HaShulchan, Orach Chayyim* 70:6).

Women and Torah

QUESTION: May women recite *Birchot HaTorah* prior to
learning Torah?

I

RESPONSE: The *Tur* (*Orach Chayyim* 47) discusses the various *berachot* that must be chanted prior to Torah study each day.
He then notes:

> There is [yet] another *berachah* over Torah; namely *Asher
> bachar banu* (translation: "which selected us [the Jewish
> people] ... and gave us his Torah"). When chanting this
> blessing one should have intention [*kavanah*] for the revela-
> tion on Mount Sinai wherein He selected us from all the
> nations, brought us to Mount Sinai and made heard His
> words ... and gave us His holy Torah, which is our life and
> treasure.

The Bach contends that the *Tur* is actually providing a
solution to a major halachic problem: namely, why does Torah
study require more *berachot* than any other *mitzvah*? Prior to
the performance of any *mitzvah* only one *berachah* is chanted;
that *berachah* is classified as a *Birchat HaMitzvah* (a blessing
chanted before the observance of a *mitzvah*). Why is it necessary

to chant the concluding *Asher bachar banu* blessing? Once the Jew has concluded his first *berachah* (the second blessing is considered by many to be an extension of the first), why mandate an extraneous *berachah*? To this Bach suggests the following:

The first *berachah* is a typical *Birchat HaMitzvah* chanted before the observance of any *mitzvah*. The second *berachah* (*Asher bachar banu*) is not a *Birchat HaMitzvah*. It is a form of thanksgiving and praise for receiving Torah on Mount Sinai. Scripture states: "Only take heed to thyself . . . lest thou forget the things which thine eyes have seen, and lest they depart from thy heart all the days of thy life, but bring them to the knowledge of thy children and thy children's children the day that thou stoodest before thy God at Horeb" (Deuteronomy 4:7–10). Thus, concludes the Bach, the second *berachah* is a means of observing the biblical mandate of never forgetting the revelation of Mount Sinai (*Orach Chayyim* 47).

Accordingly, women were definitely an integral part of *K'lal Yisrael* during the revelation at Mount Sinai. Indeed, the Torah states, *"Ko tomar l'vet Yaakov"* ("So say to the House of Jacob") (Exodus 19:3), which Rashi interprets to mean that God wished women to be addressed prior to men at Revelation. Women were therefore informed about the Torah even prior to men. Thus, women may chant the *Bachar Banu berachah* to commemorate their presence at the divine Revelation of Torah.

An interesting issue of concern is whether the pleasure associated with learning Torah is a proper emotion. The Eglei Tal (HaGaon R. Avraham M'Sochatshov) contends that as long as one recognizes that Torah learning is a *mitzvah* commanded by God, then the pleasure or enjoyment of the learning process enhances its comprehension and is definitely a proper and normal side effect of Torah learning. Should one learn Torah only because of enjoyment, however, it would be comparable to one who eats *matzah* because he loves *matzah*, rather than for the *mitzvah* of *matzah* itself (Introduction, *Eglei Tal*).

This suggests that Torah learning provides pleasure. Yet, there is a general rule that "one is prohibited enjoyment in this world unless it is preceded by a *berachah* (*Berachot* 35a). This concept serves as the rationale for obligating *berachot* prior to food. Accordingly, perhaps, it is forbidden to learn Torah without a *berachah*. If a *berachah* is the vehicle to permit personal pleasure, then even women *may be required* to recite *Berachot HaTorah* to permit them the pleasure of Torah learning.

II

Men are required to study all *mitzvot* even should they be exempt from specific observances. This means that a man who is not a *kohen*, and therefore not obligated to observe the laws pertaining to *kohanim*, is still required to learn the Torah and *mitzvot* pertaining to *kohanim*. Women, however, have no obligation to learn those *mitzvot* that are not applicable for practical observance. As a result, their scope of Torah learning is quite limited. Men, however, are directly involved in all *mitzvot* because of their mandate to study all facets of the Torah (HaGaon Rav Yosef Dov Soloveitchik, *Responsa Bet Halevi*, no. 6). Accordingly, the study by women of *mitzvot* not applicable to them would be voluntary and not required. Yet, this theory would support the position that the study of *mitzvot* that women do observe is a *mitzvah*, too.

The Bet Halevi, in his commentary on the Pentateuch (*Parashat Mishpatim*), delineates a further fine distinction between the obligations of men and women in the sphere of Torah study. He notes that Torah education has a twofold aim: the pursuit of Torah knowledge as a means to better observance of commandments and as an end in itself.

An elaboration of this distinction is as follows: To be a good Jew, carefully and scrupulously to follow the dictates of our religion, it is necessary to be well acquainted with many of its laws and customs. Indeed, it is written that an ignoramus cannot be a pious person. This is quite understandable, for a person who is ignorant of Judaism certainly cannot know whether he (or she) is doing something right or wrong. It is, moreover, practically impossible to observe the *Shabbat* if one is ignorant of the intricate, detailed laws of this holy day. Thus, Torah study serves as the vehicle to stimulate the observance of *mitzvot*. Women are involved in this facet of Torah study.

Yet there is another important aspect to the study of Torah: the obligation to study Torah for its own sake. This aspect of Torah education is not a means of observing commandments but a *mitzvah* in itself. Just as *kashrut* and putting on *tefillin* are commandments, so too is the study of Torah. This obligation is incumbent upon all Jewish men, including those who consider themselves grand masters in all aspects of the Law. Even a person who feels that he knows the entire Torah is still obligated to study Torah. The Talmud portrays this concept when it relates that a Tana asked whether someone who was well versed in all aspects of the Torah was free from the obligation to study it. The answer presented was that if one could find a period of time that was neither a part of the day nor a portion of the night, only then would he be absolved of all requirements to learn Torah (*Menachot* 99b).

It is interesting to note that there is a great practical difference between the two approaches to the study of Torah. If Torah study were simply a means of acquiring the technical knowledge necessary for an observant Jew, then it would, perhaps, be possible to free oneself from the obligation to study by retaining the services of a scholar who could outline everything one needed to know. Since men must study Torah for its own sake, however, doing this would not avail. Just as the rabbi's act of putting on *tefillin* or observing the *Shabbat* does not in any way free others from these *mitzvot*, so too the rabbi's intense scholarship does not in any way affect the requirement of others to spend a portion of their time learning Torah. Thus, the role of men in the *mitzvah* of Torah study is categorically different from that of women. Women are primarily involved in the rules relating to practical observance, while men are involved in the process of studying Torah for its own sake.

The Avnei Nezer adds an interesting nuance to this concept. He contends that since it is almost impossible to observe *mitzvot* without practical knowledge, the acquisition of such knowledge is categorized as the commencement of the performance of the *mitzvah*, rather than as part of the general principle of learning Torah. Thus, for women, the process of learning is in reality an integral aspect of the observance. They, therefore, are not considered to be involved in the general *mitzvah* of learning Torah (*Responsa Avnei Nezer, Yoreh De'ah*, 2:352).

Yet, even according to such theories, women may recite *berachot* as volunteers comparable to the *mitzvah* of *lulav* and *etrog* on Sukkot.

Keriyat HaTorah

QUESTION: Is it necessary to have a *minyan* present for *keriyat hatorah* (the public synagogue reading of the Torah).

RESPONSE: Yes. The *Mishnah* rules that *keriyat hatorah* may not take place unless a *minyan* (quorum of ten Jews) is present. The *Gemara* provides the rationale by contending that *keriyat hatorah* is a form of *kedushah* (sanctification of the Holy Name), and there is a general rule that all matters of *kedushah* require a *minyan* (*Megillah*, 23b). What is not immediately apparent is why *keriyat hatorah* is categorized as a form of *kedushah*, while the personal study of Torah is not vested with such a status. One may assume that even if a rabbi taught Torah to a thousand students, this would not transform the Torah study to a status of *Kedushah*. Wherein does *keriyat hatorah* differ from personal Torah study?

(In the previous chapter it was noted that the Bach contended that the general *berachah* each morning of "*asher bachar banu* [you chose the Jewish people]" related to the revelation of God on Mount Sinai. Namely, it was a means of remembering revelation [*Tur, Orach Chayyim* 47].)

Based upon this theory of the Bach, it is possible to clarify the *raison d'être* of *keriyat hatorah*. Since *asher bachar banu* is the basic *berachah* prior to the reading of the Torah, it is logical to assume that this blessing relates to the prime purpose of *keriyat hatorah*, namely, to keep the revelation at Mount Sinai alive in the minds of the Jewish people. The Ramban, in his commentary on Deuteronomy, specifically states that the aforementioned verse explicitly prohibits forgetting the Revelation and is one of the 613 primary *mitzvot*. (Those who dispute the Ramban contend that this verse does not relate specifically to the revelation but to a general prohibition against forgetting Torah.)

Rambam rules that Mosheh Rabbeinu enacted the original ordinance of *keriyat hatorah* (*Hilchot Tefillah* 12:1). As the greatest prophet of our people, he and his *bet din* set up *keriyat hatorah* (see *Kesef Mishnah*). The meaning appears as follows:

Mosheh Rabbeinu wished to ensure that Israel would cherish its holy legacy, the Torah. How was he to do this? The most viable means of guaranteeing the Torah was to establish a rite that would vividly emulate the Revelation, the source of all Torah. The Holy *Sefer Torah*, which had been acquired at Sinai and possessed its own *kedushah*, was the object that more than anything else symbolized the Revelation; nothing could have been better suited to a rite emulating the *kedushah* of Mount Sinai. Since *keriyat hatorah* was not a form of public Torah study but a means of emulating Sinai, it is understandable why it is classified as a form of *kedushah* and requires the presence of a *minyan*. On Mount Sinai the Torah was not given to individuals. It was granted to a people, *K'lal Yisreal*, and all of them, therefore, were in attendance. Revelation, the ultimate source of our national soul and pride, is the true seed of *kedushah*. The blessing *asher bachar banu* does not relate to the private obligations of the individual Jew. It is an affirmation that Jews are involved in Torah only because they are members of *K'lal Yisrael*. Thus *keriyat hatorah* is a means of implanting the belief that the sanctity of the Jewish people is interrelated with the sanctity of Torah.

Birchat HaTorah *for Thoughts*

QUESTION: Is a person who merely thinks Torah concepts obliged to recite a *berachah?*

RESPONSE: The *Shulchan Aruch* specifically rules that should a person just think about Torah–without any oral vocalization–such a process does not need a *berachah* (*Orach Chayyim* 47:4). This law is challenged by the Vilna Gaon, who notes that Torah learning is not restricted to an oral, vocal process. Indeed, the rationale for the ruling of the Codes requires analysis. Is not intense thought a key ingredient necessary for the acquisition of knowledge? Torah learning is not an empty ritual to be studied by rote devoid of comprehension. Indeed, as one attains a degree of scholarship, it is vital to logically and coherently think through issues.

Accordingly, thinking about Torah should be on a higher level than just reading Torah. Indeed, according to the ruling of the Codes, the following bizarre case may develop. A young child may repeat but one verse of Scripture and be required to chant a *berachah*. A venerable sage may ponder a Torah problem impacting the lives of an entire community and not be charged with a *berachah* for such efforts. Whose Torah is greater? Also, the Codes specifically note that the vehicle of writing Torah does require a *berachah* (*Orach Chayyim* 47:3). Why? Why is writing Torah more important than thinking Torah thoughts?

A basic response is that traditionally a *berachah* precedes an action. Since the process of contemplation is not an action, therefore no *berachah* is mandated. Thus, the lack of a *berachah* is not a statement regarding the value of the thought process to Torah. It relates, rather, to the structure of blessings.

An alternate response is that the ruling of the Codes alludes to an essential concept that permeates the purpose of Torah education.

Torah is not just a form of knowledge. It is a religious interlocking bridge paved to the past, lived in the present, and directed to the future. It is *mesorah*—a way of life transmitted from generation to generation with the understanding that it will be given to our children to re-create yet further links to the future.

Perhaps, this is the true meaning of the *halachah* that mandates a *berachah* only for oral or written Torah, for only through such a process may Torah be transmitted to another generation. Torah solely within one's mind may be vastly creative, analytic, and brilliant—but it remains within the individual. No one can hear such thoughts. Torah learning should emulate the tradition of Sinai. In *Pirkei Avot* it reads, "Mosheh accepted the Torah from Sinai and transmitted to Joshua, and Joshua to the elders—and they [gave it] to the prophets, who transmitted it to the men of the Great Assembly" (1:1). In other words, Torah is a gift that must be granted to others. It is not proper to obtain personal knowledge and to subsequently jealously guard such information solely for one's personal gratification. Torah has a dual responsibility. It must be learned, and it must be taught. Oral or written Torah may be overheard or studied by another. Torah thoughts remain the private domain of the thinker. They are important but lack the quality of transmission.

A *berachah* for Torah learning is required only when the process emulates the tradition of Sinai. Only such Torah that intertwines *mesorah* into its core is the type of Torah that merits a *berachah*.

The *Birchat HaTorah* emphasizes how the duality of Torah must be reenacted in each age. Each Jew must receive the benefits of Torah and strive to share its knowledge with another person.

Private Prayers

QUESTION: How does one pray for personal needs?

RESPONSE: The *Amidah* prayer has nineteen blessings. During the first three and last three no personal requests may be recited. *Halachah*, however, notes that personal prayers may be added to the middle thirteen blessings. Some guidelines:

1. Should a person be sick, he may request mercy in the *berachah* commencing with the word *Refa'einu* (heal us).

2. Should a person need a livelihood, he should make a request at the blessing beginning with the words *Bareich Aleinu* (bless us).

3. General requests, without limitation as to subject or need may be made within the blessing that starts with the phrase, *Shema Koleinu* (Hear our Voice) (*Orach Chayyim* 119:1).

From the above rules, the following may be derived.

A prayer for health may not be requested when uttering a prayer for a livelihood. Each prayer for a specific need should be noted only in the blessing relating to that need itself.

Shema Koleinu is the exception to this rule. Within it may be included all forms of need.

4. Prayers for health (or, for example, a livelihood) may be requested in their proper blessing providing the person *davening* is in present need of such help. Such prayers are not to be used for future concerns.

5. In the event a prayer is to be recited to guard one from future health hazards or future *parnasah* problems, such prayers should be recited only at *Shema koleinu*, not at other periods in the *siddur* (*Peri Megadim, Mishnah Berurah, Orach Chayyim* 119:1).

6. A personal request should follow this procedure.

A. Recite (for example) *Refa'einu* till the concluding *berachah*.

B. Insert a personal prayer.

C. Conclude *Baruch Atah HaShem*.

The rationale is that the official format should take precedence over private prayers (*Aruch HaShulchan* 119:1).

7. Permission to add a private, personal prayer in the *Shemoneh Esrei* is granted only on an infrequent occasion as a response to a specific need. It is prohibited to add a set prayer to be recited regularly within the *Shemoneh Esrei*. Such is an act of arrogance and *chutzpah* for it gives the impression that the *Anshei Kenesset HaGedolah* missed out on a prayer. The fact

that some publishers of prayer books insert texts of added prayers is not evidence of being proper. Publishers do not always hearken to rabbinic guidance. Such prayers should be added (if we so desire) after the *Yihyu LeRatzon tefillah* at the conclusion of the Amidah (*Aruch HaShulchan* 119:2).

8. The aforementioned concept provides comprehension to a talmudic principle that states, "R. Chiya b. Ashi said in the name of *Rav*—although it was laid down that a man asks for his requirements in *Shema Koleinu*—but after his prayer he may add even something like the order of the confession on Yom Kippur" (*Berachot* 31a). Of concern is the pragmatic necessity of the latter rule. May a person add such prayers such as the *Vidui* (confession) of Yom Kippur also in the *Shema Koleinu* prayers? Also, why does the Talmud use as an example of a permissible addition the Yom Kippur confessions? According to the *Aruch HaShulchan's* formulation, the citation gains new meaning. The *Vidui* is a formal litany of numerous set prayers. Such may not be part of the *Shemoneh Esrei* itself. A formal daily standard prayer can be said only after the *Yihyu LeRatzon* prayer. Indeed, even an infrequent prayer must be short, for all lengthy prayers may be recited only at the end of the *Shemoneh Esrei* (*Aruch HaShulchan* 119:4).

9. The Vilna Gaon contends that any prayer written in the plural form should not be chanted with personal intentions. It is written for the community, and communal thoughts should permeate the process. Any person who wishes to personalize the prayers should add his own words and sentiments (Commentary *Mishnayot, Berachot*, chap. 5).

Not all agree, but it is important to note.

Baruch Hu U'varuch Shemo, *Part 1*

QUESTION: During the recitation of a *berachah*, whenever God's Name is mentioned, people call out the phrase, "*Baruch Hu*

U'Varuch Shemo" (Blessed is He and Blessed is His Name). What is the source for this custom? Also, are there guidelines as to when it is to be said?

RESPONSE: The *Tur* reports that his father, Rabbeinu Asher, had such a custom. Two reasons are presented. (1) It is written, "When I proclaim the name of the Lord, ascribe ye greatness unto our God" (Exodus 32:3). (Namely, when God's Name is mentioned, others should respond by noting His glory.) (2) A human *tzaddik* is generally blessed when his name is mentioned (*Zecher tzaddik livrachah*—May the *tzaddik's* name be a blessing). As such, when God's Name is noted it certainly should be extolled (*Orach Chayyim* 124).

Magen Avraham limits this recitation to periods wherein it is permitted to interrupt the prayers. *Mishnah Berurah* pragmatizes this concept by noting that it is prohibited to be chanted during the blessings of *Keriyat Shema* and *Pesukei D'Zimrah*. In addition, should a person hear a *berachah* of which he is obliged to recite yet wishes to be included in such a blessing then *Baruch Hu U'Varuch Shemo* should not be said. It would be deemed an unwarranted interruption. In the event that *post facto* (*bidi'eved*) someone, for example, made *Kiddush* for another and the second person did indeed respond *Baruch Hu U'Varuch Shemo*, it is not necessary to stringently require the person to recite the blessing a second time (*Orach Chayyim* 124:21; see Dagul Mervavah, also Chayyei Adam, who poses the latter problem and concludes that it requires further research [*tzarech iyun*].)

Accordingly, it would be unseemly and certainly a violation of halachic principles to call out *Baruch Hu U'Varuch Shemo* during *Maariv* (evening) services. Yet, just as *Mishnah Berurah* rules that should a person included in another's *berachah* mistakenly call out *Baruch Hu U'Varuch Shemo* that he does not have to recite again the entire *berachah*, so too should be the rule for an uncalled for exclamation during *davening*. It should in no way obligate the person to repeat his prayers.

At issue is the reason for this lenient ruling. Indeed, why isn't an uncalled-for recitation of *Baruch Hu U'Varuch Shemo* classified as an interruption that should mandate one to repeat a *berachah* or *davening*?

My grandfather, the author of *Minchat Shabbat*, cites numerous sages who found no fault whatsoever in reciting *Baruch Hu U'Varuch Shemo* even when one is included in another's *berachah*. Indeed, even by *Birchat Shofar* there are sages who do not consider it wrong to say *Baruch Hu U'Varuch Shemo*. Why? The Maharam Shik (*Orach Chayyim, Siman* 81) notes that tradition has it that whoever recites Amen is deemed as if he recited the entire *berachah*. As such, the chanting of *Baruch Hu U'Varuch Shemo* is not an interruption, for the moment he says Amen it is as if he restated the entire *berachah*. The *S'dei Chemed* is cited as contending that it is preferable not to say *Baruch Hu U'Varuch Shemo* when included in another's *berachah*. However, since there is also merit in the other position, one should not scold or be harsh at those who do in fact disagree. This also suggests that *bidi'eved* one need not recite once again the *berachah* (*Minchat Shabbat* 77:15).

In addition, the person who calls out, *Baruch Hu U'Varuch Shemo* does not consider that he is interrupting the *berachah*. Just the opposite. He feels he is doing a *mitzvah*. He calls out this phrase for he feels that such is obligatory. Accordingly, it should be no worse than one who says something relating to *Kiddush* or the meal itself at a period of time when unnecessary talking is prohibited (ibid., 77:24; see *Berachot* 40a: "If he said [between the blessing and eating] bring salt, the blessing need not be repeated").

Baruch Hu U'varuch Shemo, *Part 2*

QUESTION: Should *Baruch Hu U'Varuch Shemo* be recited during the repetition of the *Shemoneh Esrei*?

RESPONSE: The *Mishnah Berurah* notes that a *shliach tzibur* should slow his pace when reciting blessings that are very brief. The examples presented are *Birchat HaShachar* and at the conclusion of each *berachah* of the *Shemoneh Esrei*. The reason is that should the *chazzan daven* at a rapid pace, then many who recite *Baruch Hu V'Varuch Shemo* would simply not hear the conclusion to the *berachah* and may not know to which specific *berachah* they are responding Amen (*Orach Chayyim* 124:23). In the *Shar HaTzion* commentary, the *Mishnah Berurah* notes that because of an apprehension that a response of *Baruch Hu U'Varuch Shemo* may overshadow or becloud the proper response of Amen, some sages such as the Vilna Gaon and others have simply not chanted *Baruch Hu U'Varuch Shemo* during such *berachot*, for Amen is definitely more important than *Baruch Hu U'Varuch Shemo*.

The *Mishnah Berurah*, however, demurs. His position is, rather, to direct the *shliach tzibur* to slow down and await the conclusion of *Baruch Hu U'Varuch Shemo* prior to concluding the blessing (see *Orach Chayyim* 124, *Shar HaTzion* 24).

The pivotal issue appears to be the pace of the *shliach tzibur*. In the event he does not slow his pace and there is a question as to which *berachah* is actually concluded, for the response of *Baruch Hu U'Varuch Shemo* drowns out the voice of the *chazzan*, then even the *Mishnah Berurah* would probably prefer not reciting *Baruch Hu U'Varuch Shemo* altogether.

The ruling of the Vilna Gaon is cited as follows: One should respond Amen after every *berachah* (of the *Amidah*). It is not necessary to be careful about reciting *Baruch Hu U'Varuch Shemo*, for the *shliach tzibur* (generally) does not await the conclusion of the responses (of *Baruch Hu U'Varuch Shemo*) and one will (therefore) lose out on the repetition of the *Amidah* (*Maasei Rav*). Why? For should one not hear the conclusion of a *berachah*, Amen should preferably not be said. Should, however, a *chazzan* await the end of all responses, then even the Gaon would probably direct all to respond *Baruch Hu U'Varuch Shemo* (see *Lekutei Dinim*).

It may be noted that there are compelling reasons to refrain from reciting *Baruch Hu U'Varuch Shemo* during the repetition of the *Amidah* that have no relationship to the pace of the *shliach tzibur.*

A person who knows how to pray may not use the services of a cantor (or *shliach tzibur*) to fulfill personal obligations (Magen Avraham, *Orach Chayyim* 124:1). *Mishnah Berurah* contends that this rule is applicable not only *ab initio* but also *post facto* (*bidi'eved*) (*Orach Chayyim* 124:1). Thus anyone who purposely relies on the prayers of the cantor would be obliged to repeat the entire *Amidah.*

Yet, there is an exception to this rule. The *Shulchah Aruch* notes that in the event a person recited the *Shemoneh Esrei* but neglected to say *Yaaleh V'Yavoh*, he may pay attention to the *shliach tzibur's* prayer and be included in that prayer (*Orach Chayyim* 124:10). The reason, says the Bet Yosef (*Orach Chayyim* 124), that a person who knows how to *daven* may rely on the *shliach tzibur* is that he at least did, in fact, pray. All he did was forget a special prayer such as *Yaaleh V'yavoh* (or *Mashiv HaRuach*) (*Mishnah Berurah, Orach Chayyim* 124:39).

The procedure for relying on the *shliach tzibur* is to listen attentively to every *berachah* he recites (*Orach Chayyim* 124:10). To the extent that most simply cannot listen so carefully, the preferred mode is to just *daven* again oneself (*Mishnah Berurah* 124:40).

The Biur Halachah cites Rav Akivah Eiger who provides an interesting nuance to the aforementioned concept. There are times when due to an error it is not necessary to repeat the entire *Amidah,* just to return to the last section, which begins with *Retzei.* Should this occur, one should not conclude the *Amidah,* but await silently for the *shliach tzibur* to recite the *Amidah.* It is, moreover, not necessary to have *kavanah* the entire *Amidah* but only from *Retzei* onward. Accordingly, it may not be so difficult to be attentive for such a short period of time.

Coupled to this is the recognition that the *shliach tzibur* definitely includes those who are not proficient in his prayers. Some say that should the *shliach tzibur* be a *chasid* who knows (and actually has) proper *kavanah* for all *berachot*, perhaps such a person can include others who compared to him and his level of spiritual *kavanah* are classified as "those who know not how to pray" (see Be'er Mosheh, *Orach Chayyim* 124:17, cited in the name of the Eishel Avraham).

Thus, there are numerous ways whereby the *Shemoneh Esrei* prayers of the *shliach tzibur* are comparable to a *Birchat HaMitzvah* in which one includes the other in the *berachah*. Just as one does not preferentially chant *Baruch Hu U'Varuch Shemo* in such cases, so too should be the mode during the repetition of the *Amidah*.

Of interest is that *Aruch HaShulchan* overtly rules that when one uses the services of the *shliach tzibur* one should not recite *Baruch Hu U'Varuch Shemo* (*Orach Chayyim*). Indeed, the *Aruch HaShulchan* in general was not overly pleased with the *Baruch Hu U'Varuch Shemo* custom. He felt there was not a compelling rationale for a communal expression of blessing when a *berachah* was chanted. Two reasons: (1) God's Name was blessed by the phrase *Barchu Atah*; therefore, there is no need to extend blessings once again. (2) If a mere recitation of God's Name requires a response, why is it not done when God's Name is mentioned not in the context of a *berachah* (*Orach Chayyim* 124:10)?

Yet, common usage of *Baruch Hu U'Varuch Shemo* during *Shemoneh Esrei* is a classic example of how custom at times overrules even logic.

Baruch Hu U'Varuch Shemo, *Part 3*

QUESTION: Is there a theological reason to refrain from saying *Baruch Hu U'Varuch Shemo* whenever God's Name is mentioned in a *berachah*?

RESPONSE: Rav Baruch HaLevi Epstein (author of the *Torah Temimah*) cites a bizarre tradition that he contends he personally heard from elder Torah scholars who imbued their wisdom from a previous generation. The tradition was that the Hebrew words *"Baruch Hu Baruch Shemo"* are the *gematria* numerical value (814) of Shabtai Tzvi's name (*shin, bet, tof, yud, tzadi, bet, yud*). The legend continues that the followers of Shabtai Tzvi covertly started the custom of reciting *Baruch Hu Baruch Shemo* whenever God's Name was mentioned. It was a devious means of bringing Shabtai Tzvi's name into the mainstream of Judaism. For this reason many rabbis simply refrained from reciting the *Baruch Shemo* phrase altogether. They did not wish to provide within our prayers even a scintilla of a reference to a false messiah who was a traitor to Jewry.

Of concern to HaRav Epstein is that the custom to recite *"Baruch Hu . . ."* was first reported by the *Tur* in the name of his father, Rabbeinu Asher, which was approximately 300 years prior to Shabtai Tzvi. (Shabtai Tzvi lived in the seventeenth century [1626–1676]; Rabbeinu Asher's life was from 1250 to 1327.) Thus the custom to recite this phrase was in effect over three centuries prior to Shabtai Tzvi's emergence. So, historically it appears that the aforementioned Shabtai Tzvi theory lacks credibility.

Perhaps, suggests HaRav Epstein, the original custom of the Rosh was to chant *Baruch Hu U'Varuch Shemo*. Note the third word begins with the Hebrew letter *vav*. Indeed, should the numerical value of *vav* (6) be added to the others, the total sum would be not 814 but 820. The disciples of Shabtai Tzvi perhaps creatively started the custom to recite the phrase without the extra *vav* prior to the third word. Their purpose was to transform a gesture extolling God's Name into a reference of their messianic ideology.

This suggests that any recitation of this phrase should scrupulously be careful to enunciate the *vav* of the third word. This pronouncement of the *vav* eliminates any reference to the false messiah. Rav Epstein concludes that he is somewhat surprised that this bizarre tale is not recorded in any of the holy *sefarim* (see *Baruch She'Amar* prayer, p. 114, *Tefillat Shemoneh Esrei*).

The Shemoneh Esrei *Prayer*

QUESTION: The silent *Amidah* prayer is commonly called *Shemoneh Esrei*, which literally means eighteen. Yet, the prayer has nineteen, not eighteen, blessings. So why does the name *Shemoneh Esrei* persist?

RESPONSE: The eighteen-blessing format of the silent prayer was set up by the Men of the Great Assembly. They not only established the number of *berachot* but also its format and proper sequence (see *Megillah* 17b). Due to an excessive amount of slanderers and/or apostates in his era, Rav Gamliel in Yavneh requested that Shmuel HaKatan develop a special prayer to combat this problem. The result is the nineteenth blessing, called *LaMalshinim* ("and to the slanderers let there be no hope") (the tenth blessing) (*Berachot* 28b). Of interest is that even after the addition of the nineteenth blessing, the prayer was and is, even in contemporary usage, still called *Shemoneh Esrei*.

HaRav Baruch Epstein was quite concerned about this issue. He notes that common parlance is to call even the silent prayers of *Shabbat* and *Yom Tov* by the name *Shemoneh Esrei*. Such prayers have much fewer than eighteen *berachot*. *Shabbat*, for example, has only seven blessings (see *Berachot* 29a). As such, the term *Shemoneh Esrei* has no relationship at all to such silent prayers.

He suggests that each silent prayer should be called by the timeframe in which it is recited. Accordingly, it should be called "silent prayer of *Shacharit*, or *Minchah* — and, for example, silent prayer of *Shabbat* morning," and so forth. Indeed, the Codes and

Rambam make such references. He also contends that perhaps the *Shabbat* services should be called *Tefillot Sheva*–the seven prayers to enunciate its specific format and number of blessings (see *Baruch She'Amar*–Prayer–Introduction to *Shemoneh Esrei*).

It should be noted that there may be some halachic basis for calling all silent prayers *Shemoneh Esrei*. Tosafot note that a person who neglected to recite *Minchah* on *Shabbat*, may make it up by chanting two silent prayers at *Maariv*. Of concern is that such a person is chanting more *berachot* than are required. On *Shabbat* he missed out on a prayer that had only seven *berachot*. On Saturday night, he recites an extra prayer containing eighteen (nineteen) blessings. To this Tosafot say that, according to law, even on *Shabbat* eighteen blessings should have been recited. The reason only seven blessings are chanted was that the sages did not mandate the long (eighteen-blessing) prayer due to their wish not to overly burden the community (*Berachot* 26b). In other words, even on *Shabbat* the eighteen-blessing format had relevance. As such, it is possible that all silent prayers were originally set up with eighteen blessings. Accordingly, even though changes occurred, the original name stayed.

Indeed, the Talmud itself suggests that the eighteen *berachot* have some relevance to *Shabbat* itself. The Talmud rules that if someone made a mistake and began to say the weekday blessing on *Shabbat*, he should finish the blessing he started. Why? For in this case "one [the man] is in reality under obligation [to say the weekday blessing] and it is the *rabbis* who did not trouble him out of respect for the *Shabbat*" (*Berachot* 21a). It is apparent that the Talmud's concern for *kavod Shabbat* and Tosafot's term of *tirchah* (excessive burden to people) relate to the same principle, namely, due to respect for *Shabbat*, efforts were made to streamline *Shabbat* services.

Another reference is the citation that R. Gamliel says, "Every day a man should say the eighteen blessings" (*Berachot* 28b). Yet, R. Gamliel is definitely aware that on *Shabbat* only seven blessings are recited (*Berachot* 29a). Again, the logic may be that originally even on *Shabbat* eighteen blessings were at one time designated to be chanted. The custom of calling all silent prayers *Shemoneh Esrei* is merely a means of pinpointing the original historical format of this prayer.

It should be noted that the rabbis who wished to elevate the respect for *Shabbat* appear to be equated to the Men of the Great Assembly as well as to Ezra and his *bet din*. In other words, all three terms relate to the same body of sages. This would harmonize the references to the formulaters of the eighteen *berachot* (that is, the Talmud gives credit to the Men of the Great Assembly—*Megillah* 17b); Rambam says it was established by Ezra and his *bet din* (Laws of Prayer 1:4). The *Gemara* notes it was developed by the rabbis (*Berachot* 21a). The *Siftei Chachamin* (*Berachot* 21a) further suggests that perhaps the Men of the Great Assembly were the *bet din* of Ezra.

Notes

1. Deuteronomy 15:7 and 15:8. Translation of Torah, Jewish Publication Society, 1962.
2. Deuteronomy 15:7 and 15:8. Linear translation of the Pentateuch, trans. by Abraham ben Isaiah and Benjamin Sharfman (Philadelphia: S. S. and R. Publishing Co., Inc., Press of the Jewish Publication Society, 1949).

   In both translations, the Hebrew term *evyon*, which is almost synonomous with the Hebrew term *oni*, which means a poor person, is translated to be a needy person. There is even a translation that calls him a "necessitous person." See Samson Raphael Hirsch, *Pentateuch*, vol. 5, Deuteronomy, rendered into English by Isaac Levy, 2nd ed. (New York: Judaica Press Inc., 1971).
3. *Sifre*, Deuteronomy 15:7 and 8, also *Ketubot* 67b.
4. *Sifre*, Deuteronomy 15:7–8.
5. Tosefta, *Pe'ah*, chap. 4.
6. *Ketubot* 67b (tr. JSC).
7. Ibid.
8. Tosefta, *Pe'ah*, chap. 4.
9. R. Yitzchok of Fez (Rif), *Ketubot*, chap. 6.
10. *Pe'ah* 8:7.
11. *Ketubot* 67b (free translation – see Rashi).
12. *Pe'ah* 8:7.
13. Psalm 145 – a literal translation.
14. *Ketubot* 67b (free translation – see Rashi). This story is not written in the Codes.
15. In *Ketubot* 67b it is recorded as the third case. For clarity, it was herein written as the fourth.
16. R. Shmuel Eliezer Halevi Aydels, Poland and Austria (Maharsha), *Ketubot* 67b.

17. R. Menachem Hameiri (Bet HaBechirah), *Ketubot* 67b. Raba's case could, according to this interpretation, merely have been an act of piety.
18. See n. 3.
19. Tosefta, *Pe'ah*, chap. 4.
20. Hameiri, *Ketubot* 67b.
21. *Pe'ah* 8:7.
22. See commentary of R. Shmuel Avigdor of Carlin (Minchat Bekurim), Tosefta, *Pe'ah* 4:10. Without even consideration of the limiting definition of the Bible, he states that the requirement of actually feeding the poor is only when the poor person is weak by nature and thus requires such treatment.
23. Theory of Gaonim–quotation Shitah Mekubetzet Collection of Commentaries on *Ketubot* 67b, ed. R. Bezalal Ashkenazi.
24. Commentaries on *Ketubot*: Commentary of R. Asher mentions only case of Hillel. Commentary of Tosafot Rid (early commentary) mentions only case of Hillel. Commentary of R. Alfas–R. Yitzchok of Fez (Rif) mentions only case of Hillel.
25. *Pe'ah* 8:7.
26. Maimonides, Gifts to the Poor 7:3.
27. *Tur, Yoreh De'ah* 250:1. *Shulchan Aruch, Yoreh De'ah* 250:1.
28. See Commentary of Bach, *Tur, Yoreh De'ah* 250:1; also Commentary of Shach and *Shulchan Aruch, Yoreh De'ah* 250:1.
29. *Ketubot* 50a.
30. *Pe'ah* 1:1; *Shulchan Aruch, Yoreh De'ah* 249:1.
31. Rema, *Shulchan Aruch, Yoreh De'ah* 250:1; also *Tur, Yoreh De'ah* 250:1.
32. Commentary of R. Shabse Kohan (Shach), *Shulchan Aruch, Yoreh De'ah* 250:1.
33. Commentary of R. Yitzchok of Fez, *Ketubot* 67b.
34. Commentary of R. Yoshe Volk Katz (Drishah), *Tur, Yoreh De'ah* 250:1.
35. Hameiri, *Ketubot* 67b.
36. Commentary of Tosafot Rid, *Ketubot* 67b.
37. Hameiri, *Ketubot* 67b.
38. Ibid.
39. *Shulchan Aruch, Yoreh De'ah* 250:3.
40. Commentary of R. David b. Shmuel Halevi of Austria (Taz), *Shulchan Aruch, Yoreh De'ah* 250:1.
41. Shach Shulchan Aruch, *Yoreh De'ah* 250:6. See Bach, *Shulchan*

Aruch, Yoreh De'ah 250:6; *Tur, Yoreh De'ah*, chap. 250. Since Maimonides places this law in chap. 7, which deals with individuals, and not in chap. 9, which deals with *kupah* funds, the implication is that Maimonides refers only to individuals.

This entire law is based on an incident in *Bava Batra* 9a; also stated in *Sifre*, Deuteronomy 133.

42. Rashi, *Bava Batra* 9a.
43. Rashi, *Shabbat* 118a.
44. This is not a major analysis of this form of communal response to poverty but merely a brief description of its existence. For detailed description see Maimonides, Gifts to the Poor, chaps. 1–5.
45. Maimonides, Gifts to the Poor 1:15; *Pe'ah* 1:2.
46. Maimonides, Gifts to the Poor 2:12; *Shabbat* 23a–b.
47. Maimonides, Gifts to the Poor 4:1; *Pe'ah* 4:10.
48. Maimonides, Gifts to the Poor 5:1; *Pe'ah* 5:7.
49. Maimonides, Gifts to the Poor 6:1–5.
50. *Maimonides*, Commentary, *Pe'ah* 8:7.
51. Ibid. *Bava Batra* 8b; Maimonides, *Mishneh Torah, Zera'im*, Gifts to the Poor 9:1, 3,6; *Shulchan Aruch, Yoreh De'ah* 256:1, 4.
52. See Maimonides, Gifts to the Poor 4:1: "The communal agents take from each person what he is capable of giving." See same language in *Shulchan Aruch, Yoreh De'ah* 256:1. This appears to be based on a statement of the Talmud that Rava coerced Rav Nathan bar Ami to give 400 *zuzim* to charity after he was assessed to be wealthy and capable of providing such funds. See *Bava Batra* 8b – Commentary of Rabbeinu Gershon. See also Commentary of Tosafot, *Bava Batra* 8b.
53. Rav Alfus (Rif), Commentary on *Bava Batra* 5b. See also Commentary of Rabbeinu Asher (Rosh), *Bava Batra* 8b.
54. Rabbeinu Gershon, Commentary, *Bava Batra* 8b.
55. *Bava Batra* 8b; *Shulchan Aruch, Yoreh De'ah* 256:3; also 248:2.
56. Rabbi David ben Zimrah (Radbaz), Commentary on Maimonides, Gifts to the Poor 9:6.
57. Rav Shabse Kohan (Shach), *Yoreh De'ah* 256:11; *Shulchan Aruch, Yoreh De'ah* 256:5.
58. Rav Alfasi (Rif), Commentary on *Bava Batra* 5b; Maimonides, Gifts to the Poor 9:12.
59. Rabbi Dovid ben Zimrah, Maimonides, Gifts to the Poor 9:12. See Tosefta, *Pe'ah* 4:9 – a poor person who resided in town 30 days can acquire funds from the *kupah*.

60. *Bava Batra* 8a. Rabbeinu Gershon, Commentary, *Bava Batra* 8a.
61. See *Bava Batra* 8b; Maimonides, Gifts to the Poor 9:6; *Shulchan Aruch, Yoreh De'ah* 256:4.
62. Notes of Rema, *Shulchan Aruch, Yoreh De'ah* 256:5.
63. Maimonides, Gifts to the Poor 9:1 (the term food is used); *Shulchan Aruch, Yoreh De'ah* 256:6 (the term sustenance is used).
64. *Shabbat* 118a; *Pe'ah* 8:7; Maimonides, Gifts to the Poor 9:13. *Shulchan Aruch, Yoreh De'ah* 253:1.
65. Maimonides, Commentary to *Pe'ah* 8:7; see also Nekudot Hakesef (Shach), *Shulchan Aruch, Yoreh De'ah* 253:1.
66. Commentary, Rashi, *Shabbat* 118a.
67. Ibid.
68. See, for example, the communal *tomchui, Bava Batra* 8b; Maimonides, Gifts to the Poor 9:2.
69. *Bava Batra* 8b; *Shulchan Aruch, Yoreh De'ah* 256:4.
70. See *Pe'ah* 8:7; *Shabbat* 118a; *Shulchan Aruch, Yoreh De'ah* 253:1.
71. See n. 61.
72. *Bava Batra* 8b; *Shulchan Aruch, Yoreh De'ah* 256:1, 3.
73. See *Shulchan Aruch, Yoreh De'ah* 256:1.
74. Ibid.
75. Maimonides, Commentary on *Pe'ah* 8:7.
76. *Bava Batra* 8b; *Shulchan Aruch, Yoreh De'ah* 256:1, 4; Maimonides, Gifts to the Poor 9:2, 6.
77. *Bava Batra* 8b; *Shulchan Aruch, Yoreh De'ah* 256:4.
78. Maimonides, Gifts to the Poor 9:1. See also *Shulchan Aruch, Yoreh De'ah* 256:1; also, Rabbi David ben Zimrah, Maimonides, Gifts to the Poor 9:1.
79. See n. 55.
80. *Bava Batra* 8b; *Shulchan Aruch, Yoreh De'ah* 256:3.
81. Ibid.
82. Rabbeinu Gershon, Commentary on *Bava Batra* 8b.
83. See n. 80.
84. See n. 80.
85. See n. 55.
86. See n. 70.
87. Rashi, *Shabbat* 118a (he who goes from place to place—and does not sleep in town).
88. Tosafot, *Bava Batra* 9a.
89. *Shabbat* 118a; Maimonides, Gifts to the Poor 7:8; *Shulchan Aruch, Yoreh De'ah* 250:4.

90. Rashi, *Bava Batra* 8b.
91. See n. 58.
92. See n. 60.
93. Maimonides, Gifts to the Poor 9:3; *Shulchan Aruch, Yoreh De'ah* 256:1.
94. Rabbi David ben Zimrah (Radbaz), Maimonides, Gifts to the Poor 9:12.
95. *Shabbat* 117b, 115a.
96. HaRash M'Shantz, Commentary on *Pe'ah* 8:7.
97. Maimonides, Commentary on *Pe'ah* 8:7.
98. *Pe'ah* 8:8; Maimonides, Gifts to the Poor 9:13.
99. *Shulchan Aruch, Yoreh De'ah* 253:1.
100. Commentary of R. Shimshon of Shantz, *Pe'ah* 8:8. This theory is also noted in the Commentary of R. Ovadiah of Bartenura, *Pe'ah* 8:8.
101. Ibid.; also nn. 52 and 53.
102. R. Yitzchok Isaac Yehudah Yechiel of Komarno, Commentary on *Pe'ah* 8:8.
103. Leviticus 27:3 (JPS, 1947).
104. Leviticus 27:8.
105. Rashi, ibid.
106. Leviticus 25:35.
107. Leviticus 25:39.
108. Leviticus 27:8.
109. *Kiddushin* 17a.
110. *Pisekta of Rav Kahana, Piska* 11. R. Hanina said: "All *shekelim* of the Bible are *sela'im.*"
111. See for development of this theory biblical Commentary of R. Meir Simcha HaKohen of Dvinsk, *Meshech Chochmah, Parshat Re'eh.*
112. Maimonides, Commentary on *Pe'ah* 8:7.
113. *Pe'ah* 8:8.
114. Ibid.
115. Ibid., Jerusalem Talmud.
116. *Ketubot* 68a.
117. Commentary of Rav Alfasi (Rif), *Ketubot* 29b.
118. *Ketubot* 68a.
119. Rif, *Ketubot* 68a; also *Shulchan Aruch, Yoreh De'ah* 253:1.
120. *Shulchan Aruch, Yoreh De'ah* 253:1; Maimonides, Gifts to the Poor 9:14.

121. Ibid. See Commentary of Rabbi David ben Zimrah (Radbaz) on Maimonides, Gifts to the Poor 9:14.
122. Rabbi David ben Zimrah, ibid., deduces from Maimonides' terminology the implication that as long as a person takes from private sources, he is not decreasing communal funds. See also Maimonides, Commentary on *Pe'ah* 8:8.
123. Rashi, *Bava Kamma* 7a.
124. Rashi, *Ketubot* 68a.
125. Rashi, *Shabbat* 118a.
126. See Codes of R. Asher, *Ketubot* 6.
127. Rema, *Shulchan Aruch, Yoreh De'ah* 253:4.
128. Though in Tosafot *Ketubot* 68a, the name R. Tam is quoted, see glossary of Tiferet Samuel and Karban Netanel on the Codes of R. Asher, *Ketubot* 6, who maintain the correct version of R. Channiel. Also notes of Bach, *Ketubot* 68a.
129. Tosafot *Ketubot* 68a.
130. Comments of Karban Netanel, *Ketubot* 6.
131. See nn. 119 and 120.
132. *Pe'ah* 8:9; Maimonides, Gifts to the Poor 9:13; also *Shulchan Aruch, Yoreh De'ah* 253:1.
133. Commentary of Maimonides on *Pe'ah* 8:9.
134. *Pe'ah* 8:8; Maimonides, Gifts to the Poor 9:13; *Shulchan Aruch, Yoreh De'ah* 253:1.
135. Commentary of Pinchas Kahati, *Pe'ah* 8:8.
136. *Pe'ah* 8:7; see Commentary of R. Shimshon of Shantz (Rosh), *Pe'ah* 8:8.
137. *Responsa* of R. Moses Sofer, *Shulchan Aruch, Yoreh De'ah* 239.
138. Commentary of *Mishnah Rishonah, Pe'ah* 8:8.
139. Commentary of Tosafot, *Bava Kamma* 7a; also *Tur, Yoreh De'ah* 253; see notes of Shach, ibid.; see *Bava Kamma* 7a-b.
140. Rashi, *Bava Kamma* 7a.
141. Ibid., 7b.
142. *Bava Kamma* 7a.
143. Rashi, *Bava Kamma* 7a.
144. Maimonides, Gifts to the Poor 9:16; also *Shulchan Aruch, Yoreh De'ah* 253:3; also Shach, ibid.
145. Ibid.; see view of R. Yerucham (Shach).
146. Rif, *Bava Kamma* 7a-7b; see *Shulchan Aruch, Yoreh De'ah* 253, also notes of Rama, *Shulchan Aruch, Yoreh De'ah* 253.
147. Commentary of Rif, ibid.; also *Shulchan Aruch, Yoreh De'ah* 253.

148. Rashi, *Bava Kamma* 7a.
149. *Pe'ah* 5:4.
150. Maimonides, Gifts to the Poor 9:15; *Tur, Yoreh De'ah* 253; *Shulchan Aruch, Yoreh De'ah* 253:4.
151. See n. 149.
152. *Pe'ah* 5:3.
153. Commentary of R. Yaakov David of Slutzk (Ridbaz), *Pe'ah* 5:3.
154. Commentary of R. Moses Margolis (P'nei Moshe), *Pe'ah* 5:3. See also commentary of R. David Oppenheim of Nikolsburg (HaRaDa), *Pe'ah* 5:3.
155. See variants Jerusalem Talmud, *Pe'ah* 5:3 (edition published by Press Inc. and Polk Brothers, New York).
156. Commentary of R. Moshe Sofer, *Pe'ah* 5:3.
157. See n. 150.
158. Ibid.; see notes of Rema, *Shulchan Aruch, Yoreh De'ah* 253:4.
159. *Aruch HaShulchan, Yoreh De'ah* 253:11.
160. Maimonides, Commentary on *Pe'ah* 5:4.
161. See n. 105.
162. See *Pe'ah* 5:4.
163. See n. 105.
164. Commentary of R. Shlomo Hedan (Melechet Shlomo), *Pe'ah* 5:4.
165. *Bava Kamma* 8a; Maimonides, Gifts to the Poor 9:12; *Shulchan Aruch, Yoreh De'ah* 9:12; *Tur, Yoreh De'ah* 256; *Shulchan Aruch, Yoreh De'ah* 256:5.
166. *Aruch HaShulchan, Yoreh De'ah* 256:15.
167. *Bava Batra* 9a. See Commentary of Rashi and R. Gershon.
168. Maimonides, Gifts to the Poor 7:6; *Tur, Yoreh De'ah* and *Shulchan Aruch, Yoreh De'ah* 251:10.
169. Maimonides and *Tur*, ibid. See note of R. Eliyahu of Vilna, who quotes source as Tosefta, *Pe'ah* 8.
170. *Aruch HaShulchan, Yoreh De'ah* 251:12.
171. *Pe'ah* 8:8.
172. Maimonides, Gifts to the Poor 10:7.
173. Ibid., Law 8.
174. P'nei Moshe, *Pe'ah* 5:13; also *Mishnah Shekalim* 5:4.
175. Tosefta, *ibid.*, quoted by commentary of Caro, *Tur, Yoreh De'ah* 249. (It is interesting that several sources discuss the process of contribution to the silent fund, and each utilizes a different term to describe the contributor.) *Mishnah Shekalim*, 5:4 "those who feared sin"; Maimonides, Gifts to the Poor 10:7, "righteous people";

Tur, *Yoreh De'ah* 249, "pious people." The source for each city having such a fund is questioned by R. David ben Zimra, commentary on Maimonides, Gifts to the Poor 10:8.

176. *Tur, Yoreh De'ah* 249.
177. *Tur, Yoreh De'ah* 253:2.
178. *Shulchan Aruch, Yoreh De'ah* 253:2.
179. See notes of Gaon of Vilna, ibid., n. 6, R. Shlomo ben Aderet (1235–1310).
180. See n. 178.
181. See notes of Gilyon Maharsha, *Shulchan Aruch, Yoreh De'ah* 253:2.
182. See n. 178.
183. See Deuteronomy 15:7, 15:8.
184. Rashi, Deuteronomy 15:4.
185. Hirsch, *Pentateuch*, Deuteronomy 15:4.
186. *Avot* 4:1.
187. See commentary of R. Yona of Gerona (thirteenth century), *Avot* 4:1.
188. R. Moshe ben Yosef Metrani, *Keriyat Sefer*, Laws, Gifts to the Poor 9.
189. See nn. 116–128.
190. Rabbi Moshe Feinstein, *Iggerot Mosheh – Responsa*, vol. 1 (Brooklyn, NY: Balshon Printing, 1959), pp. 296–299, *Responsa, Yoreh De'ah* 149.
191. *Ketubot* 16b–17a.
192. The numbers are presented merely for purposes of clarification and do not represent historical epochs.
193. See wording of Maimonides, Gifts to the Poor 7:2; also *Shulchan Aruch, Yoreh De'ah* 250:1 vs. language of *Ketubot* 67b.
194. See Deuteronomy chaps. 6, 7, 8; also 11:29 and chap. 12.
195. Deuteronomy 15:7–8.
196. For mention of division of land and distribution according to families, see Joshua 15:20, 16:5, 8, 17:2, 18:27, 19:1, 19:10, 19:17, 19:24, 19:32, 19:40.
197. Numbers 26:54 and 55.
198. Judges 8:30, 31, 9:1–3.
199. Deuteronomy 14:22–29 and chap. 15.
200. See Judges, 1 Samuel, 2 Samuel.
201. Joseph Klausner, *To Paul*, trans. from the Hebrew by William F. Stinespring (Boston: Beacon Press, 1961), p. 8.
202. Avigdor Tscherikower, *HaYehudim vehaYevanim baTekufah ha-Hellenistit* (Tel Aviv, 1931), pp. 340–353.

203. Klausner, op. cit., pp. 23–25.
204. David Weiss, "Talmud," *Encyclopaedia Britannica,* vol. 21 (Chicago: *Encyclopaedia Britannica,* 1971), pp. 641–643.
205. Ibid.
206. Ferdinand Tonnies, *Gemeinschaft und Gesellschaft, Community and Society,* trans. and ed. by Charles P. Loomis (New York: Harper Torchbook, Harper & Row, 1963), pp. 33–34.
207. Ibid., pp. 42–43.
208. Ibid., p. 253.
209. Ibid., p. 192.
210. Ibid., p. 206.
211. Ibid., p. 208.
212. Ibid., p. 189.
213. Ibid., p. 227.
214. Ibid., pp. 33–34.
215. Ibid., p. 252.
216. Ibid., p. 35.
217. Ibid., p. 65.
218. Ibid., p. 77.
219. Ibid., p. 79.
220. Ibid., p. 189.
221. Deuteronomy 15:7–8.
222. *Bava Batra* 10a.
223. Rabbi Yehudah Loew ben Bezalel (Maharal of Prague) (sixteenth century), *Netivot Olam* (New York: Chorav Printing), *Netiv Ha-Tzadkah,* chap. 2, pp. 171–172.
224. *Bava Batra* 9a.
225. The Hebrew word *ger* literally means a stranger and by tradition is assumed to imply a proselyte.

See *Reishit Chochmah,* chap. 4, Modesty. It is stated that the prohibition concerning the observance of the Sabbath is repeated in the Bible 28 times, the injunction against idol worship is reiterated 28 times, and the laws requiring fair treatment for *Gerim* (strangers, proselytes) is also repeated 28 times. The author, therefore, maintains that the laws dealing with the treatment of proselytes are as vital and important to Judaism as those relating to the observance of the Sabbath and the belief in monotheism.

See *Yalkut Shimoni, Parshat Mishpatim* 349, wherein it states that R. Eliezer HaGadol said that the injunction against harsh treatment to a *ger* is mentioned 36 times. Others are quoted as saying it is mentioned 46 times.

See *Tosafot, Bava Metzia* 59b. There it is noted that the number 46 includes phrases where the word *ger* is mentioned in the Bible but not in the form of a command.

See *Tosafot, Kiddushin* 70b. Here a source is quoted that maintains that the word *ger* is repeated only 24 times. See R. Yitzchok Barcelona, *Sefer HaChinuch*, commandment 3, who states that the injunction relating to a *ger* is repeated 21 times.

226. Rabbi Yehudah Rozanes, *Perashat Derachim, Derech Tzedakah*, chap. 17. (This is the author of the famous *Mishnah LeMelech* on Maimonides.)
227. Genesis 15:9.
228. Oscar Lewis, "Further Observations on the Folk-Urban Continuum and Urbanization with Special Reference to Mexico City," in *The Study of Urbanization*, ed. Philip M. Hauser and Leo F. Schaure (New York, London, Sydney: John Wiley and Sons, 1967), p. 499.
229. *Sifre*, Deuteronomy 15:7–8; *Shulchan Aruch, Yoreh De'ah* 251.
See Rema, *Shulchan Aruch, Yoreh De'ah* 251; Maimonides, Gifts to the Poor 7:13.
230. *Shulchan Aruch, Yoreh De'ah* 257:8.
231. *Nedarim* 65b.
232. Commentary of Tosafot, *Nedarim* 65b.
233. Commentary of R. Asher, *Nedarim* 65b.
234. *Shulchan Aruch, Yoreh De'ah* 250:1 (clearly noted).
235. Ibid.; see comments of Schach, *Shulchan Aruch, Yoreh De'ah* 250:1.
236. Maimonides, Gifts to the Poor 8:18; *Shulchan Aruch, Yoreh De'ah* 251:9.
237. See *Responsa* of Chacham Tzvi, *Responsum* 70.
238. *Shulchan Aruch, Yoreh De'ah* 250:5.
239. R. Shlomo ben Aderet, *Responsa*, part III, 380.
240. *Aruch HaShulchan, Yoreh De'ah* 250:10–12.
241. See *Tur, Yoreh De'ah* 253; also *Shulchan Aruch, Yoreh De'ah* 253:2.

Glossary

Acharonim. Latter-day sages (after the fifteenth century).

Achilat matzah. The concluding phrase of the blessing for eating of *matzah*.

Adar. Name of the Hebrew month wherein Purim takes place.

Af al pi ken. Nevertheless.

Al HaNisim. (literally, for the miracles) Special prayer on Chanukah detailing the miracles.

Aliyah. (literally, to go up) To be called to read in the Torah.

Am Yisrael chai. The nation Israel lives forever.

Amelek. First nation to war upon Israelites after the Exodus.

Amidah. (literally, standing) Silent prayer (*Shemoneh Esrei*).

Amud HaShachar. The morning star.

Anan Sadi. We assume.

Anshei Kenesset HaGedolah. Men of the Great Assembly.

Anveihu. I will adorn or beautify Him.

Aron. Casket; container; also Ark in synagogue for Holy Scrolls.

Arvut. Jewish solidarity; concern for an interdependent cohesive relationship.

Asher bachar banu. (literally, which you [divinely] selected us) Phrase used in blessing before reading in the Torah or learning Torah each day.

Aufruf. Ceremony when bridegroom is called to the Torah on the *Shabbat* prior to his marriage.

Avodah Zarah. (literally, strange worship) Idolatry.

Azur. Will help.

Baal Koreh. Reader of the Holy Scroll.

Baal Mum. Blemished person.

Baal Teshuvah. (pl. *Baalei Teshuvah*) Penitent.

Badecken. The unveiling of the bride prior to the marriage ceremony to attest to her identity.

Bamidbar. Numbers (fourth book of the Pentateuch).

Bar. Son.

Bar mitzvah. Age of male religious maturity: 13 years for a boy.

Baruch Atah HaShem. (literally, blessed are You, God) Beginning phrase of all blessings.

Baruch Hu U'Varuch Shemo. Blessed is He and Blessed is His Name.

Bat Kol. Heavenly voice.

Bat mitzvah. Age of female religious maturity: 12 years.

Becher. Wine goblet.

Bechor. Firstborn son.

Bedavka. Specifically (because).

Ben. Son.

Bensch. To say Grace after Meals, *Birchat HaMazon.*

Ben Torah. (literally, son of Torah) Scholar.

Ben tovim. Member of a highly regarded family.

Berachah. (pl. *berachot*) Blessing.

Berachah achronah. Blessing recited after such food as cake.

Berachah levatalah. A blessing made in vain.

Berachamav. With his mercy.

Berav am (hadrat melech). In the multitude of people, the King's glory.

Beshalach. When (He) sent; name of Torah portion when Jews departed from Egypt.

Bet din. Rabbinical court.

Bet hamidrash. House of religious study.

Bet HaMikdash. The Holy Temple.

Bet Mishteh. Banquet, party (drinking party).

Bidi'eved. After the fact (*post facto*).

Birchat Erusin. The first two blessings recited under a marriage canopy.

Birchat HaMazon. Grace after Meals.

Birchat HaMitzvah. Blessing recited prior to the performance of a *mitzvah.*

Birchat HaShachar. Morning blessings mandated to be chanted prior to prayers.

Birchat HaShevach. A blessing of appreciation.

Birchat HaTorah. Blessing recited before reading or learning Torah.

Birchat Kohanim. The blessings of the *Kohanim* (those Jews who descend from Aaron the High Priest).

B'nei. Children of.

Boneh Berachamav Yerushalayim, Amen. (literally, rebuilds Jerusalem with His mercy, Amen) Third blessing of Grace after Meals.

Brisk. (Brisker Torah) Town of Brest-Litovsk, which became famous due to its renowned rabbis. A form of highly analytical textual study of Torah.

Chai Adam. Life of a person.

Challah. (pl. *challot*) Twisted, braided loaves of bread used at Shabbat and holiday meals.

Chanukah. Festival of Lights.

Chas veshalom. Heaven forbid.

Chashivut. Formal importance.

Chatan. Bridegroom.

Chavilot. Bundles.

Chayyei she'ah. Short period of time to live.

Chayyim shel Yisrael. Life of a Jew.

Chazal. Rabbinical sages.

Chazzan. (pl. *chazzonim*) Cantor.

Cherem. Excommunication.

Chesed. Kindness.

Chevrah Kadisha. (literally, Holy Society) Society that cares for burying the dead.

Chilul HaShem. Profanation of the Holy Name of God.

Chinuch. Education.

Chumash. Pentateuch.

Chuppah. Canopy for marriage.

Churban. The destruction of the Holy Temple.

Chutzpah. Audacity.

Daven(ing). Praying.

Devar Torah. Torah message.

D'oraita. Biblical *mitzvot*.

D'vei Haseir. Introductory prayer added to the *Birchat HaMazon* recited for a bride and bridegroom.

Efod. Breastplate worn by High Priests in the Holy Temple.

Eidei Mesirah. Witnesses observing the transference of documents.

Ein Mekablin Oto. We do not accept him.

Elul. Hebrew month prior to Rosh Hashanah.

Erev. Eve of (*Shabbat* or *Yom Tov*).

Eruvin. (sing. *Eruv*) Symbolic enclosure to permit carrying on *Shabbat*.

Etrog. Citron.

Evyon. A poor person (a necessitous person).

Frum. Truly observant.

Gabbai. Agent, surrogate.

Gadol. Adult, or great scholar.

Gadol HaBayit. Head of the household.

Gamur. Complete.

Gaon. Title granted to great sages.

Gedolei Hador. Outstanding sages of the generation.

Gehinnom. Purgatory.

Gemara. Talmud.

Gematria. Process of comparing words having similar numerical values of their Hebrew letters (Hebrew letters have specific numerical values).

Ger. Convert.

Get. A Jewish religious divorce granted by a religious court.

Gezeirah. A rabbinic ban.

Givonim. Nation that tricked Joshua into believing they lived far from Israel.

Gosses. A person in the throes of death.

Grevoi. Dole or repossessing.

HaChinuch. The education.

Haftorah. Portion of Prophets read in the synagogue on Saturdays and holidays.

Haggadah. Guide for Passover evening.

Halachah (halachic). (pl. *hilchot*) Jewish law.

Hallel. Prayer of thanksgiving and praise.

Hamavarech. Person who recites a blessing.

Ham'lavah et ha'orei'ach. Escorting a guest.

Hamotzei Mechaveiro alav hareiyah. Onus of proof is the responsibility of the claimant.

Hamotzi. Who brings forth (bread); blessing before eating bread.

HaNavi. The prophet.

HaNeirot Halalu. (literally, these candles) Prayer recited on Chanukah during kindling of *Menorah*.

HaShem. God.

Hashmona'im. Family of *Kohanim* who served as leaders during the era of Chanukah.

Hasid. (pl. *hasidim*) Pious follower of Baal Shem Tov and his disciples.

Havdalah. Concluding prayer of *Shabbat*.

Havivah hi me'od. Very dear.

Hechsher mitzvah. Preparation prior to actual performance of *mitzvah*.

Hefsek. Undue interruption.

Heh. Fifth Hebrew letter, phonetically sounded as an "h."

Hiddur mitzvah. Beautification of the *mitzvah.*
Ikar k'dinah. Such is the basic law.
Isur M'dorayta. Biblical injunction.
Kabbalah. Mysticism.
Kabbalat Mitzvot. Commitment to observe commandments.
Kabbalat Shabbat. Welcoming the Sabbath.
Kabbalist. Jewish mystic.
Kaf (כ). Letter in Hebrew alphabet, with numerical value of 20, phonetic equivalent of "k."
Kail. God.
Kallah. Bride.
Kara'it. (pl. *karitut*) Extirpation.
Kavanah. Proper intention.
Kavod. Honor, homage.
Kavod habriyut. Concern for respect and propriety.
Kavod HaTorah. Homage to Torah scrolls or Torah scholars.
Kavod HaTzibur. Homage to the congregation.
Kavod Shabbat. Homage to *Shabbat.*
K'daishe. A promiscuous woman.
Kedushah. Holiness.
Kedushat Shabbat. The sanctity of *Shabbat.*
Kehillah. Community.
Kelayim. Prohibited mixture of wool and linen.
Keriyat HaTorah. The public reading of the Torah.
Ketoret. Incense.
Ketubah. Ancient marriage contract.
Keviut. Permanency.
Kibud. Honor.
Kibud av. Honoring a father.
Kiddush. Sanctification of *Shabbat* and holidays.
Kiddushin. Marriage.
Kiddush Levanah. Prayers sanctifying the New Moon.
K'lal Yisrael. Jewish nation.
Ko'ach. Strength.
Kodshim. Animals sacrificed at the Holy Temple.
Kohen. (pl. *Kohanim*) Priest, descendent of Aaron.
Kohen Gadol. High Priest.
Kol HaMarbeh. Whoever increases.
Korban. (pl. *korbanot*) Animal sacrifice.
Kos. Goblet.

Kosher. (adj.; noun, *kashrut*) Jewish dietary laws.

Kos Shel Berachah. Goblet used for the performance of a *mitzvah*.

Ko tomar levet Yaakov. So say to the House of Yaakov (Exodus 19:3).

Kriah. Rending of a mourner's garment.

Kupah. Charity fund (weekly).

Laasot. To observe (*mitzvot*).

Lag B'Omer. The thirty-third day of the *Omer*. A date celebrated as a semi-holiday.

LaMalshinim. To the slanderers (opening phrase of prayer added to the eighteen benedictions of the *Amidah*).

Lashon hara. Gossip; negative tidings about people.

Lechah Dodi. (literally, Go out my dear) Friday evening prayer.

Lechalotam. To destroy them.

Lechatchilah. *Ab initio.*

Lechem mishneh. Double portion of *challot* (for Shabbat and holidays).

Lefi re'ot enei hamoreh. According to the purview of each rabbi's judgment.

Lehachis. To incite hateful behavior.

Leharich. To prolong.

Lehashmid. To utterly destroy.

LeMishpechoteihem. According to their families.

Letei'avon. Personal pleasure.

Lilmod Al minat laAsot. Learning Torah in order to perform *mitzvot*.

Lo maasti. I have not hated (them).

Lo plug. General rule, no distinctions.

Lo ta'amod. Do not stand (idly) by.

Lo yaavor. Do not (permit) afterwards.

Lu'ach. Jewish calendar.

Lulav. Palm (used on Sukkot).

Maamar. Saying (generally, an ethical or theological discourse).

Maariv. Evening prayers.

Maaseh Bet Din. Formal act of a rabbinic court.

Maaseh Mitzvah. Process of actually performing a *mitzvah*.

Maaseh rav. Pragmatic action of a teacher.

Maasim tovim. Good deeds.

Maftir. The *Shabbat* Torah portion is divided into seven portions. After seven people are called up to the Torah, part of the last portion is repeated and is called *Maftir*. The one called to *Maftir* also reads the prophetic portion.

Magid she'ur. A Torah lecturer.

Mah Nishtanah. Why is (this) different?

Mamzer. Bastard; child born from incestuous or adulterous relationship (pl. *mamzerim*).

Maror. Bitter herbs.

Matan Torah. Revelation.

Matzah. Unleavened bread used on Passover.

Matzeivah. Memorial stone.

Mazel Tov. Good luck.

Mechallel Shabbat befarhesiah Dino Ke'akum. One who publicly desecrates *Shabbat* is to be treated as a non-Jew.

Me'eit la'eit. Till the actual time itself.

Megillah. Scroll.

Megillat Esther. Scroll of Esther.

Mekubalim. Mystics.

Melachah. Action prohibited on *Shabbat*.

Melavah malkah. Saturday night meal.

Menorah. Candelabra for Chanukah (eight lamps).

Menshlichkeit. Jewish decency, gracious humanity.

Mesader Kiddushin. Officiating rabbi at a wedding.

Mesorah. Tradition.

Met Mitzvah. A dead Jewish body with no available person to insure burial.

Metziut. Reality, human nature.

Mezuzah. Biblical portion of the *Shema* (on parchment) placed on doorposts.

Mi Maamakim. Out of the depths (Psalms 130).

Midah keneged midah. Measure for measure.

Middot. Moral character.

Midrash. Biblical legends.

Mikvah. (pl. *mikva'ot*) Ritualarium.

Milah. Circumcision.

Min HaTorah. Biblically.

Minchah. Afternoon prayer.

Minhag. Custom.

Minhag ra. Bad custom.

Minyan. Quorum of ten Jews.

Mishloach manot. Edible presents given on Purim.

Mishpatim. Social laws.

Mishpato. His judgment.

Mishteh. Drinking party.

Mita bedei Shamayim. Death by the hand of heaven (a divine punishment).

Mitoch. Law that states that once an item is permitted on *Yom Tov* for food purposes, it is also permitted for nonfood purposes.

Mitoch devar halachah. By way of a halachic statement.

Mitzvah. (pl. *mitzvot*) Commandment, good deed.

Mitzvah derabim. A public *mitzvah*.

Mizbe'ach. Altar.

Morah. Awe.

Motzi. To include others in a *mitzvah*.

Muktzah. Item forbidden to move on Shabbat or holidays.

Mumar. Apostate.

Musar. Religious ethics.

Muvhak. Proficient, an expert.

Nazir. One who is prohibited to shave or drink alcoholic beverages.

Nesu'in. Completion of marriage.

Netzach Yisrael. Jewish eternity.

Nidah. Menstruant.

Niddui. Excommunication (thirty days).

Oleh. Ascend.

Omer. Offering brought to the Holy Temple on the sixteenth of *Nisan*; subsequently new harvest was permissible to eat.

Panim chadashot. Person who did not attend a wedding and is accordingly "a new face"; Special person who enhances the festive meals held throughout the first week of marriage (*sheva berachot*).

Parashah. Torah portion.

Parashat HaShavua. Torah portion of the week.

Parashat Zachor. Portion of Torah read before Purim dealing with Amelek.

Parnasah. Livelihood.

Peri HaGafen. (literally, fruit of the vine) Concluding phrase of wine blessing.

Peru Uvru. Be fruitful and multiply.

Pesach. (Passover) Holiday commerating Exodus of Jews from Egypt.

Pesak. Halachic decision; final law.

Pesak Din. A rabbinic decision; a decision of a rabbinic court.

Pesukim. Verses.

Pidyon shevuim. Ransoming captive Jews.

Pikuach nefesh. Life-threatening condition.

Pilegesh. Common-law wife; wife not sanctified by Jewish wedding.

Pilpul. Incisive talmudic logic.

Pirsum hanes. Publicizing and popularizing the *mitzvah*.

Po'alo. His deeds; actions.

Posek. (pl. *poskim*) Decisor of Jewish law.

Purim. Holiday commemorating victory of Mordechai and Esther and the Jews of ancient Persia over their enemy, Haman.

Rachamim. Mercy.

Rachatz. The washing of hands with the blessing at the Passover seder.

Racheim. Have mercy.

Rasha. (pl. *rasha'im*) Wicked person.

Rasha gamur. Absolutely wicked person.

Rav Muvhak. Primary rabbi or teacher.

Rav. Rabbi.

Rebbe. Hasidic rabbi; teacher, mentor.

Refa'einu. (literally, Heal us) First word of eighth blessing in the *Amidah*.

Reish (ר). Letter of Hebrew alphabet corresponding to "r" (numerical value, 200).

Revi'it. A measurement; a quarter of a "lug" (three ounces).

Rishonim. Early sages; after period of Gaonim till fifteenth century.

Rosh Chodesh. First day of Hebrew (lunar) month.

Rosh HaShanah. Jewish new year.

Rosh HaYeshivah. Head of a rabbinical academy.

Rosh Kollel. Head of a *kollel*. A *kollel* is an advanced talmudic institute for married scholars.

Safek. Doubt.

Safek berachot l'eKula. Doubt (of requirements) pertaining to blessings, decided leniently.

Safek derabbonim lekula. Doubt of rabbinic law, decided leniently.

Sakanah. (pl. *sakanot*) Life-threatening danger.

Sanhedrin. Supreme Jewish Court of Law.

Sechitah. Squeezing liquid.

Seder. Order, Passover eve service.

Sefer Torah. (pl. *Sifre Torah*) Torah scroll.

Sefirah. The counting of the *omer*, commencing the second night of Passover and continuing for forty-nine days.

Segol. Sign for phonetic sound "eh."

Segulah. Charm, potent for good tidings.

Seudah. Meal.

Seudat mitzvah. Meal where a *mitzvah* is observed.

Sevarah. Common sense, logic.

Shabbat. Sabbath, Saturday.

Shabbosdik. Conforming to the high spirituality of *Shabbat*.

Shacharit. Morning prayer.

Shalom. Hello, good-bye, peace.

Shalosh seudah. (pl. *seudot*) The third meal eaten by Jews on *Shabbat* (the meals are Friday night, after evening religious services; *Shabbat* morning, after religious services; and *Shabbat* afternoon [after *Minchah*]).

Shas. Talmud.

Shaveh lakol. Practiced by all.

Shecheinav. His neighbor.

Shechitah. Kosher form of religious slaughter of animals.

Sheki'ah. Sunset.

Shema. First word of verse *Shema Yisrael*—Hear O Israel.

Shemoneh Esrei. Silent prayer, *Amidah*.

She'ur. Torah class or seminar.

Shev v'al taaseh. Sit still and do nothing; a passive status.

Sheva berachot. Seven blessings (performed at marriage and seven days subsequently at meals).

Shevuot. (literally, weeks) Holiday commemorating the giving of the Torah on Mount Sinai.

Shinui. Altered, not common mode of action.

Shivah. Seven, generally the seven days of mourning.

Shliach. Agent or surrogate.

Shliach Tzibur. Agent of congregation, *chazzan*.

Shlitah. Acronym signifying "may he live to a long and good life."

Shloshim. Thirty-day period of mourning from time of death.

Shomer Shabbat. Sabbath observant.

Shulchan Aruch. Code of Jewish laws.

Shuvah. Return.

Simchah. Happy event; party; happiness.

Simchat Torah. (literally, happiness of Torah) Last day of Sukkot holiday, featuring dancing with *Sifre Torah*.

Sin, Shin (ש, שׁ). Letters of Hebrew alphabet—*sin* = s sound; *shin* = sh sound (numerical value, 300).

Sotah. Woman suspected of adultery by her husband.

Sukkah. (pl. *sukkot*) Tabernacle; frail booth; holiday after Yom Kippur.

Tadir. Frequent.

Takanah. Rabbinic decree.

Talmid Chacham. Torah scholar.

Talmud. Repository of oral Torah traditions and debates.

Talmud Torah. *Mitzvah* of learning Torah.

Tanach. Jewish Bible; Pentateuch, Prophets, and Holy Writings (*Torah*, *Nevi'im*, *Ketuvim*).

Tanna. Sage mentioned in the *Mishnah*.

Ta'ut. Mistake, error.

Tefillin. Phylacteries.

Teshuvah. Repentance.

Tevillah. Immersion.

Timche. Blot out.

Timche et Zeicher Amelek. Blot out the remembrance of Amelek (Deuteronomy 25:9).

Tirchah. Excessive burden.

Tisha B'Av. Ninth of *Av* (fast day commemorating the destruction of the Holy Temple).

T'noyim. Engagement contract prior to marriage.

Tomchui. Daily charity (food) fund.

Torah. Jewish Bible, written and oral tradition.

Torah Tzivah Lanu Mosheh. The Torah that Moses commanded us (Deuteronomy 33:4).

Torato umanuto. A professional Torah sage; one who constantly learns Torah.

Tosafot Shabbat. Time added to the *Shabbat* observances.

Toveil. Dip, immerse.

Tractate. Section of the Talmud.

Tzaddik. (pl. *tzaddikim*) Saintly, pious person.

Tzait HaKochavim. When the stars come out (at night).

Tzar. Sorrow, pain, trouble.

Tzarich iyun. It requires further clarification.

Tzedakah. Charity.

Tzeireh. Phonetic name of long a sound.

Tzibur. Community, congregation.

Urim VeTumin. Special attire of High Priest (made up of brilliant stones).

V. In front of word indicates "and."

Vav (ו). The sixth letter of the Hebrew alphabet (numerical value, 6).

V'ish lo yaamod. No man shall stand.

Vekidashto. "And you shall keep him holy"; biblical command to provide special treatment to *kohanim* (descendents of Aaron, the High Priest).

Velo heh'e'luhu. And no one brought him out.

Veshamru. And [the children of Israel] shall keep [the *Shabbat*].

Vidui. Confession.

Yahrzeit. Anniversary of death.

Yarad. [He] went down.

Yarmulkah. Skullcap.

Yeshivah. (pl. *yeshivot*) Torah rabbinical or talmudic institute.

Yetzer hara. Inclination for sin; evil impulse.

Yichus. Lineage.

Yihyu Leratzon. Prayer – May it be the [divine] will.

Yisrael Gedolim. Adult Jews.

Yom Iyun. Day of intense [Torah] study.

Yom Kippur. Fast of Atonement.

Yom Tovah. Festive day party.

Zayit. (pl. *zaytim*) (Size of an) olive.

Zechut. Privilege, advantage.

Zemirot. Songs of *Shabbat* and holidays.

Zimun. Special introductory prayer added to Grace after Meals when three or more adult males are in attendance.

Z"l. *Zichrono Levrachah* – May his memory be a blessing.

References

Ahiezer. See R. Grodszensky.

Am HaTorah, contemporary Torah periodical published by Agudat Israel.

Arieli, R. Yitzchok See *Einayim LeMishpat.*

Avnei Chaifetz. See R. Aaron Levin.

Aruch HaShulchan, novellae and halachic rulings on the Codes. R. Yechiel Michal Epstein. Belorussia (1829–1908).

Asher ben Yechiel, Rabbeinu (Rosh), talmudist and codifier of Jewish law. Germany (1250–1327).

Ashkenazi, R. Shimon. See *Yalkut Shimoni.*

Ateret Zekeinim, R. Menachem Mendel Orbach, halachic decisor. Vienna, Krakow, Kurishtan (1620–   ).

Avnei Meluim, R. Arye Leib b. R. Yosef Hakohen, talmudist (1775–1813).

Avnei Nezer, responsa, R. Avraham ben Ze'ev Nachum Bornstein. Sochaczew, Poland (1839–1910).

Baal Hatanya. See *Shulchan Aruch HaRav.*

Babbad R. Yosef. See *Minchat Chinuch.*

Bach, commentary on Codes of R. Yaakov b. Asher (*Tur*), R. Yoel Sirkes. Poland (1561–1640).

Baruch HaLevi Epstein, R. Bible commentator. *Torah Temimah, Tosefot Berachah,* also commentary on the prayer book and *Avot, Baruch She'Amar.* Russia (1860–1942).

Be'er Heitiv, commentary on *Shulchan Aruch,* R. Yehudah Ashkenazi. Frankfurt, Germany (1730–1770).

Bet Shmuel, R. Shmuel b. R. Or Shraga Faivish, commentary on Codes. Lvov, Shidlov (d. 1694).

Bet Yosef, commentary on Codes of R. Yaakov b. Asher (*Tur*) (R. Yosef ben Ephraim Caro, author, *Codes of Jewish Law:* [*Shulchan Aruch*], which is divided into four sections: *Orach Chayyim* (prayers and holidays); *Yoreh De'ah* (*Kashrut*, Torah, mourning); *Even HaEzer* (marriage, divorce); *Choshen Mishpat* (torts, jurisprudence). Spain; Safed, Israel (1488–1575).

Binyan Tzion, halachic *responsa.* R. Yaakov Etinger. Manheim, Altuna, Germany (1788–1862).

Birkai Yosef, R. Chayyim Yosef David Azulai (Chida), halachist, kabbalist. Glosses to *Shulchan Aruch.* Jerusalem (1724–1806).

Biur Halachah, commentary on author's halachic codes, *Mishnah Berurah* (also *Chofetz Chayyim*). Radin, Poland (1838–1933).

B'air Yaakov, commentary on codes of *Orach Chayyim,* R. Chayyim Yaakov Halevy Krauser. Dalina (early twentieth century).

R. Yosef Caro. See *Bet Yosef.*

Chacham Tzvi, responsa, R. Tzvi Hirsch b. Yaakov. Amsterdam (1660–1718).

Channiel b. Chushiel, Rabbeinu, talmudic commentator and halachic scholar. Rome (d. c. 1056).

Chatam Sofer, R. Moshe Sofer, halachic scholar, *responsa, Torat Moshe,* Pentateuch. Pressburg, Czechoslovakia (1763–1830).

Chav'at Yair, responsa, R. Yair Chayyim b. Moshe Shimshon Bachrach. Germany (1638–1702).

Chayyei Adam, code on *Orach Chayyim,* R. Avraham Danzig(er), also author of *Chachmat Adam,* code on *Yoreh De'ah.* Danzig, Vilna (1748–1820).

Chayyim Sonnenfeld, R., scholar, *responsa, Simlat Chayyim.* Jerusalem (1849–1932).

Chidah, halachic scholar, kabbalist, R. Chayyim Yosef Dovid Azulai. Jerusalem (1724–1806).

Chidushei HaRim, R. Yitzchak Meir Alter, chasidic *rebbe,* author of talmudic commentaries. Gur, Poland (1799–1867).

Chofetz Chayyim. See *Biur Halachah.*

Chok Yaakov, commentary on Codes, R. Yaakov Yosef Reicher, also author of *Iyun Yaakov,* commentary on *Aggadah* and *responsa, Shev'ut Yaakov.* Austria (d. 1737).

Cohen, R. Yosef, contemporary Dayan, Jerusalem; grandson of R. Tzvi Pesach Frank, former chief rabbi. Jerusalem.

Daat Torah, commentary on Codes, R. Shalom Mordechai b. Moshe Shvadron (Maharsham—Moreinu haRav Shalom Mordechai). Galicia (1835–1911).

Darkei Teshuvah, Commentary on Codes, R. Tzvi Hirsch Shapira. Munkach (1850–1914).

Derech HaChayyim, Codes, R. Yaakov ben Yaakov Moshe of Lissa. Lorberbaum, Poland (1760-1832) (Published in prayer books).

Divrai Malkiel, responsa, R. Malkiel Tzvi Halevi. Lomza, Poland (early twentieth century).

Drishah uPrishah, commentary on Codes of the *Tur*, R. Yehoshua ben Alexander Hakohen Falk. Lublin, Poland; Lemberg, Germany (1555-1614).

Dushinsky, R. Yosef Tzvi, *responsa, Ma'haritz*. Chust, Galanta, Czechoslovakia; Jerusalem (1864-1948).

Eglei Tal (analysis of *Shabbat* principles). See *Avnei Nezer*.

Eiger, R. Akivah, talmudist. Eisenstadt, Austria; Posen, Poland-Lithuania (1761-1837).

Ein Yaakov, commentary on legends of the Talmud. R. Yaakov ben Solomon ibn Habiv. Spain (1445?-1515/16).

Einayim LeMishpat, talmudic commentaries. R. Yitzchok Arieli, contemporary dean, Yeshiva Merkaz HaRav. Jerusalem (published 1947).

Eishel Avraham, commentary on Codes (Mahadura Tenina). R. Avraham Wharman. Butchatch, Ukraine (1771-1840).

Engel, R. Yosef, halachic and talmudic scholar. *Gilyonai HaShas – Bet HaOtzur*. Cracow, Poland (1859-1920).

Epstein, R. Baruch. See R. Baruch.

Ezra, R. Avraham ibn, biblical commentator. Spain (1089-1164).

Ezrachi, R. Baruch Mordechai, *responsa, Birchat Mordechai*, contemporary Jerusalem *rosh yeshivah* (Bayit Vagan) Ateret Yisrael, former *Rosh Yeshivah*, Hebron.

Feinstein, R. Moshe, renowned contemporary halachic scholar, *responsa, Iggerot Moshe*. Russia; New York (1895-1986).

Frank, R. Tzvi Pesach, halachic scholar (*Eretz Tzvi*, also *Mikra'ei Kodesh*), former chief rabbi. Jerusalem (1873-1960).

Gershon b. Yehudah, Rabbeinu. Major German talmudic scholar (960-1028).

Gilyon Maharsha, R. Shlomo Eiger ben R. Akivah Eiger, commentator on Talmud and Codes. Warsaw (d. 1852).

Grodszensky, R. Chayyim Ozer, rabbinic leader and sage, *responsa, Achiezer*. Vilna, Lithuania (1863-1940).

H'Admor of Lubavitch, Rabbi Menachem Mendel Schneerson, international spiritual leader of *Chabad chasidim*. Brooklyn, New York, (b. 1902).

Hagaot Maimuni, commentary on Rambam, R. Meir Hakohen. Rottenburg (end of thirteenth century).

HaGra (Vilna Gaon), halachic scholar (*Siddur, Likutei Dinim, Glosses on Codes, Divrei Eliyahu* [Prophets]. R. Eliyahu b. Shlomo Zalman. Vilna (1720–1797).

Hanisu'im Kehalachah, contemporary compendium on laws of marriage. R. Binyamin Adler (Jerusalem, 1985).

HaRada, R. Dovid Oppenheim, talmudist. Nikolsburg, also Prague (1664–1736).

Haviv, R. Moshe b. Shlomo ibn, talmudic commentator, *Kapot Temarim*. Turkey (1654–1696).

Henkin, R. Yosef Eliyahu, halachic decisor, *Eidut LeYisrael, Lev Ivrah* (synagogue Luach). Belorussia; New York (1880–1973).

Heden, R. Solomon (*Melechet Shlomo*).

Hirsch, R. Samson Raphael, German Orthodox leader (biblical commentaries). Frankfurt (1808–1888).

Hurowitz, R. Pinchas b. Tzvi Hirsh HaLevi (*Haflah* and *HaMakneh*), talmudic commentary, *Panim Yafot*; Bible commentary. Frankfurt, Germany (1730–1805).

Hoffman, R. Dovid Tzvi, *rosh yeshivah*, Hildesheimer Seminary, halachic authority, *responsa Melamid LeHo'il*. Berlin (1843–1921).

Hutner, R. Yitzchok, contemporary *rosh yeshivah*, Rabbi Chaim Berlin Rabbinical Academy (*Pachad Yitzchok*). New York (1905–1980).

Imrai Ash, responsa (talmudist) R. Meir Ash, *rav* in the city of Ungvar in 1833 (d. 1852).

Iyun Yaakov. See *Chok Yaakov*.

Katz, R. Yosef, b. R. Mordechai Gershon, *rosh hayeshivah*, Cracow, 40 years. *Responsa She'erit Yosef*. Direct ancestor of author (1481–1561).

Kav HaYashar, R. Tzvi Hirsh Koidnover, *tzaddik*, ethical and mystical discourses (d. 1712).

Kesef Mishneh. See *Bet Yosef*.

Kitzur Shulchan Aruch, popular abridged Codes. R. Shlomo ben Yosef Ganzfried. Ungar, Hungary (1804–1886).

Klein, R. Menashe, contemporary halachic scholar, *responsa, Mishnah Halachot*. Ungvar (USSR); New York; Jerusalem.

Kluger, R. Shlomo, halachic scholar, *responsa, Tuv Taam veDaat, HaElef Lecha Shlomo, Hagaddah*. Brody, Russia (1785–1869).

Kol Bo, anonymous halachic guide to ritual laws, liturgy, customs. First printed in Naples (1490–1491).

Kol Ram (biblical interpretations cited in the name of his *rebbe*, Rav Moshe Feinstein), Rabbi Avraham Fishelis, contemporary author. New York.

Korban Netanel, R. Netanel Viel, talmudic and halachic scholar. Prague (1687-1769).

Kotler, R. Aaron, founder and *rosh yeshivah* of Bet Medrash Govoha, Lakewood, New Jersey (1892-1962).

Kotler, R. Shneur, son of R. Aaron Kotler. Contemporary *rosh yeshivah*, Lakewood, New Jersey.

Kovner Rav, R. Avraham Duber Kahanah Shapira, *responsa, Devar Avraham*. Warsaw (1902).

Landau, R. Yechezkal b. Yehudah, halachic authority, *responsa, Noda B'Yehudah, Dagul Mervavah, Tzlach* (commentary on the Talmud). Prague, Czechoslovakia (1713-1793).

Levin, R. Aaron b. Natan, communal leader and halachic scholar, *responsa, Avnei Chaifetz*. Poland (1879-1941).

Levush commentaries, R. Moshe Mordechai Epstein, *rosh yeshivah*, Slabodka, Hebron (1866-1935).

Levi Yitzchok, R., hasidic leader, *Kedushat Levi*. Berditchev (1749-1810).

Luria, R. Shlomo b. Yechiel (Rashal), talmudic commentator and halachic scholar (*Yam shel Shlomo* and *Chachmat Shlomo*). Poland (1510?-1574).

Mabit, R. Moshe b. Yosef Mitroni, *responsa*; also commentary on Rambam. Safed (1505-1585).

Machattzit HaShekel, commentary on the *Magen Avraham*, Rabbi Samuel haLevi Kolin. Bohemia (1720-1806).

Madani Shmuel (Laws of Pesach); *Minchat Shabbat* (Laws of Shabbat), R. Shmuel HaKohen Burstein. Shatava, Ukraine (1860-c. 1920). Author's paternal grandfather.

Magen Avraham, halachic commentator on *Shulchan Aruch*, R. Avraham Abeli Gombiner. Poland (1637-1683).

Magid Mishneh, R. Vidal Yom Tov of Tolosa. Commentary on Rambam's codes. Spain (second half of fourteenth century).

Maharal of Prague, halachic scholar and kabbalist, R. Yehudah Loew b. Bezalel. Prague, Czechoslovakia (1525-1609).

Maharam Shick, R. Moshe b. Yosef Shick. Rabbi and halachic scholar. Hungary (1807-1879).

Mahari Berunah, Rabbi Yisrael ben Chayyim. German *rav*, Berunah and Regensburg (1400-?).

Maharil, Rabbi Yaakov ben Moshe, head of German, Austrian, and Bohemian Jewish communities (1340?–1427).

Maharsha, commentator, Talmud R. Shmuel Eliezer Halevi Aydels. Poland and Austria (1555–1631).

Maharsham. See *Daat Torah*.

R. Moshe Margolis, *P'nei Moshe* (commentary on the Jerusalem Talmud). Died in Brody, on the way to Israel (1710–1781).

R. Meir Loeb b. Yechiel (*Malbin*), commentary on Pentateuch and prophets. Volhynia (1809–1879).

R. Meir Simcha HaKohen, talmudic and halachic sage, *Meshech Chachmah* (biblical Commentary), commentary on Rambam. Dvinsk, Lithuania (1843–1926).

Meiri, talmudic commentator, R. Menachem b. Shlomo Meiri (HaMeiri), *Bet Habechirah*. Provence, France (1249–1316).

Mechilta, R. Shimon Bar Yochai (halachic *midrash*, Exodus).

Meshech Chachmah. See R. Meir Simcha.

Midrash Rabbah, oldest Amoraic classical *midrash* on the Pentateuch and the *Megillot*.

Minchat Chinuch, commentary on *Chinuch* (list of biblical mitzvot), R. Yosef Babad. Tarnopol, Russia (nineteenth century).

Minchat Elazer, R. Chayyim Elazar Shapira, *responsa*. Munkach (1882–1947).

Minchat Shabbat. See *Madani Shmuel*.

Mishnah, compendium of Oral Torah (redacted by R. Yehudah HaNasi) (latter half of the second century and beginning of third century C.E.).

Mishnah Berurah. See *Biur Halachah*.

Rabbi Mordechai b. Hillel HaKohen, German rabbinical authority (1240–1298).

Nachalet Tzvi. See *Pitchei Teshuvah*.

Naeh, R. Avraham Chayyim, contemporary Jerusalem halachic scholar, *Ketzot Hashulchan*, commentary on codes of *Shulchan Aruch HaRav*. Israel (b. 1925).

Natroni Gaon, R. Sura (ninth century C.E.).

Nitziv, talmudic and halachic scholar (*Meromei Sadeh*, commentary on Talmud), R. Naftali Tzvi Hirsch. Berlin; Volozhin, Russia (1817–1893).

Or HaChayyim, Bible commentator, R. Chayyim Michel (1792–1846).

Perashot Derachim, talmudic essays, R. Yehudah Roznis, author, *Mishneh LeMelech*, commentary on the Rambam. Turkey (1658–1727).

Peri Megadim, commentary on Codes, R. Yosef b. Meir Teomim. Lvov, Russia (Ukraine) (1727–1792).

Pitchei Teshuvah, halachic digest, R. Avraham Tzvi Hirsch b. Yaakov, Eisenstadt. Grodno, Kovno, Russia (1813–1868).

P'nei Yehoshua, talmudic commentary, R. Yaakov Yehoshua. Lvov, Berlin, Frankfurt, Germany (1681–1756).

Prishah. See *Drishah uPrishah.*

Raavid, R. Avraham b. Dovid, notes on text of Rambam's codes, major Spanish halachic scholar. Posquieres, Provence, Spain (1125–1198).

Rabbeinu Tam, tosafist, R. Yaakov b. Meir Tam. France (1100–1171).

Radbaz, halachic authority, *responsa,* R. David ben Zimrah. Egypt (1479–1573).

Rambam, halachic authority, R. Moshe b. Maimon, *Yad Halachah, Sefer HaMitzvot.* Egypt (1135–1284).

Ramban, Bible commentator and halachic scholar, R. Moshe b. Nachman. Verona, Italy (1194–1270).

Ran, halachic scholar, R. Nissim b. Reuven Gerondi. Barcelona (fourteenth century).

Rashal. See R. Shlomo Luria.

Rashash, R. Shmuel Shtarshon, talmudic commentary. Vilna, Poland (early twentieth century).

Rashi, Bible and Talmud authority, R. Shlomo b. Yitzchok. Troyes, France (b. 1040).

Reishit Chachmah, R. Eliyahu Di Vidash b. R. Moshe Di Vidash, pietist, mystic. Safed; Hebron (1550–1587).

Rema, halachic scholar, R. Moshe b. Yisrael Isserles. Cracow, Poland (1525- or 1530–1572).

Ridbaz, R. Dovid, of Slutzk, R. Yaakov Dovid Wilubaski, served as rabbi in Babroisk, Vilna, Wilkoner and Slutsk, New York, and Chicago (1845–1914).

Rif, R. Yitzchok b. Yaakov Alfasi, talmudic and halachic scholar. Fez, Morocco (1013–1103).

R. Yosef Rosen, halachic and talmudic scholar, *responsa, Tzafnot Paanei'ach.* Rogachov, Poland (1858–1936).

Rosh. See Rabbeinu Asher ben Yechiel.

Sedei Chemed, halachic encyclopedia, Rabbi Chayyim Chezekiah ben Raphael, *Eliyahu Medini* (Sephardic author). Constantinople (1832–1904).

Semak (Sefer Mitzvot Katan), R. Yitzchok MeKurvil, analysis of commandments. France (d. 1280).

Shaarei Teshuvah. See Rabbeinu Yonah.

Shach, commentary on Codes, *Nekudat HaKesef,* R. Shabbetai b. Meir HaKohen. Lithuania (1621–1662).

Shelah HaKodesh (the holy *Shelah*), R. Yeshia b. Avraham Halevi, kabbalist, rabbinic leader. Frankfurt; Prague; Jerusalem (1565?–1630).

Shem Rokei'ach, R. Elazar Rokei'ach, halachic sage, talmudic commentary (1758–1837).

Shemesh Tzedakah, R. Shimon Murpugo, halachic scholar. Italy (1682–1740).

Shevut Yaakov. See *Chok Yaakov.*

Shibolei Haleket, compendium of halachic decisions and customs, R. Zedkiyahu HaRofeh. Rome (thirteenth century).

R. Shimshon of Shantz, French *tosafot* also known as HaSar (the "Prince") of Shantz. France (late twelfth–early thirteenth centuries).

Shita Mekubetzet, digest of talmudic commentaries, R. Bezalel b. Avraham Ashkenazi. Safed, Israel; Egypt (1520–c. 1591).

Shmirot Shabbat Kehilchata (published Jerusalem, 1979), compendium of laws of *Shabbat,* R. Yehoshua Yeshia Noibert. Jerusalem.

Shmelke, R. Shmuel, of Nikolsburg, rabbi and kabbalist, disciple of Dov Baer, the Maggid of Mezrich (1726–1778).

Shulchan Aruch. See *Bet Yosef.*

Shulchan Aruch HaRav, codes of Jewish law, R. Shneur Zalman of Laidi, founder of *Chabad* Chasidism (Baal HaTanya). Belorussia (1745–1813).

Sifre, halachic *midrash* to the Books of Numbers and Deuteronomy (first printed in Venice, 1545).

Siftei Chachamim, commentary on Rashi, R. Shabtai Strimmer. Prague (d. 1709).

Soloveitchik, R. Yosef Dov, talmudist, Brisk, *responsa, Bet Halevi.* Brest Litovsk (1820–1892).

Spector, R. Yitzchok Elchonon, rabbinic author, *responsa, Bet Yitzchok.* Kovna, Lithuania (1817–1896).

Sridei Eish, responsa, R. Yecheil Weinberg, last *rosh yeshivah,* Berlin Rabbinical Academy (1885–1966).

Taamei Minhagim (customs), R. Avraham Yitzchak Sperling. Lvov (1928).

Talmud, Babylonian. The interpretation and elaboration of the *Mishnah* (first half of third century C.E. to the end of the fifth century).

Avodah Zarah (idolatry)	*Ketubot* (wedding contracts)
Bava Batra (real estate)	*Megillah* (Purim)
Bava Kamma (damages)	*Menachot* (animal sacrifices)
Bava Metzia (torts)	*Moed Katan* (mourning)
Bechorot (first-born)	*Pesachim* (Passover)
Berachot (blessings)	*Shabbat* (sabbath)
Bikurim (first fruit)	*Sotah* (woman suspected of adultery)
Eruvin	*Taanit* (fast days)
Horayut	*Yevamot* (Levirate marriage)
Kiddushin (marriage)	*Yoma* (Yom Kippur)

Taz (Turei Zahav), commentary on *Shulchan Aruch*, R. David b. Shmuel Halevi. Cracow, Poland; Posen, Poland-Lithuania; Vohynia, Russia (1586–1667).

Terumot Hadeshen, R. Yisrael Iserlun, halachic sage. Bomberg, Germany (1390–1460).

Tiferet Yisrael, R. Yisrael b. R. Gedalya Lipshitz, commentary on *Mishneh*. Community rabbi, scholar. Danzig (d. 1840).

Tosafot, commentators on Talmud. France and Germany (1100–1300).

Tosafot Rid, R. Yeshia b. Mal. di Trani, commentaries on Talmud. Italy (1200–before 1260).

Tukachinsky, R. Yechiel Michal, contemporary halachic scholar, *Gesher HaChayyim* (volumes on laws dealing with death). Jerusalem (d. 1955).

Tur, Codes on Jewish law, R. Yaakov b. R. Asher. Germany; Toledo, Spain (1270–1340).

Tzirelson, R. Yehudah Leib (*Responsa Marchei Lev*), chief rabbi Kishinov and Bessarabia (1932).

Unterman, R. Isar Yehuda, former Ashkenazi chief rabbi, Israel, *Responsa Sheivet Yehudah* (1886–1964).

Usiel, R. Ben Zion Hai, former Sephardi chief rabbi of Israel, halachic authority, *Piskei Usiel*. Tel Aviv (1935).

Vilna Gaon. See HaGra.

Weingart, R. Sol (Shaul), rabbinic scholar, disciple of R. Weinberg, graduate of rabbinical seminary in Berlin. Montreux, Switzerland (1915–1947).

Yalkut Shimoni, collection of talmudic and midrashic material arranged on relevant verses, edited by R. Shimon Ashkenazi. Frankfurt (fourteenth century).

Yehudi HaKadosh, R. Yaakov Yitzchok b. Asher (the Holy Jew), founder of Pshischah *Chasidim* in Poland (1766–1814).

Yerucham bar Meshulam, Rabbeinu, medieval halachic scholar, Provence; Toledo (fourteenth century).

Yerushalmi, Palestinian Talmud.

Yitzchok Isaac Yehudah Yechiel, R., (Safrin) Komarno. Chasidic mystic, scholar, Commentary on *Mishneh* (1806–1874).

Yonah, Rabbeinu, commentator, Talmud, halachic scholar (*Shaarei Teshuvah, Gates of Repentance*), R. Yonah b. Avraham Gerondi. Toledo, Spain (1200–1263).

Yossef, R. Ovadia, contemporary scholar, former Sephardi chief rabbi, Israel (b. 1920).

Zolti, R. Bezalel, contemporary Ashkenazi (former) chief rabbi, Jerusalem, *Responsa Mishnat Ya'vitz*.

Index

About the Author

Rabbi Jack Simcha Cohen is the spiritual leader of Congregation Shaarei Tefila in Los Angeles, California, and is a scion of eighteen generations of rabbis. He is the founder of a national rabbinic think tank, and serves at the helm of several national and local rabbinic and communal organizations. His column, *Halachic Questions*, appears in *The Jewish Press*. Rabbi Cohen is the author of four previous works: *Timely Jewish Questions, Timeless Rabbinic Answers, Intermarriage and Conversion: A Halachic Solution, The Jewish Heart,* and *The 613th Commandment.* His writings have been acclaimed as "remarkable achievements" that "succeed in creating genuine Torah excitement."